In this provocative and original study, Alan Richardson examines
an entire range of intellectual, cultural, and ideological points of
contact between British Romantic literary writing and the pioneering brain science of the time. Richardson breaks new ground in two
fields, revealing a significant and undervalued facet of British
Romanticism while demonstrating the "Romantic" character of
early neuroscience. Crucial notions like the active mind, organi-
cism, the unconscious, the fragmented subject, instinct and intuition, arising simultaneously within the literature and psychology of
the era, take on unsuspected valences that transform conventional
accounts of Romantic cultural history. Neglected issues like the
corporeality of mind, the role of non-linguistic communication,
and the peculiarly Romantic understanding of cultural universals
are reopened in discussions that bring new light to bear on
long-standing critical puzzles, from Coleridge's suppression of
"Kubla Khan," to Wordsworth's perplexing theory of poetic
language, to Austen's interest in head injury.

ALAN RICHARDSON is Professor of English at Boston College. He
has published extensively on the literature and culture of the British
Romantic period. His books include *A Mental Theater: Poetic Drama
and Consciousness in the Romantic Age* (1988) and *Literature, Education and
Romanticism* (Cambridge University Press, 1994), which won the
American Conference on Romanticism Book Prize for 1994.

CAMBRIDGE STUDIES IN ROMANTICISM 47

BRITISH ROMANTICISM
AND THE SCIENCE OF
THE MIND

CAMBRIDGE STUDIES IN ROMANTICISM

This series aims to foster the best new work in one of the most challenging fields within English literary studies. From the early 1780s to the early 1830s a formidable array of talented men and women took to literary composition, not just in poetry, which some of them famously transformed, but in many modes of writing. The expansion of publishing created new opportunities for writers, and the political stakes of what they wrote were raised again by what Wordsworth called those "great national events" that were "almost daily taking place": the French Revolution, the Napoleonic and American wars, urbanization, industrialization, religious revival, an expanded empire abroad, and the reform movement at home. This was an enormous ambition, even when it pretended otherwise. The relations between science, philosophy, religion, and literature were reworked in texts such as *Frankenstein* and *Biographia Literaria*; gender relations in *A Vindication of the Rights of Woman* and *Don Juan*; journalism by Cobbett and Hazlitt; poetic form, content and style by the Lake School and the Cockney School. Outside Shakespeare studies, probably no body of writing has produced such a wealth of response or done so much to shape the responses of modern criticism. This indeed is the period that saw the emergence of those notions of "literature" and of literary history, especially national literary history, on which modern scholarship in English has been founded.

The categories produced by Romanticism have also been challenged by recent historicist arguments. The task of the series is to engage both with a challenging corpus of Romantic writings and with the changing field of criticism they have helped to shape. As with other literary series published by Cambridge, this one will represent the work of both younger and more established scholars, on either side of the Atlantic and elsewhere.

For a complete list of titles published see end of book

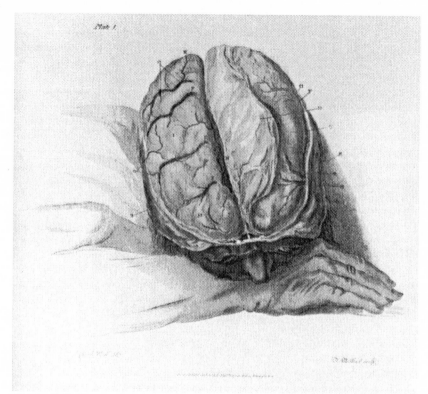

Charles Bell, *Anatomy of the Brain, Explained in a Series of Engravings* (London, 1802), plate 1.

BRITISH ROMANTICISM
AND THE SCIENCE OF
THE MIND

ALAN RICHARDSON

Boston College

CAMBRIDGE
UNIVERSITY PRESS

CAMBRIDGE UNIVERSITY PRESS
Cambridge, New York, Melbourne, Madrid, Cape Town, Singapore, São Paulo

Cambridge University Press
The Edinburgh Building, Cambridge CB2 2RU, UK

Published in the United States of America by Cambridge University Press, New York

www.cambridge.org
Information on this title: www.cambridge.org/9780521781916

First published 2001
This digitally printed first paperback version 2005

A catalogue record for this publication is available from the British Library

Library of Congress Cataloguing in Publication data

Richardson, Alan, 1955–
British Romanticism and the science of the mind / Alan Richardson.
p.   cm. – (Cambridge studies in Romanticism ; 47)
Includes bibliographical references and index.
ISBN 0 521 78191 4 (hardback)
1. English literature – 19th century – History and criticism.   2. Literature and science – Great
Britain – History – 19th century.   3. Brain – Research – Great Britain – History – 19th century.
4. Neurosciences – Great Britain – History – 19th century.   5. Romanticism – Great Britain.
6. Mind and body in literature.   7. Psychology in literature.   I. Title.   II. Series.

PR468.S34 R53   2001
820.9′356 – dc21   00-050356

ISBN-13 978-0-521-78191-6 hardback
ISBN-10 0-521-78191-4 hardback

ISBN-13 978-0-521-02040-4 paperback
ISBN-10 0-521-02040-9 paperback

For Deborah

It is not an easy task to reconcile two subjects so far apart in the minds of most readers as Anatomy and the Fine Arts; but if prejudices early imbibed, be thrown off, it will be found that there is no science, taken in a comprehensive sense, more fruitful of instruction, or leading to more interesting subjects of inquiry, than the knowledge of the Animal body.

Charles Bell, *The Anatomy and Philosophy of Expression*

Contents

Illustrations

Preface

The secondary literature devoted to William Wordsworth, by now extensive enough to stock a small library, has found no room to discuss a most
remarkable feature of the poet's sensory life. Wordsworth's critics and
biographers alike have made little or nothing of an intriguing psychophysiological oddity attested to both in Robert Southey's 1822 reminiscences and in Christopher Wordsworth's 1851 *Memoirs*: the poet "had
no sense of smell."[1] Perhaps the near-total silence regarding Wordsworth's
sensory deficit ever since is understandable. For many critics, at least
until recently, it might have been seen as having anecdotal value at best,
good perhaps for a donnish lecture joke. ("'All the mighty world / Of eye
and ear,' – but not, sadly, of nose.") In the present critical climate,
however, with unprecedented attention to the centrality of sensation, of
"organic sensibility," perception, and the body within Romantic writing,
Wordsworth's limitation to four of five external senses seems at least
worth noting. If, as an influential critic has declared, Wordsworth's
poetic project is "grounded in a regimen of the senses,"[2] does the ground
shift when one considers Wordsworth's alienated relation to at least one
of those senses?

Put more directly, did his lifelong experience of a congenitally
damaged sensorium affect the way Wordsworth himself understood
sense experience, the sensory organs that variously channel it, the mind
that anticipates, shapes, and interprets it? Wordsworth came of age,
after all, at a time when the bodily – and hence mutable – nature of the
mind had been boldly asserted by Joseph Priestley, when the medical and
physiological account of mind developed in Erasmus Darwin's *Zoonomia*
had caught the fancy of avant-garde intellectuals, and when sensory and
cognitive deficits gave fuel to arguments for the mind's dependence on,
if not identity with, the brain. Wordsworth was exposed to these new
ideas in the formative 1790s, a time of close collaboration with
Coleridge, himself thoroughly caught up in questions of perception,

epistemology, and mind–body interaction. Radically modular accounts of mind and sensation were just on the horizon, most notoriously the "organology" of Gall, whose brain-based psychology would soon be described for the English public in a pamphlet by Wordsworth's friend Henry Crabb Robinson. By 1851 Harriet Martineau, a recent convert to the phrenology movement that had given Gall's ideas wide currency, would cite Wordsworth's defective sense (and his momentary, perhaps apocryphal, recovery of it) in the context of a modular, anti-dualistic, embodied theory of mind and sensation.[3] Martineau came late (though with characteristic zeal) to a Romantic fascination with the brain, the nerves, and the continuity between body and psyche. For the half century conventionally associated with literary Romanticism (1780–1830) had also witnessed the rise and first flourishing of a biological science of mind.

Any number of motifs, ideals, and "discoveries" routinely attributed to literary Romanticism – including the split or fragmented psyche; the revaluation of feeling, instinct, and intuition; the active mind; developmental models of subject formation; the unconscious; even a new, more humane construction of "idiocy" – feature prominently in the era's emergent biological psychologies as well. In the chapters that follow, I argue that these common focal points reveal an important though neglected area of overlap between Romantic-era literary and scientific representations of the mind as situated in and lived through the body. The new biological psychologies of Darwin, Gall, and other radical brain scientists constitute a crucial segment of the Romantic discursive field; they give new dimensions to terms like "sensibility," "nervous," "organic," "natural," "universal," and "brain" that reverberate through the fictional works and poetic theories of their literary contemporaries. Rediscovering the extensive commerce between literary and scientific investigations of mind in the Romantic era does more, however, than open up a vital new area for research in the history of literature and esthetics. It also presents a fertile site for examining cultural and ideological conflict, looking back to a time when an immaterial and indivisible conception of mind seemed an indispensable prop to established religious doctrine and even political stability.

These claims may seem surprising, and the elaborate network of discursive connections and historical contacts that supports them came initially as a surprise to me. I was taught to think of Romantic-era brain science, when at all, as a vaguely comical affair of phrenological bumps and Hartleyan vibratiuncles. The early psychological theories of Darwin or Gall might provide matter for the sociologist of science, but could hold little interest in themselves or in relation to the larger intellectual culture of the period. It was through the lens of contemporary neuroscience, which has returned (in its own way) to one after another concern of Romantic psychology – from the modular mind to facial expression theory – that I began to see how innovative, exciting, and threatening the theoretical and experimental work of leading Romantic-era brain scientists might once have appeared. (That it did strike contemporaries as momentous can be seen in the comments from reviews, lectures, notebooks, letters, and other sources cited throughout this book.) Although I develop my argument primarily through the interplay of archival research and textual analysis associated with "new" historicist literary criticism, I have deliberately preserved traces of its beginnings in the unexpected parallels I noticed between the brain science of the Romantic era and that of our own period. Given that the past can never be addressed from an entirely neutral or detached position, I have thought it best to be candid about the interests that launched me into this subject. In certain cases, as with the "cognitive unconscious" or the "basic" level of conceptual categorization, where formulations from cognitive neuroscience can enrich or clarify an understanding of notions or terms within Romantic discourse, the parallels are made explicit.

I cannot, all the same, claim this study as an exercise in what John Sutton has christened "historical cognitive science," though I share his conviction that research into certain "strange, neglected" traditions in neuropsychology gains immeasurably from the perspective of recent cognitive and neuroscientific theory. (I also find aid and comfort in Sutton's avowal of the "virtues and pleasures of superficially silly old theories," "weird old views" that seem considerably less so in the wake of the cognitive revolution).[4] My methodological sympathies here lie closer to what Nicholas Roe, in his revealing study of Keats, terms "literal archaeology," an attempt to recover the ideological as well as scientific and cultural valences of key terms and ideals usually limited to a range of literary meanings.[5] Nevertheless, I hope this book will find readers beyond its primary audience of British Romantic scholars, among historians of psychology and neuroscience, and even among cognitive scientists seeking to learn from the "prehistory" of their field. It may also appeal to those beginning to bring methods and findings from cognitive science to bear on the study of literature, by demonstrating how the interplay between literary and neuroscientific models and representations has a rich past as well as a robust future.

As I have presented sections of the work below to various audiences, I have learned to anticipate several recurring questions, some addressed in the course of the argument, others best dealt with up front. One sort of question concerns my use of a neuroscientific lexicon to clarify and highlight aspects of Romantic-era texts, especially non-scientific texts, that I read in terms of what I call "embodied" or "corporeal" accounts of mind. The anxiety, as I understand it, is that I illicitly borrow an aura of authority from the sciences, especially when I point to parallels (however rough) with recent neuroscience, thus implicitly claiming a special validity for my interpretations. I would emphasize in response, first, that in drawing on models and formulations from recent neuroscience in order to add clarity and point to my discussions of "weird old views," I make no claim for the validity of these views, old or new. To the contrary, I am quite aware that among the recent scientific conceptions I allude to here and there in the text and notes, at least some are sure to prove invalid, since some of them contradict or cancel out others. I have borrowed eclectically (but not, I hope, promiscuously) from cognitive theory and neuroscience in trying to give new life to old ideas, but the resonance I hear between the Romantic era and the past few decades does not in itself speak to the truth value of either past or current findings and models. The sciences of mind, perpetually reinventing themselves, can circle back to reopen promising paths abandoned for no good reason, or can return to the mistaken, even perverse windings of the past in (temporarily) compelling new ways. I do think that the brain science of the Romantic era has been badly undervalued, both in terms of its cultural weight in its own time and its intellectual interest for the present, but (some very general trends apart) I would not want to claim that it has been "vindicated."

Those who look here for full-scale interpretations of literary works will in any case be disappointed. My aims are more modest, concerned with contradictions, cruxes, and charged moments in selected texts rather than with comprehensive readings of them. I try to show that by shifting and extending notions of historical context to include the context of brain science, one detects new meanings in certain key terms ("organic," "unconscious"), discovers new approaches to longstanding problems (Coleridge's un-Coleridgean preface to "Kubla Khan," some of the knotty points in Wordsworth's poetic theory), and finds new philosophical and ideological significance in a familiar topic (blushing and related psychophysiological events in Keats). Even the chapter devoted to Austen's *Persuasion* looks primarily at selected incidents and stylistic issues, leaving many aspects of the novel undisturbed. In proposing and selectively illustrating new ways of thinking about British Romantic culture, I have tried to be provocative rather than definitive or synoptic. Other texts, authors, and issues might well have been taken up in light of the embodied approaches to mind being worked out in the scientific and literary discourses of the period. I hope other scholars will find cause to help fill in the picture, and I welcome in advance the gains in nuance and complexity that further critical discussion will add to the new perspectives offered below.

For crucial support in the course of researching and writing this book, I thank, first of all, the John Simon Guggenheim Memorial Foundation for a Fellowship in 1997–98. Boston College generously supplemented the fellowship in numerous ways, including a Summer Research Grant in 1997, a Research Expense Grant in 1998, and Undergraduate Research Assistant Grants in 1998 and 1999. Thanks to these programs, I had the pleasure as well as profit of working with three talented research assistants, Beth Bradburn, Stellar Kim, and Sara Hart. Research for this book was also significantly aided by the librarians and staffs at the O'Neill Library at Boston College (especially Brendan Rapple), the Widener Library at Harvard, and the Countway Rare Books collection at the Harvard Medical School (especially Jack Eckert).

I am particularly grateful for the opportunities given me to present, discuss, and circulate parts of this work at various stages of its progress. Earlier versions of chapters 2 and 4 were published (respectively) in the journals *Romanticism* and *Poetics Today*. I wish to thank the anonymous readers and especially the editors I worked with, Nicholas Roe and Meir Sternberg, for their suggestions. The American Conference on Romanticism twice gave me venues for presenting aspects of this work at annual meetings held at the University of Georgia and at Indiana University; thanks to the interdisciplinary and comparatist ethos of this group, and the lively and attentive audiences it fosters, I learned a great deal in each case. No less instructive were the more intimate (but no less lively!) exchanges sponsored by the ELH seminar series at Johns Hopkins University and the seminar on Romantic Literature and Culture at the CLCS (now the Humanities Center) at Harvard University. The latter has provided me with an academic second home for many years and I am especially grateful to Sonia Hofkosh for helping to keep the seminar as collegial as it is challenging. I cannot imagine more informed or more stimulating audiences for the chapters on Coleridge and Wordsworth than those I found in 1998 at the Coleridge Summer Conference at Cannington and the Wordsworth Summer Conference at Grasmere. I am also thankful for opportunities to lecture closer to home at Dartmouth University and the University of New Hampshire. Though I cannot individually acknowledge all of those who helped me with questions, comments, or suggestions, I hope they will find their interventions bearing fruit below.

Those who provided indispensable early encouragement for this project include William Keach, Ti Bodenheimer, Frederick Burwick, Marilyn Butler and Chuck Rzepka. Chuck also proved a generous and demanding reader of various chapters in draft, along with Mary Crane, Richard Matlak, Bruce Graver, Marilyn Gaull, Francis Steen, Beth Lau, Ash Nichols, Brian Richardson, John Mahoney and, not least, David Miall. Josie Dixon provided exceptionally valuable editorial guidance in the early stages of this project and her successor, Linda Bree, brought her own keen attention and high scholarly standards to bear on its completion. I am immensely indebted to Roy Porter and to a second reader (who remains anonymous) for their detailed, scrupulous, and stimulating responses. I am also grateful for the careful attention of Christine Lyall Grant, who brought a much-appreciated combination of rigor, professionalism, and tact to copyediting the final manuscript. Most of all, I wish to thank Deborah Blacker. This book grew indirectly out of many conversations with her, and it continued to grow literally under her hands as she read and commented on every page as I wrote and rewrote it. Dedicating the book to her is a small enough return for making it, and for making so much else, possible.

Abbreviations

AP	Charles Bell, *The Anatomy and Philosophy of Expression As Connected with the Fine Arts*, 7th edn. (London: George Bell, 1877).
BL	Samuel Taylor Coleridge, *Biographia Literaria, or Biographical Sketches of My Literary Life and Opinions*, ed. James Engell and W. J. Bate, 2 vols. (Princeton University Press, 1983).
Essays	Charles Bell, *Essays on the Anatomy of Expression in Painting* (London: Longman, Hurst, Rees, and Orme, 1806).
FB	François Joseph Gall, *On the Functions of the Brain and of Each of Its Parts: With Observations on the Possibility of Determining the Instincts, Propensities, and Talents, or the Moral and Intellectual Dispositions of Men and Animals by the Configuration of the Brain and Head*, tr. Winslow Lewis, 6 vols. (Boston, MA: Marsh, Capen, and Lyon: 1835).
HW	William Hazlitt, *The Complete Works of William Hazlitt*, ed. P. P. Howe, 21 vols. (London, Dent: 1930–34).
JkL	John Keats, *The Letters of John Keats 1814–1821*, ed. Hyder Edward Rollins, 2 vols. (Cambridge: Harvard University Press, 1958).
JKNB	John Keats, *John Keats's Anatomical and Physiological Note Book*, ed. Maurice Buxton Forman (Oxford University Press, 1934).
LL	Samuel Taylor Coleridge, *Lectures 1808–19 on Literature*, ed. R. A. Foakes, 2 vols. (London and New York: Routledge & Kegan Paul, Princeton University Press, 1987).
LPZ	William Lawrence, *Lectures on Physiology, Zoology, and the Natural History of Man, Delivered to the Royal College of Surgeons* (London: Benbow, 1822).
Outlines	Johann Gottfried von Herder, *Outlines of the Philosophy of the History of Man*, trans. T. Churchill (1800; rpt. New York: Bergman, 1966).
P	J. G. Spurzheim, *Phrenology, or, The Doctrine of the Mind; and of the Relations Between Its Manifestations and the Body*, 3rd edn. (London: Charles Knight, 1825).

PS   J. G. Spurzheim, *The Physiognomical System of Drs. Gall and*
          Spurzheim; Founded on an Anatomical and Physiological Examination of
          the Nervous System in General, and of the Brain in Particular; and
          Indicating the Dispositions and Manifestations of the Mind, 2nd ed.
          (London: Baldwin, Cradock, and Joy, 1815).

R   Pierre-Jean-George Cabanis, *On the Relations Between the Physical*
          and Moral Aspects of Man, tr. Margaret Duggan Saidi, ed.
          George Mora, 2 vols. (Baltimore: Johns Hopkins University
          Press, 1981).

STCL   Samuel Taylor Coleridge, *Collected Letters of Samuel Taylor*
          Coleridge, ed. E. L. Griggs, 6 vols. (Oxford University Press,
          1956–71).

SW   Samuel Taylor Coleridge, *Shorter Works and Fragments*, ed. H. J.
          Jackson and J. R. de J. Jackson, 2 vols. (London and New York:
          Routledge & Kegan Paul, Princeton University Press, 1995).

TT   Samuel Taylor Coleridge, *Table Talk*, ed. Carl Woodring, 2 vols.
          (London and New York: Routledge & Kegan Paul, Princeton
          University Press, 1990).

WP   William Wordsworth, *The Prose Works of William Wordsworth*, ed.
          W. J. B. Owen and Jane Worthington Smyser, 3 vols. (Oxford:
          Clarendon Press, 1974).

Z Darwin, *Zoonomia: or, The Laws of Organic Life*, 2 vols. (London:
          J. Johnson, 1794–96).

Quotations from poems by Blake, Darwin, Keats, and Wordsworth, unless otherwise noted, follow these editions: *The Complete Poetry and Prose of William Blake*, ed. David Erdman, rev. edn. (Garden City: Anchor Press, 1982). *The Poetical Works of Erasmus Darwin, M.D., F.R.S.*, 3 vols. (London: J. Johnson, 1806). *The Poems of John Keats*, ed. Jack Stillinger (Cambridge: Harvard University Press, 1978). *William Wordsworth: The Poems*, ed. John O. Hayden, 2 vols. (Harmondsworth: Penguin, 1977) excluding the 1798 *Lyrical Ballads*, which follows *Wordsworth and Coleridge: Lyrical Ballads 1798*, ed. W. J. B. Owen, 2nd edn. (Oxford University Press, 1969) and *The Prelude*, which follows *The Prelude 1799, 1805, 1850*, ed. Jonathan Wordsworth, M. H. Abrams, and Stephen Gill (New York, Norton, 1979); 1805 is preferred unless 1799 is being explicitly discussed. Line numbers are given for quotations from longer poems only.

CHAPTER ONE

Introduction: neural Romanticism

This is a book about Romantic literary culture and the brain in Great Britain, from the 1790s to around 1830. It argues both that the pioneering neuroscience of the era manifests a "Romantic" character, and that literary Romanticism intersects in numerous and significant ways with the physiological psychology of the time. It aims, in short, to give the brain a central place in the history of the Romantic mind. But what, you may already be wondering, could the brain have to do with British Romanticism? To look at the relevant literary and cultural histories, not much. Fifty years ago one could publish a book reducing the psychological thought of the era to "the psychology of the association of ideas," Hartleyan associationism stripped of the neural substrate Hartley had welded to it.[1] Things are not much different now, although a half-century of psychoanalytically inspired literary analysis has piqued scholarly interest in Mesmerism and other Romantic-era anticipations of depth psychology.[2] Most work on the Romantic mind continues to be informed by a disembodied version of associationism, by psychoanalysis, or by epistemological issues that link Romantic literary figures to a philosophical tradition running from German idealism to phenomenology and its deconstruction.[3] The Romantic brain, however, has been left almost wholly out of account.

The history of science and medicine tells quite a different story. Historians of neuroscience, of biological psychology, and of neurology concur in viewing the late eighteenth and early nineteenth centuries as a crucial period for the emergence of an unprecedented series of hypotheses and discoveries concerning the brain and nervous system.[4] Only in the Romantic era, in fact, was the brain definitively established as the organ of thought, although this seemingly inevitable notion would continue to be challenged on religious and other grounds well into the 1820s. Equally important – and controversial – developments included the rise of comparative neuroanatomy, the framing of adaptationist and

I

functionalist analyses of specific features of the mind and brain, a fundamental redefinition of the brain as an assemblage of parts or "organs" rather than an undifferentiated whole, and anti-dualistic psychological models founded on the mind's embodiment, placing novel emphases on automatic and unconscious mental processes and on body–mind interaction. Sociological approaches to the history of brain science have only intensified interest in the period, detailing how widely disseminated, politically charged, and ideologically suspect were the new materialist and naturalistic models of mind in a period of revolution and reaction, when to challenge orthodox notions of the mind and soul meant implicitly to challenge the social order.[5] If the Romantic period can indeed be seen as an age of revolution, its iconoclastic brain science played a major role in the ideological ferment of the time.

Students of Romantic literature and culture have much to gain by looking to the era's revolutionary science of the mind, however underappreciated it has been to date. To begin with, no account of Romantic subjectivity can be complete without noting how contemporary understandings of psychology were either grounded in, deeply marked by, or tacitly (when not explicitly) opposed to the brain-based models of mind being developed concurrently in the medical sciences. Moreover, a whole range of topics and concerns typically associated with Romanticism – the relation of mind to body, the relation of human beings to the natural world, the new emphasis on human difference and individuality, the environmental role in shaping mind and behavior, the status of various materialist ideologies, even such staples as sensibility and the creative imagination – reveal unsuspected facets and interconnections when placed in the context of contemporary work on the brain and nerves. Exploring some of the many connections between the brain science and literary culture of the period in detail constitutes the main task of this book. This chapter will sketch out some of the more important figures and developments in Romantic-era brain science, particularly those most relevant to the literary culture of the time, and pose some fundamental links and working assumptions along the way.

THE RETURN OF THE BRAIN-MIND

It is no coincidence that the history of neuroscience has rediscovered the Romantic era at a time when biological approaches to psychology and materialist models of the mind have seen a major revival, from the "cognitive revolution" beginning in the 1950s to the recent "decade of the brain." A figure like F. J. Gall seems a good deal less quaint, his thought a good deal more intriguing, once a prominent cognitive scientist has proclaimed an "honored" place for Gall in the history of psychology – a sentiment that has become almost standard in popular expositions of recent neuroscience.[6] This is not to suggest, of course, that historians of medicine and psychology have been remaking the early history of brain science in the image of current research. The best studies exhibit an exemplary wariness of false parallels, forced connections, misplaced emphases, and imaginary lines of descent between then and now. But recent work on the brain has been instrumental in throwing Romantic-era developments into new relief and in restoring a certain cultural weight – one certainly felt widely at the time – to figures and ideas that had long seemed of antiquarian interest at best. As Anne Harrington has written, a "lively interest in the sciences of mind and brain in one's own era" does not license the use of history as a "vehicle to hunt for the present in an earlier age," but it may legitimately inspire a renewed interest in the "cognitive goals" of an earlier era's scientific culture.[7]

In relation to the Romantic era, recent work on the brain and mind can help scholars to perceive distinctions, register nuances, and appreciate moral and philosophical repercussions that might have seemed non-existent, elusive, or simply not worth pursuing a few decades ago. It can also help reveal how certain issues and questions hung together for Romantic-era writers, but not because these issues and questions are identical to those that have come to occupy cognitive scientists at the turn of the twentieth century. How could they be? Rather, the connections between, say, adaptationist accounts of mind and the hypothesis of a modular brain, or anti-dualistic cognitive theories and an emphasis on the unconscious and emotive aspects of rational thought, have returned in a different but comparable manner. I have not hestitated to point to such parallels and recurrences when they seem needful to sharpen the lineaments or convey the richness of an issue that might otherwise remain murky or undervalued. Indeed, I have become convinced that informed comparison with models, findings, and controversies from the present are needed to help bring certain Romantic-era developments and debates into focus. It is less a matter of insisting on resemblance than of listening for resonance, and allowing that resonance to help reopen avenues for scholarly investigation that have long remained untrodden.

Let me illustrate by quoting from a letter that Coleridge sent to Godwin in September of 1800:

I wish you to write a book on the power of words, and the process by which human feelings form affinities with them – in short, I wish you to *philosophize* Horne Tooke's System, and to solve the great Questions – whether there be reason to hold, that an action bearing all the *semblance* of pre-designing Consciousness may yet be simply organic, & whether a *series* of such actions are possible – and close on the heels of this question would follow the old "Is Logic the *Essence* of Thinking?" in other words – is *Thinking* impossible without arbitrary signs? & – how far is the word "arbitrary" a misnomer? Are not words &c part and germinations of the Plant? And what is the Law of their Growth? – In something of this order I would endeavor to destroy the old antithesis of *Words* and *Things*, elevating, as it were, words into Things, & living Things too. (*STCL* 1: 625–26)

Already "often-quoted" when William Keach analyzed it so tellingly in his essay "Words Are Things," Coleridge's letter has informed a great deal of important speculation on Romantic theories of language and on the difficulties of Coleridge's various theories of mind.[8] Until a few years ago, however, it remained difficult to fully appreciate the important links between the quite astounding series of tasks blithely set by Coleridge for Godwin and the "great Questions" being posed by the brain scientists of their day – questions that have again become prominent within the cognitive neuroscience of the past decade. Can a conscious act of volition be reduced, as the Churchlands, Crick, and others have argued, to organic brain activity at the neuronal level, and is it possible to theorize and empirically validate a working model of consciousness along such lines? Is the mind, as first-generation cognitive scientists proposed, best understood as a computational device and thinking as the processing of arbitrary symbolic representations? Is it, as cognitive linguists in both the Chomskian and Lakoffian traditions have suggested, misleading to call linguistic signs entirely "arbitrary"? What do models like Edelman's "neuronal group selection" theory tell us about how words and conceptual categories might be reconceived along organic and dynamic lines, and can neuroscience yield us rules for their development? And, to return to Coleridge's initial question, what does work like that of the Damasios on the role of the limbic system in linguistic production and comprehension reveal about the process by which human feelings form affinities with words?

At the risk of anachronism, I have tried to provoke a new sense of the interpretive possibilities for this letter, and by extension for Coleridge's thought on the mind and language more broadly, by updating his provocative series of questions in the language of recent neuroscience. My point is not to claim Coleridge as a poet-prophet of late twentieth-century work on the brain and mind, but rather to elicit several initial hunches from the consonance we can hear between his questions and ours. One is that these questions are linked for Coleridge by an "organic" or embodied notion of mind, however fitfully or anxiously he may have entertained it.[9] A second is that Coleridge here, as elsewhere, is more deeply engaged with the brain science of his era than has generally been acknowledged and is in this way representative of any number of writers we now call "Romantic." A third, perhaps the most important, is that noting how questions of language, volition, logic, organic development, and non-"arbitrary" elements of linguistic and cultural activity have become linked in recent cognitive science can help us to follow comparable links in the nascent psychology of Coleridge's day, while taking care to avoid simply conflating his era's science with our own. Language, free will, the connections among ideas, the organic development of the mind both in the human species and in each human individual, and the constraints that a shared physiology and anatomy might place on linguistic difference: these were all profoundly related issues for various Romantic-era thinkers. They had become closely intertwined through a whole set of postulates, theories, and research agendas that came to prominence in the work of a handful of influential writers on the brain-mind in the late eighteenth and early nineteenth centuries who collectively established the precedent for a biological psychology.

ROMANTICISM IN A NEUROSCIENTIFIC CONTEXT

The group of brain scientists whose work challenged and helped transform the psychological thinking of their time includes, most prominently, F. J. Gall in Austria, Pierre-Jean-George Cabanis in France, and Erasmus Darwin and Charles Bell in England. As particularly important popularizers of a brain-based psychology (especially for Great Britain) Sir William Lawrence, J. G. Spurzheim (Gall's errant disciple), and George Combe also demand new attention. And certain postulates and lines of investigation had been established earlier in the eighteenth century by David Hartley, Denis Diderot, Julien Offray de La Mettrie, and J. G. von Herder, among others. Significantly, all of the writers just mentioned, with the exception of Herder and Diderot, were medical doctors; all were committed to the biological account of the mind and its functioning that was becoming standard in medical education.[10] Although anything but a coherent movement – the list includes detractors as well as advocates of phrenology, vitalists as well as materialists, avowed skeptics and devout Christians – these doctors, philosophers, and proto-psychologists together altered the terms and changed the terrain for theorizing about the mind. Their work not only provided new directions for medical research, but helped fundamentally to recast the great questions on the mind in terms of new theoretical and scientific work on the brain.

From their varied writings one can abstract not a consensus but a constellation of roughly affiliated theoretical positions, each held by most of the Romantic-era figures, a few by all of them, but the whole set by no one thinker. There is enough overlap, however, that one can meaningfully group them together under the rubric of "Romantic psychologies," a shorthand expression I will use at times in relation to Darwin, Gall, Cabanis, Bell, and their associates, built though it is from two terms rarely used in their modern sense at the time.[11] All of them agree in locating the mind in the brain, the "cerebral organ" or organ of thought. They all emphasize that the mind is an active processor, rather than passive register, of experience, holding this in common with German idealist philosophy and with Scottish "common sense" psychology but uniquely seeking to elucidate the active mind in neurological terms.[12] Most posit the constant activity of the brain, even during sleep. They also share a biological rather than mechanistic conception of physiological and mental functioning, here (as in their active conception of mind) departing from Hartley and Locke (another doctor–philosopher important in the eighteenth-century background). They all stress the complexity of the brain, often envisioning it as a collection of "organs," and exhibit a cautious fascination with the role of electricity in neural transmission. Other common assumptions include the continuity between human beings and other animals (with a corresponding penchant for comparative anatomy and physiology), an ecological approach to studying humans in their natural and social environments, and a ruling interest in human development. This last broadens into a concern with the development of the human species, often giving rise to evolutionary or proto-evolutionary speculation and always involving adaptationist explanations for anatomical features and psychological functions, which in turn inspire a novel biological understanding of human universals. All develop anti-dualistic accounts of the brain-mind, though Bell does so in his own pious fashion, and all but Bell were attacked as "materialists," though only Lawrence willingly accepted the charge – until forced to recant.

A series of stunning scientific developments helped to fuel speculation on the brain and to inspire widespread fascination with the new biolog-

ical accounts of mind. Most important in establishing the new climate
was Galvani's demonstration of "animal electricity," which he described
in print first in 1791.[13] Although the criticism Galvani received from
Volta kept fellow scientists wary, it also kept his theory of electrical nerve
transmission, with its far-reaching implications for biological psychologies, in the public mind. As John F. W. Herschel wrote in his popular
Romantic-era exposition of science, with the "principle once established, that there exists in the animal economy a power of determining
the development of electric excitement, capable of being transmitted
along the nerves . . . it became an easy step after that to refer the origin
of muscular motion in the living brain to a similar cause; and look to the
brain, a wonderfully constituted organ, for which no mode of action
possessing the least plausibility had ever been devised, as the source of
the required electrical power."[14] Spurzheim's flair for publicity – including his popular neuroanatomy demonstrations – helped disseminate a
second important development, the pioneering brain dissection techniques that he and Gall had perfected in the 1780s and 1790s. Their anatomical methods and discoveries won praise even from their critics,
revealing neural structures in unprecedented clarity and complexity and
eventually finding their way into Hazlitt's art criticism and Keats's "Ode
to Psyche." A series of pathbreaking neurological discoveries included
Soemmerring's tracing of the cranial nerves in 1778, Vicq D'Azir's
description of the cerebral convolutions in 1786, and the roughly con-
temporaneous discovery, by Bell in England and Magendie in France, of
the basic distinction between sensory and motor nerves, first described
by Bell in a privately printed work of 1811. Neurological research and
speculation was carried out in the context of a distinctively international
scientific culture, one that seeped readily into the philosophical and literary discourses of the age. Not only national borders, but the equally
conventional boundaries between the sciences and the humanities,
between legitimate and "pseudo" science, and between intellectual and
popular culture all need to be bracketed in order to develop a feeling for
the intellectual climate of the Romantic era. It was a time when poets
(like Coleridge) consorted with laboratory scientists and when philosophical doctors (like Darwin) gave point to their scientific theories in
verse, when phrenology and mesmerism gained adherents across the
medical community, when Bell could work out his physiological psychology in a series of lectures to London artists, scientists could perform as
showmen, and Galvani's experiments with "animal electricity" could be
replicated by an eager public "wherever frogs were to be found."[15]

In suggesting that the cultural tendencies we associate with "Romanticism" bear a significant relation to speculation on the central nervous system, I am picking up the thread of an argument posed some years ago by G. S. Rousseau. In "Nerves, Spirits, and Fibres: Towards Defining the Origins of Sensibility," Rousseau located a paradigm shift in European accounts of mind – a "revolution in sensibility" – set in motion by the work of the seventeenth-century physiologist Thomas Willis, the "first scientist clearly and loudly to posit that the seat of the soul is strictly limited to the brain, nowhere else."[16] This "brain-nerve revolution," with its daring reduction of the "totality of human feeling" to "motion in the nerves," led, via the sensationalism of Locke (Willis's student at Oxford) and an ensuing succession of "cults of sensibility," at last to "that most puzzling of modern enigmas, Romanticism," now to be reconsidered in terms of its "specific neurological legacy."[17] Although scholars of Romanticism did not rush to take up his challenge, recent criticism has circled back to some of the connections Rousseau posited some thirty years ago. Isobel Armstrong, for example, suggests that the "speculations on the nervous system" of early nineteenth-century physiologists share with certain texts by Romantic-era women poets a model of sensibility as "action in the body" – "We must feel to think" as Letitia Landon puts it.[18] And Jerome McGann, in *The Poetics of Sensibility*, has described how writers from Locke to Priestley, from Montagu to Robinson, register in increasingly dramatic ways the "stakes involved in overturning the traditional understanding of the relations of mind and body."[19] Romantic-era developments in brain science, however, greatly intensified the revolution in understanding mind–body relations outlined by Rousseau, bringing Romantic writers into a productive (though not always explicit) creative and critical dialogue with the neuroscientific thinking of their time. Knowledge of these developments was readily available not only to literary figures like Coleridge (with his scientific connections), Joanna Baillie (born into a celebrated medical family), and John Keats (trained as a surgeon), but to a surprisingly wide and diverse audience. Male and female writers alike, of a broad stripe of ideological and philosophical allegiances, can often be found making common cause with contemporary speculation on the brain and nerves. Particularly in its association with materialism, however, brain science also inspired a good deal of hostility and anxiety, remaining open throughout the period not only to the embrace of literary writers but to their attacks as well.

A CHAOS OF ASSOCIATION: COLERIDGE, HARTLEY, AND THE CORPOREAL MIND

When Coleridge sets out to discredit a brain-based account of mind in the *Biographia Literaria*, he chooses as his foil not Gall or Darwin – though he had studied the ideas of both – but Hartley. This fits the narrative trajectory of Coleridge's literary autobiography nicely: Hartley's early attempt (often considered the first) to frame a physiological psychology is presented as a youthful intellectual infatuation that must be left behind for Coleridge's mature philosophy of mind to develop.[20] The extended attack on Hartley serves the polemical aims of the book just as well, however, by allowing Coleridge to evade the full weight of the challenge posed by contemporary biological accounts of mind while using the weaknesses of Hartley's dated materialist psychology to discredit any such speculation in advance. Hartley's theory of mind, and Coleridge's critique, together convey a good sense of the intellectual ground that Romantic psychologies would occupy, some of the major challenges they had to overcome, and the ideological stakes they would raise. In the *Observations* (1749) Hartley attempted no less than to explode post-Cartesian dualism and reground philosophy of mind in the brain and nervous system. Building on sensationalist and associationist principles derived from Hobbes and Locke, he attempted to reduce all mental functioning to the single principle of association. Drawing on hints in the second edition of Newton's *Principia* and in the works of early neurologists like Willis, he simultaneously proposed a material process of "vibrations" in the brain and nerves that undergirded the workings of association and provided a physiological explanation for psychological phenomena. "Motions" from the external environment, Hartley proposed, bombard the senses in such a way as to cause vibrations, which run along the "medullary substance" of the nerves, solid but porous cords with "infinitesimally small particles" of Newtonian ether diffused throughout. These vibrations or oscillations then trigger corresponding tiny vibrations ("vibratiuncles") in the medullary substance of the brain. (By "medullary substance" Hartley means what is now called the "white" or axonal matter of the brain, a common usage throughout the period.) Vibratiuncles could persist in the brain as "dispositions," particularly if reinforced directly (by repeated exposure to the sensory data) or indirectly (by association).[21]

Although Hartley claimed both that his theory could be reconciled with Scriptural authority and that the doctrine of vibrations was

ultimately expendable (viii, 416), he nevertheless speaks throughout the
work of the "corporeal" nature of thought and even posits a "material"
soul, pointing out that there is no necessary connection between the
soul's immortality and its immateriality (511–12). Like Diderot, La
Mettrie, and other eighteenth-century thinkers then widely considered
"materialists," Hartley argues for the material embodiment of the mind
in the brain, the "Organ of Organs" (62), pointing to the mental effects
of intoxicating substances like alcohol and opium, the relation between
neurological insults (like concussion) and disrupted mental functioning,
and citing more exotic phenomena like phantom limb pains that seemed
to demand a brain-based theory of mind (7–9, 32, 374). He anticipates
the anti-dualistic psychology of the Romantic era in stressing the importance of unconscious mental functioning and hinting at the salient role
of "internal" sensations (sensations from within the body) in mental life,
both areas all but entirely neglected within earlier accounts of associationism developed by Hobbes and Locke. Hartley touches as well on the
lessons to be learned from visual illusions (9–10) and the continuities
among the "nervous Systems of Animals of all Kinds," including human
beings (404), topics that will become standard in expositions of brain
science in the Romantic era (and in the present one). Throughout
Hartley advances what would now be termed a "medical model"
psychology, one aimed at securing the "common Consent of Physicians
and Philosophers" (33).

Coleridge had read the *Observations* in the 1790s with great enthusiasm,
naming his first son after Hartley and claiming (in a letter to Southey) to
"go farther than Hartley and believe the corporeality of *thought* – namely,
that it is motion" (*STCL* 1: 137). This was by no means an idiosyncratic
stance at the time, especially among the radical set that Coleridge ran
with. Coleridge's friend John Thelwall, for example, gave a lecture in
1793 on "The Origin of Sensation," purporting to explain the "phenomena of mind . . . upon principles *purely Physical*."[22] Priestley, in his 1775
and 1790 expositions of Hartley's thought, had jettisoned the vibration
theory not because he opposed materialist accounts of mind but because
he thought a better one was at hand, with the emergent dynamic conception of matter and the new physiology together suggesting a more
powerful model of thought as a "property of the *nervous system*, or rather
of the *brain*."[23] Galvani's electrophysiological experiments had suggested
a credible model of rapid neural transmission much superior to
Hartley's vague sense of (possibly electric) vibrations and oscillations,
and Darwin was updating key notions derived from Hartley and supple-

menting them with the new physiological research and biological thinking of the time in *Zoonomia* (1794–96).[24] Coleridge was in good company
in the 1790s in finding Hartley to have been right in principle but held
back by the limitations of his era's science. Within a few years, however,
Coleridge would begin turning from Locke and Hartley and, by 1817 in
the *Biographia*, would note with obvious satisfaction that "It is fashionable
to smile at Hartley's vibrations and vibratiuncles," with only the vaguest
reference to the more recent developments that might have been used to
buttress and update his belief in the corporeality of mind (*BL* 1: 110).
Hartley's theory, with its canny anticipation of Donald Hebb's "rever-
berating cell-assemblies" in "vibrations" and of "long-term potentia-
tion" in its brain "dispositions" seems less risible today, but for Coleridge
in 1817 the notion of a "disposition in a material nerve" had become patently "absurd" (*BL* 1: 109).[25] At best it was purely "hypothetical" (*BL* 1:
106) – a charge posed by Thomas Reid as well, who noted that the "infin-
itesimal particles of the brain and nerves" described by Hartley had to
be taken on faith, remaining well out of reach of the limited microscopes
then available.[26]

Some of Coleridge's criticisms hit harder, and pointed to the same
impasses in Hartley's theory that his Romantic-era heirs were attempting to move beyond. Hartley's system suffered, first, from the "passive"
and mechanical approach to perception and other mental acts that
limited associationist accounts generally; Hartley's formulations implied
a "senseless and passive memory," a cognitive process characterized by
"mere lawlessness."[27] Because Hartley, in Coleridge's view, saw the brain
as a complex but functionally undifferentiated organ (an understandable
but somewhat misleading reading of his theory), Coleridge argued that
it also would have no way of organizing perceptions and memories, no
way of successfully functioning, but would instead be characterized by a
"phantasmal chaos of association" (*BL* 1: 111, 116).[28] Because his commitment to sensationalism left Hartley with no recourse to innate faculties, it could not account for functions like willing and reasoning, neither
of which, Coleridge claimed, could be generated from a passive,
mechanical, and insufficiently differentiated process of association (*BL*
1: 128). These were fundamental flaws that would reduce mental functioning to a "blind mechanism" and leave the mind devoid of "distinct
powers" (*BL* 1: 116).

Coleridge also condemned Hartley on moral and ideological grounds,
advancing a series of related criticisms that would recur throughout the
Romantic period in attacks on Gall, on Lawrence, and on brain-based

psychology generally. For all Hartley's avowed (and undoubtedly sincere) piety, his system, in Coleridge's view, left no necessary function or identifiable locus for the soul, reducing it to a "mere ens logicum" and failing to account for the "imperishable" nature of human thought (*BL* 1: 114, 117). In its mechanistic and materialistic account of mental life, it left no room for the intervention of an "infinite spirit, an intelligent and holy will," no appeal to divine agency (*BL* 1: 120). Nor did it provide a convincing account of human agency or even of stable identity, implying that the conscious will would be constantly overridden by blindly working unconscious processes and ultimately exposing the conscious self as an illusion, the "poor worthless I" stripped down to physical relations of *"extension, motion, degrees of velocity,"* and their *"copies"* in the brain (*BL* 1: 90, 119). One readily begins to see how high indeed were the stakes of neuroscientific speculation in the era: no less than the existence of the soul, the necessity of God, and the integrity of the self were in question. This is the ground that Coleridge's theory of imagination would set out to reclaim, implicitly taking up the challenge posed by a resurgent physiological tradition in psychology building upon Hartley but moving beyond his mechanistic approach.

ERASMUS DARWIN AND THE ORGANIC MIND

On at least one major issue, Coleridge could have made common cause with the innovative brain science of his own time: the fundamental postulate of an "active" mind that "by perceiving, creates" the phenomenal world around it (*BL* 1: 118). Darwin had in fact advanced such a conception in 1794, meeting one of the major objections to Hartley's brain-based, associationist psychology head on. In the first volume of *Zoonomia*, dedicated to "all those who study the Operations of the Mind as a Science," Darwin begins by exhibiting the brain as an "active organ," functionally differentiated through its complex links with the various "sensory organs," internal as well as external (*Z* 1: 16). He demonstrates the active character of perception much as do popular works on neuroscience today, by confronting the reader with a series of visual illusions (inserting colored plates into the text for this purpose) that together suggest how much active – and unconscious – processing must take place for the brain to produce the images we consciously see. In addition to providing the means for a series of visual afterimage effects ("ocular spectra"), he invites the reader to experience a related illusion by spinning around until dizzy, and then noticing how the "spectra of the ambient objects continue to present themselves in rotation" (Z 1: 20) due to the brain's briefly continuing efforts to compensate for the body's movement. Wordsworth, another proponent of the active mind, might well have found something familiar in these perceptual experiments when he, like Coleridge, read *Zoonomia* in the 1790s. He describes a related practice of his own in *The Prelude*, when he would skate rapidly and then suddenly stop short to watch the "sweeping" scenery on either side continue to "wheel" by, "even as if the earth had rolled / With visible motion her diurnal round" (1: 481–86). Such self-experiments, along with more exotic phenomena like phantom limb pains, demonstrate for Darwin that "all our ideas are excited in the brain, and not in the organs of the sense" (Z 1: 28), although our sense organs are crucial in gathering and translating sensory data into cognizable information. Because the brain receives not "mechanical" impressions (as in Hartley and earlier associationist psychology) but actively processes "animal motions or configurations of our organs of sense," it is subject neither to the "lawlessness" nor the "chaos of association" that Coleridge saw as inherent in Hartley's theory. Percepts do not flow directly into sensory channels to be automatically processed, but are gathered and translated into various kinds of "sensory motions" (neural impulses) by highly specialized organs to be selected and arranged and further transformed by a dynamic and functionally designed brain.

The brain is intimately connected not only to the sensory organs, however, but to the body as a whole via the nervous system. Darwin sees the mind as fundamentally embodied, a *"sensorium"* denoting "not only the medullary part of the brain, spinal marrow, nerves, organs of sense, and of the muscles; but also at the same time that living principle, or spirit of animation, which resides throughout the body, without being cognizable to our senses, except by its effects" (Z 1: 10). This "spirit of animation" is made not of transcendental mind-stuff but of "matter of a finer kind" that we "possess in common with brutes" (Z 1: 109), analogous to electricity or magnetism and perhaps an "electric fluid" as Galvani's researches had suggested (Z 1: 64, 10).[29] Indivisible from the sensorium through which it flows, the spirit of animation is a bodily energy expressed in the four primary "sensorial powers" of irritation, sensation, volition, and association. Its materiality, its habitation in the brain and nervous system, and its functional differentiation (demonstrated by visual illusions and the like) keyed to various bodily organs breaks down the distinction between body and mind. Ideas are not immaterial, immutable entities (as Coleridge insists in the *Biographia*) but "animal motions of the organs of sense" processed in the brain. Because mind and body interpenetrate one another, ideas are in turn manifested bodily, as in heart palpitations from fear, salivating at the sight of food, or the "glow of skin in those who are ashamed" (Z 1: 23, 39).

This intimate connection between the brain-mind and organs such as the stomach, the heart, and the skin works in both directions. The mind receives "sensory motions" not only from the organs attuned to the external world, but from organs located *within* the body as well. Darwin's discussion of the senses therefore includes the internal senses or "appetites": hunger, thirst, the "want of fresh Air, animal Love, and the Suckling of children" (Z 1: 124–25). The behaviors generated by these "appetites" are not instinctive, but rather a matter of habit (*"repeated efforts of our muscles under the conduct of our sensations or volitions"*); however, the *"sensations or desires"* that ultimately drive those behaviors are *"natural or connate"* (Z 1: 136–39). Despite his debt to Hartley in particular (largely unacknowledged but evident throughout the book) and to the Lockean tradition in general, Darwin here departs from Locke in several important ways: by granting a salient role to the *internal* senses, by the opening thus made to *innate* desires with a profound (though not direct) effect on behavior, and by a related emphasis on *unconscious* mental processes guided by habit and "natural" desire. These ideas are not incompatible with sensationalist psychology and in fact comprise key aspects of David Hume's critique of Locke from within sensationalist and associationist principles. Darwin's revision of the Lockean tradition differs significantly, however, in its physiological and organic commitments and in the optimistic rather than skeptical attitude with which Darwin regards the mind's literal incarnation in the body.

Darwin's equanimity regarding the mind's corporeality, its subjection to *"connate"* desires, and indeed its success in organizing the flow of sensory data into a reasonable approximation of the external world all stem from his embrace of an adaptationist and evolutionary view of nature. "Our senses are not given us to discover the essences of things," he writes, quoting Malebranche, "but to acquaint us with the means of preserving our existence" (Z 1: 108). But who gave us our senses? An evolutionary process reaching back to the beginnings of life and guided by the "general efforts of nature to provide for the continuation of her species of animals" (Z 1: 485), relying both on sexual reproduction (which weeds out harmful traits) and on Lamarckian-style inheritance (which preserves helpful ones) (Z 1: 480). All living forms, he writes in *The Temple of Nature* (1802), "Arose from rudiments of form and sense / An embryon point, or microscopic ens" (Canto 1: 13–14). Unlike mechanical creatures ("Self-moving Engines"), the robots of their time, which can function but not adapt, living animals improve over the ages: "Each new Descendant with superior powers / Of sense and motion speeds the transient hours" (Canto II: 21, 33–34). Grafting (asexual reproduction) and inbreeding, in their failure to weed out "hereditary" diseases, underscore the virtue of "connubial powers"; the poem proceeds to hail the "DEITIES OF SEXUAL LOVE" and its presiding genius is Eros (Canto II: 175–80, 244). Charles Darwin would minimize the intellectual debt he owed to his grandfather (whose evolutionary theory seems crude enough by comparison), but there is no doubt that the elder Darwin's science of mind was undergirded by his sketchy notions of inheritance and adaptation. Guided by the "firm immutable immortal laws" of nature, "Organic Life began beneath the waves" and embarked on a gradual, inevitable course of improvement (Canto I: 234). It is this natural process, not some divine fiat, that ultimately produced the marvels of human cogntion: "the fine nerve to move and feel assign'd, / Contractile fibre, and etherial mind" (Canto I: 217–18).

Darwin's answer to the problem of mental function and design, then, was a materialist one, or at least one thoroughly compatible with materialism, and it was attacked as such. Although Darwin had prudently begun *Zoonomia* by stating his belief in "two essences or substances," spirit and matter (Z I: 5), his theory of mind struck contemporaries as unorthodox, materialistic, and all too much in keeping with his other avant-garde and radical views, duly pilloried by the *Anti-Jacobin* in "The Loves of the Triangles" in 1798.[30] Thomas Brown's critical *Observations on the Zoonomia of Erasmus Darwin, M.D.*, published the same year, was more genteel, even collegial, in tone, yet still arraigned Darwin's system as "materialist" in tendency, opposed to the author's (and the establishment's) "mentalist" allegiances.[31] The Church and King riots of 1791, in which a "loyalist" mob had invaded Priestley's home and destroyed his scientific equipment, had demonstrated a connection even in the popular mind between political radicalism and unorthodox science at the very beginning of the period of anti-jacobin reaction. By the early nineteenth century, any theory that "so much as hinted" that the mind arose from "corporeal organization" was branded as "atheistical and politically subversive," in other words, "French-inspired."[32] Darwin's psychological views had accompanied him into dangerous ideological territory, and his reputation suffered greatly as a result.[33]

Darwin's response to some of the other problems that Coleridge identified in Hartley was no less distasteful to orthodox sensibilities. Human identity ("the poor, worthless I") consists not in divinely vouchsafed consciousness of self but in the sum of our unconscious sensations and routinized behaviors, "our acquired habits or catenated trains of ideas and muscular motions" (Z 1: 133). The fundamentally embodied nature of the mind also gives rise to our sense of location in the world and of its substantiality, literally fleshing out our sense of personal identity. "The medulla of the brain and nerves has a certain figure; which, as it is diffused through nearly the whole of the body, must have nearly the same figure of that body" (Z 1: 111). This "figure" and our lived experience of it forms our primary cognitive reference point for abstractions like solidity and motion, time and place, space and number; because the mind is known only in and through the body, the body informs the basic categories of perception and cognition.[34] In both *Zoonomia* and *The Temple of Nature* the will, which (as Coleridge argued) Hartley had failed to rescue from an avowedly mechanistic psychology, also finds its ground in the dynamic unity of body, nerves, and brain. Volition for Darwin, however, can be unconscious and episodic rather than the exertion of a unified conscious subject:

> Next the long nerves unite their silver train
> And young SENSATION permeates the brain;
> Through each new sense the keen emotions dart,
> Flush the young cheek, and swell the throbbing heart.
> From pain and pleasure quick VOLITIONS rise,
> Lift the strong arm, or point the inquiring eyes.   (Canto II: 269–74)

Keats would do this sort of thing better. But Darwin's poem on the adapted, organic, nervous, embodied mind and the "origin of society" made some of the key ideas of *Zoonomia* accessible to at least the avant-garde segment of the poetry-reading public. As Darwin's seemingly materialist and vaguely French-sounding ideas became increasingly suspect, however, in the period of "anti-Jacobin" reaction and conservative retrenchment, naturalistic, brain-based accounts of mind began to take on a radical, even sinister cast. This could not have been helped by the independent development of a compatible theory of mind by Cabanis, one of the French "Ideologues" and a prominent supporter of the French Revolution.

CABANIS: SENSIBILITY AND THE EMBODIED MIND

Cabanis, like Darwin, had been schooled in the fine points of sensationalist and associationist philosophy, particularly as developed by

Condillac. He drew equally, however, on a French anti-dualist tradition, exemplified by Diderot, La Mettrie, and the Montparnasse physicians, that located the mind in the body and sought the explanation for its "wonderful and incomprehensible" abilities not in an intangible soul but in the "specific organisation of the brain and of the whole body."[35] His major work, *On the Relations Between the Physical and Moral Aspects of Man* (*Rapports du physique et du moral de l'homme*), was read to the Revolutionary Institute in 1796–97 and published in 1798, with six further "memoirs" added in 1802. Cabanis, long unavailable in English, was not well known to the first generation of British Romantic writers, though a faithful sketch of his most important ideas had been published as early as 1801 in the *Monthly Review*. (The reviewer, no doubt thinking of Darwin in particular, remarks that few of Cabanis' arguments and views "will be new to those who have studied the writings of the English material-ists.")[36] Cabanis would become an important source for Percy Shelley in the 1810s and his ideas would eventually reach a wide British public through William Lawrence's notorious lectures on physiology and the "natural history of man." Working independently, but from many of the same sources and with similar aims in mind, Cabanis developed a physiological psychology that overlapped significantly with that of Darwin.[37] The "First Memoir" begins, in fact, as does *Zoonomia*, by stressing the centrality of the "cerebral organ" as an active processor, rather than passive register, of sensory data (*R* 1: 50), a position that puts Cabanis at odds with Condillac and links him instead to Darwin, Gall, and the Romantic poets.

Cabanis' most famous (or infamous) statement, in fact, that the brain "digests" impressions as the stomach digests food, is not the reductive analogy it was sometimes taken for, but rather makes part of his attempt to convey the active, complex, organic character of the brain-mind. The brain is the product of natural and adaptive (but not evolutionary) design, a "special organ designed to produce thought" as the "stomach and intestines are designed to operate the digestion" (*R* 1: 116). Cabanis' inability to explain just how the brain accomplishes its task does not demand reference to an immaterial principle, since important aspects of digestion remain mysterious as well. Thinking will eventually be under-stood, however, as a complex and dynamic organic process rather than the passive and mechanical one implied by Condillac. "We also see the impressions arrive at the brain, through the nerves; they are then isolated and without coherence. The organ enters into action; it acts on them, and soon it sends them back changed into ideas, which the language of physiognomy and gesture, or the signs of speech and writing, manifest outwardly. We conclude, with the same certainty, that the brain digests, as it were, the impressions, that is, that organically it makes the secretion of thought" (*R* 1: 117). Mind is not a thing apart but rather an expression of the "continuous activity" of the brain and nervous system, and cognitive performance can be altered by material substances like narcotics and alcohol or disrupted by brain lesions and other neurological insults (*R* 1: 96, 129, 138).

As it does for Darwin, however, the brain for Cabanis forms the center of a neural system dispersed throughout the body. In place of Darwin's notion of the "sensorium," Cabanis develops the analogous one of "sensibility," a physical process (probably linked to "galvanism" or animal electricity) that "radiates" from the brain, "unceasingly traversing the nervous system" (*R* 1: 277, *R* 2: 547, 553). Sensibility is not limited to what we receive from the senses attuned to the external world (as in Locke and Condillac) but also involves "impressions received in the internal organs" (*R* 1: 92). The internal impressions remain largely unconscious, although they have an "extensive" (and usually unnoticed) effect on cognition (*R* 2: 568). The internal organs are instrumental in stimulating and modifying instinctive "tastes, inclinations, desires" (*R* 1: 101) that can be witnessed already in newborns and that "undoubtedly are engraved in the cerebral system at the very moment of the formation of the fetus" (*R* 2: 580). Wondering how the stomach or the "genital organs" can "transmit, or contribute to awakening" these innate inclinations, Cabanis leaves a space for what would eventually be called the neuroendocrine system, though to him, of course, it remains mysterious, a pressing subject for "physiology and medicine" to pursue (*R* 1: 98). He can state with certainty, however, that the prevalence of unconscious and instinctive processes in mental life is "extremely favourable to the preservation and well-being of animals," including human beings. "Nature has exclusively reserved for herself the most complicated, the most delicate and the most necessary operations" (*R* 1: 98). Nurture is given a significant role in human development, but bodily self-regulation, nutrition, basic defenses, and propagation are too important to be left entirely or even mainly to socialization.

The mind is no less fundamentally embodied for Cabanis than for Darwin. Criticizing the mechanistic assumptions behind Condillac's supposition of an animated statue (a kind of thinking machine) to analyze distinct sensory impressions, Cabanis stresses instead both the embodied character of human cognition and its gradual development in a living, desiring being. "How could these various operations be executed without the organs whose special action or cooperation is essential to the production of the simplest sensitive act, of the vaguest intellectual combination and desire, [or] be developed by degrees, unless they had already, by that sequence of movements that nascent life impresses on them, acquired the type of progressive instruction that alone makes them fit to fulfill their proper functions and to associate their efforts by directing them toward the common goal" (*R* 2: 568). Cognitive activities like perception and reason are adaptively shaped and constantly modified by innate inclinations (like the instinct for self-preservation), visceral feelings, and routinized behaviors: "How could the habits of the entire sensitive system, those of the internal organs or of the other main organs, and the nature of their sympathies with the cerebral center, remain foreign to that chain of coordinated and delicate movements that takes place within it for the formation of thought?" (*R* 2: 570).[38] Cabanis also agrees with Darwin in grounding identity in the body, distinguishing the sensibility from the *conscious* subject or "MOI." The MOI resides in a "common center" where all sensations, including internal ones, converge, but it lacks access to many of those sensations. In this way autonomic functions may "very sensibly and quickly" modify one's "entire realm of ideas and emotions" in the absence of any explicit awareness, and emotions and "unperceived judgments" can color ideas and thought processes via the body's silent pathways to the brain (*R* 2: 547–8, 551, 590). Descartes was wrong in separating mind from body, reason from emotion, and in grounding identity on thought and not sensibility. "From the moment at which we feel, we are" (*R* 1: 51).

GALL'S ORGANOLOGY

Gall shared a good deal of common ground with Cabanis, as Gall himself notes in his later works (*FB* 1: 111, 2: 20).[39] His own version of a brain-based psychology or "organology," however, was developed independently in the 1780s and 1790s. Gall was struck already in adolescence by the different character types and cognitive strengths among his schoolmates, despite commonalities in education and social class. He became convinced that innate dispositions and propensities, rooted in the specific organization of the brain, accounted in large part for differences among human beings, while at the same time accounting for the basic "uniformity" of human nature found across cultures and throughout history (*FB* 1: 148). In Herder Gall found the outlines of an "*organic*"

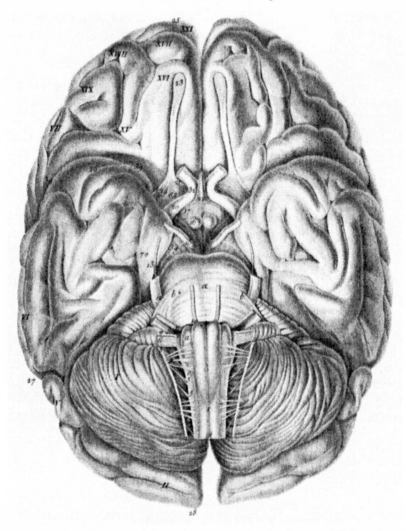

1 F. J. Gall and J. G. Spurzheim, *Atlas* accompanying the "large work," *Anatomie et Physiologie du Système nerveux en général* (Paris, 1810), plate IV (ventral surface).

approach to the mind, a defense of instinctive and unconsciously motivated behavior, an affirmation of the continuity between humans and other animals, and a recourse to comparative physiology and neuroanatomy for tracing the "various evolutions and changes" that culminated in the "*structure of the brain*" and the "*elaboration* of its parts," Nature's finest work (*Outlines* ix, 8, 76). But whereas Herder gives a primary role in mental life to the soul, acting "conformably to her organs, and in harmony with them," but according to her own *"psychological laws"* (*Outlines* 117–18), Gall's psychology is thoroughly materialistic. For Gall, the brain is the "source of all perception, the seat of every instinct, of every propensity, of all power, moral and intellectual" (*FB* 1: 73–4). If there is an immortal soul (Gall claims that his research has no bearing on the question), "every thing indicates" that in this life, from conception to the last breath, the "soul is in dependence on the material organs" and the distinction between mind and body is an artificial and misleading one (*FB* 1: 88).

What most distinguishes Gall from Cabanis and Darwin (and what triggered the Gall revival in recent years) is his greater emphasis on the complexity of the brain, envisioned not as a single organ but "an assemblage of particular organs" with distinct functions and discrete anatomical locations (*FB* 1: 92). The brain's complex organization accounts, better than could any *"tabula rasa"* model (*FB* 1: 95), for its ability to construct a coherent object world; purely sensationalist psychologies imply a passive, mechanistic mind at the mercy of "external fortuitous and versatile objects" rather than one that can organize and successfully negotiate a human-scaled world from the givens of sensory data (*FB* 1: 109).[40] Like Cabanis, Gall stresses the importance of "interior sensations" as well, linking them to the pervasive role of *"instinctive tendencies"* in cognition and behavior (*FB* 1: 111). These too are actively (though unconsciously) constructed and interpreted by various brain organs, and different mental "dispositions" are "transmitted from family to family" along with distinctive types of brain "organization" (*FB* 1: 185). The organic, ultimately hereditary character of mental differences can also be witnessed in development, as various capacities, bents, and desires emerge at discrete periods of life keyed to the development of the brain and nervous system (*FB* 1: 174). Despite differences (including selective differences between the sexes), however, the "new physiology of the brain" (*FB* 2: 83) also explains why all human beings "in all countries and in every age, have essentially the same propensities and the same faculties," as all human brains, if not "naturally defective," exhibit the "same parts and the same principal convolutions" (*FB* 2: 113).

Brain functions cannot, however, be explicated apart from the entire bodily system, and Gall's notion of the self is, as in Darwin and Cabanis, an essentially embodied one. "Life, *moi*, consciousness of the existence of the world, begins with sensation, with the nervous apparatus. When the individual perceives, that it is distinct from surrounding things, it has

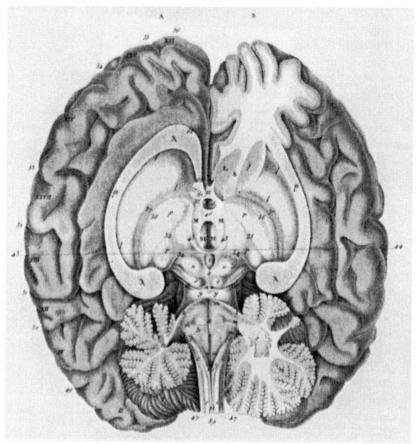

2 Gall and Spurzheim, *Atlas*, plate VI (midline dissection).

a *moi* whose capacity will be in proportion to the variety and intensity of its sensations; and consequently, to the number and energy of the organs of internal sensibility and external relations" (*FB* 1: 288). The mind, brain, and body make up a single system and mind-body reciprocity is the rule rather than the exception. This very integration, however, undermines the stability of the self or *moi*, which changes over time along with changes in the body and its brain (*FB* 3: 76). Being material, the mind is readily affected by opiates and other narcotic substances, by lesions and concussions, by diseases that reach the brain; certain lesions can even result in the experience of two distinct selves (*FB* 2: 164) and mental illness generally can be attributed to brain disfunction (*FB* 2: 122–4). The large (and adaptive) role of innate, largely unconscious drives in mental life undermines any clear distinction between will and instinct, or any absolute gap between human beings and their fellow animals (*FB* 6: 259).[41] If opponents to a brain-based psychology were looking for ideological ammunition, they could readily find it in Gall.

RADICAL BRAIN SCIENCE: FROM GALL TO LAWRENCE

They did find it, and more. Gall made a particularly tempting subject for attack thanks to his conviction that the various brain organs he hypothesized would manifest their differences in prominence (or degree of development) through corresponding differences in the shape of the skull; hence his science of craniology, popularized by Spurzheim and others as phrenology. Even the contemporary brain scientists who accepted Gall's general approach to the "physiology of the brain" and who acknowledged his anatomical discoveries and the superiority of his dissection techniques tended to dismiss his "organology," as Gall himself pointed out (*FB* 3: 66). His system was readily open to critique, even ridicule, on three main points: the notion that the skull would "conform" to the brain in a predictable and demonstrable manner; the functional division of the brain into precisely twenty-seven discrete "organs" that seemed both ill-assorted (there is one for self-preservation and one for poetry) and arbitrarily chosen; and his insistence on precise, bounded anatomical locations for each. Worse, Gall and Spurzheim were transparently lacking in empirical rigor when adducing various proofs of the cranial manifestation of one or another organ. This despite their claim to "neither deny nor affirm anything which cannot be verified by experiment," an irony that was not lost on their reviewers (*PS* 250).

Gall's theories were widely discussed in the contemporary journals, nearly always critically, often with a tone of mockery. By 1826 Francis Jeffrey could begin a typically dismissive account (in *The Edinburgh Review*) by remarking that "Every one, of course, has heard of Dr. Gall's Craniology."[42] Thanks, in part, to the *Edinburgh Review* itself, which had devoted long critical articles to Gall and Spurzheim already in 1803 ("of Dr. Gall, and his skulls, who has not heard?") and again in 1815.[43] The *Quarterly Review* took on phrenology in 1815 as did the *Monthly Review* in 1808, 1815, and 1821.[44] *Blackwood's* devoted an article in its first issue (1817) to lambasting the "new system" of Gall and Spurzheim (already "very fully detailed and discussed in all the literary journals of this country"), and returned to the attack in 1819, twice in 1821, and twice again in 1823.[45] This is just a sample.[46] But if Gall and Spurzheim's system was simply a farrago of "exaggerated and dogmatical assertions" as Hazlitt (who contributed three critiques of his own) insisted in *The Plain Speaker* of 1826, why did the most influential reviews of the day continue to attack it, rather than dismissing it once and for all (*HW* 12: 139)?[17]

Hazlitt provides one answer in pointing to the absence of a "superintending or *conscious* faculty or principle" in phrenological theory, of a "rational and moral agent," an integral and executive "I" rather than the fragmented, unstable, largely unconscious "*moi*" of Gall and Spurzheim (*HW* 12: 150–51). This recalls Coleridge's principal criticism of Hartley; although Hazlitt's answer is not a transcendental, divinely supported ego but a "general faculty modified by experience," he still insists that "the mind is one" (*HW* 12: 143). Jeffrey similarly holds that the mind is "one and indivisible" and, unlike Hazlitt, argues extensively against the notion that mental operations could be "unconscious" and the faculties or organs that perform them unavailable to introspection (256, 261). The "whole brain" may rightly be called the "organ of the whole mind" (though Jeffrey, true to his age, considers the "whole body" a better candidate), yet the mind cannot be reduced to the action of "material organs" (257, 261). The *Quarterly Review* insists on the "single and indivisible" nature of the mind as well, while rejecting any reduction of mind to the brain and nervous system, and an 1815 review in the *Edinburgh* argues that there is no proof that the "brain *is* the organ of intellect" and takes particular umbrage at Gall's doctrine of "innate and determinate" mental functions and faculties.[48]

The attacks on Gall and Spurzheim reignited the furor over materialistic theories of mind that had met Priestley and Darwin in the 1790s, again linking brain science to political subversion. Critics of phrenology often cited the dubious precedent of Darwin's corporeal psychology and evolutionary theory, as in an 1826 pamphlet consigning Gall to the "fungus school" of Hartley and Darwin.[49] Renewed opposition to materialism, the defense of the conscious and "superintending" ego, and the affirmation of a quasi-divine ("one and indivisible") mind, reveal a significant area of ideological consensus among reviewers who generally take opposite political positions, liberals like Hazlitt and Jeffrey for once finding common cause with the conservative writers for *Blackwood's* and the *Quarterly*. The establishment consensus asserts itself most vocally in the public hounding of Lawrence, whose openly materialist doctrines were seen as both dangerously subversive and brazenly outspoken. When Jeffrey, in the 1826 review, equates the rhetorical style of Gall and

Spurzheim with that of radicals like Cobbett and Owen, the comparison is neither incidental nor ideologically neutral (281). It demonstrates, rather, that in the wake of the Lawrence controversy, an association between brain-based psychology and radical ideologies could again be taken for granted in the mind of the common reader.

Lawrence has received attention of late as the friend (and physician) of the Shelleys, a member of the Godwin circle, the chief "materialist" in the early nineteenth-century materialist–vitalist debates, and, as Marilyn Butler has shown, a "household name" by 1820 as a proponent of "radical science" vaguely but ominously linked with libertine poets and political agitators.[50] Scholarship has yet to note, however, the extent to which Lawrence's perceived threat to the social order was bound up with his views regarding the brain. If some pamphleteers stressed his politics – *The Radical Triumvarite; or, Infidel Paine, Lord Byron, and Surgeon Lawrence, colleaguing with the Patriotic Radicals to emancipate mankind from all laws, human and divine* – others attacked him more squarely on psychological grounds: *Thought, not a function of the brain: a reply to the arguments for materialism advanced by W. Lawrence, in his Lectures on physiology.*[51] Lawrence's lectures on comparative anatomy and on "life," delivered to the Royal College of Surgeons in March of 1816 and published later that year, attempted to wrest John Hunter's legacy from those who, like John Abernethy, would use it to reconcile the new physiology with orthodox religious conceptions of an immaterial soul. For Abernethy, Hunter's speculations on life implied an immaterial, or at least supersensible, "vital" force that distinguished living from nonliving beings and provided the ultimate energy for physiological and mental functions alike. Lawrence, to the contrary, argued that Hunter's work taught that the "functions are an offspring of the structure – or the life is the result of the organization." A key issue, then, would be to argue the dependence of thought, traditionally associated with the transcendent mind or immaterial soul, on the organization of the brain.[52]

The title of Lawrence's augmented series of lectures, published in 1819, already suggests his debt to the new science of the mind: *Lectures on Physiology, Zoology, and the Natural History of Man*. Human beings are continuous with the other animals; not only are comparative anatomy and physiology needful for understanding human psychology, but "man" is properly approached as an "object of zoology" (*LPZ* 103). All nature is a "great system of organisation" and man, as a fully "natural" creature, must be understood ecologically in terms of his relation to the physical as well as social environment around him, and zoologically in terms of

the commonalities between his organization and that of like animals.
Though man, for Lawrence, is not a primate, he is closest to the
"monkey race" in design and much could be learned about human
beings from studying monkeys, especially apes (*LPZ* 110, 114). Indeed, the
reasoning abilities readily seen in other animals suggests that if the
human mind relies on an "immaterial principle," so does the animal
mind; a more elegant theory would instead regard the "phenomena of
mind . . . physiologically merely as the functions of the organic apparatus contained in the head" (*LPZ* 95–96, 164). The lessons of human
development and the "hereditary transmission" of "moral" as well as
physical qualities lead to the same conclusion (*LPZ* 397), as do the well-
known effects of head injuries and the "material organic" causes of
insanity (*LPZ* 6, 98).

In arguing for the material basis of mind Lawrence draws heavily,
though for the most part tacitly, on both Cabanis and Gall. Other ideas
are taken over from Darwin, though Lawrence's rejection of the vague
"electro-chemical" character of Abernethy's vital force would seem to
apply equally to Darwin's "sensorial" fluid or Cabanis' analogous conception of "sensibility" (*LPZ* 11). Lawrence does, however, adopt
Cabanis's most notorious analogy for thought: "There is no digestion
without an alimentary cavity; no secretion without some kind of liver;
no thought without a brain" (*LPZ* 53). Moreover, he counters the tradition of charging Cabanis with gross reductionism by correctly spelling
out the point of the analogy. "Shall I be told that thought is inconsistent
with matter; that we cannot conceive how medullary substance can perceive, remember, judge, reason? I acknowledge that we are entirely
ignorant how the parts of the brain accomplish these purposes – as we
are how the liver secretes bile, how the muscles contract, or how any
other living purpose is effected" (*LPZ* 91). There is nothing unique, as
Cabanis had argued, about the inability to give a complete physiological account of cognition. But the evidence of recent advances in neuroanatomy and physiology would suggest, at the same time, that the brain,
in its complexity, its newly apparent division into functionally distinct
"parts," its privileged relations with the rest of the body, and its eminently protected situation, was more than capable of performing its
function without the aid of an occult "immaterial substance" (*LPZ* 92).
Dualistic accounts reveal an almost comic ignorance of the new anatomical, physiological, and adaptationist work on the brain. "This large
and curious structure, which, in the human subject, receives one fifth of
all the blood sent out from the heart, which is so peculiarly and delicately

organised, nicely enveloped in successive membranes, and securely lodged in a solid bony case, is left almost without an office, being barely allowed to be capable of sensation. It has, indeed, the easiest lot in the animal economy: it is better fed, clothed, and lodged than any other part, and has less to do" (*LPZ* 92).

Correlations between brain development and psychological growth, another important element of the new brain science of the 1790s, gives Lawrence (a witty as well as fearless polemicist) further ammunition. "Examine the mind, the grand prerogative of man. Where is the mind of the fetus? Where that of the child just born? Do we not see it actually built up before our eyes, by the action of the five external senses, and of the gradually developed internal faculties? Do we not trace it advancing by a slow progress through infancy and childhood, to the perfect expression of its faculties in the adult; – annihilated for a time by a blow upon the head, or the shedding of a little blood in apoplexy; – decaying as the body declines in old age" (*LPZ* 6). Like his reference to the complex organization and "parts" of the brain, Lawrence's balancing of the external senses with their "internal" counterparts and his emphasis on organic development reveals how dated the mechanistic, sensationalist psychology of eighteenth-century associationism had become within the London medical community. Indeed, thanks to Darwin, to the phrenology movement, and to Lawrence himself, mechanistic approaches to psychology were becoming dated in the intellectual world at large. Lawrence again bears witness to the new "biology" of mind (he is among the first English writers to use the term) in his rejection of the "sensorium commune" that Coleridge had shown to be problematic in Hartley's psychology. "Physiologists have been much perplexed to find out a common centre in the nervous system, in which all sensations may meet, and from which all acts of volition may emanate; a central apartment for the superintendent of the human *panopticon*; or, in its imposing Latin name, a *sensorium commune*. That there must be such a point they are well convinced, having satisfied themselves that the human mind is simple and indivisible, and therefore capable of dwelling only in one place . . . this assumed unity of the sentient principle becomes very doubtful, when we see other animals, possessed of nervous systems, which, after being cut in two, form again two perfect animals. Is the immaterial principle divided by the knife, as well as the body?" (*LPZ* 77)

Lawrence's pointed alignment of the central, executive self with the overseer of Bentham's idealized disciplinary institution – a connection he poses a good century and a half before Foucault – marks only the

most striking of the many explicitly political passages scattered throughout the *Lectures*. Lawrence contrasts the relative freedom of thought in
America with the reactionary, post-Waterloo climate in Europe, a time
of "combinations, or conspiracies of the mighty, which threaten to
convert Europe into one great state prison" (*LPZ* 33) – presumably to be
managed on panoptical principles. The triumph of a naturalistic
psychology will accompany an era of the "complete emancipation of
mind: the destruction of all creeds and articles of faith; and the establishment of full freedom of thought and belief" (*LPZ* 84). These were
words not to be taken lightly in the England of 1819. The *Quarterly Review*
moved swiftly to attack Lawrence's "open avowal" of "materialism,"
made as it was in the "British empire, in lectures delivered under public
authority."[53] Lawrence is targeted as the popularizer he was, a "mere
copyist" from the "free-thinking physiologists of the German school"
and their Gallic counterparts, the "French physiologico-sceptical
school" (4, 8), with a dash of "Dr. Darwin" to boot (14). Among the
"fearful" doctrines being promulgated in the medical heart of the
empire, the review singles out the assertion, "as if it were a known and
acknowledged truth," that "'*medullary substance* is capable of sensation
and of thought'" (3), that man is "only a superior kind of brute, an
ourang-outang or ape" with "more 'ample cerebral hemispheres'" (27,
30). Suggesting that early developmental accounts of mind, now often
seen as "disciplinary" and normative in tendency, could at the time seem
downright subversive, the reviewer complains that for Lawrenece the
mind is gradually "*built up*" and not an "immaterial," "original part of
the human being" (17).

The *Quarterly* portrays Lawrence's psychology as no less dangerous
than his politics, and finds the two difficult to distinguish in any case. His
belief that the "material brain is the source of thought and of all the
other faculties" undermines the Established Church by denying the
necessity for an "immaterial and immortal soul" (8, 17), a "conscious
being" residing within and animating the brain (24). His (Erasmus)-
Darwinian notion that "there is no other difference between a man and
an oyster, than that the one possesses bodily organs more fully developed
than the other" mocks the immortal part and the special creation of man
in a single gesture (14). (In his own response to Lawrence, the essay on
the "Theory of Life," Coleridge distinguished the uniquely human
"rational and responsible soul" from the "functions and properties,
which man possesses in common with the oyster and the mushroom" –
yet another jab at Darwin and the "fungus" school as well [*SW* 1: 501].)[54]

The providence, Revelation, and "superintendance of a Being infinitely benevolent and just" are all cast into doubt, the review in the *Quarterly* concludes (32). Lawrence must "strictly abstain" from declaring his materialist principles in the future and "expunge" them from his published works (34).

Within a few years Lawrence had done both, though his recanting failed to save him his lectureship. After he officially withdrew his published lectures, they lived on in pirated editions, cheaper and more readily available to the radical lower-class readers who found much to admire in a brain-based theory of mind. Lawrence's public defeat meant that the tradition of "materialist psychology" running from Darwin to Lawrence now had to move "underground," as Edward Reed has argued, or to be shorn of its more radical implications and reconciled with religious sentiment and the new bourgeois ethos, as Roger Cooter details in his study of the phrenology movement.[55] Public and open agreement with Lawrence was left to figures on the radical fringe like Richard Carlile, who helped keep Lawrence's lectures in print while promoting the discoveries of Gall and Spurzheim as "new and invincible proof of the good foundation of the science called Atheism or Materialism."[56] It might seem that the anti-dualistic, neurophysiological approach to the mind that had surged from the 1790s to the end of the 1810s was, at least temporarily, moribund as far as mainstream intellectual culture was concerned. And yet Charles Bell was continuing to advance a conception of the embodied mind that significantly overlapped with the theories of Gall, Cabanis, and Darwin, without provoking ideological attacks. In fact, some of the very notions that seemed dubious or patently absurd to the *Edinburgh Review* in its series of attacks on phrenology – that the brain was the "presiding organ of the bodily frame," that comparative anatomy located man's "ennobling" consciousness in "his superior Nervous system," that the "intricate fibrils" of the medullary (white) matter originated in the brain's "grey substance," even that there might be "several" integrated cognitive systems rather than a unified central knower – would be endorsed by the same journal in a review of Bell in 1828.[57] The new brain science was still a force to be reckoned with.

BELL'S NEW ANATOMY AND THE BODILY CREATION OF MIND

Bell's career demonstrates how quickly any retrospective division between Romantic-era "materialists" and "vitalists" becomes misleading.

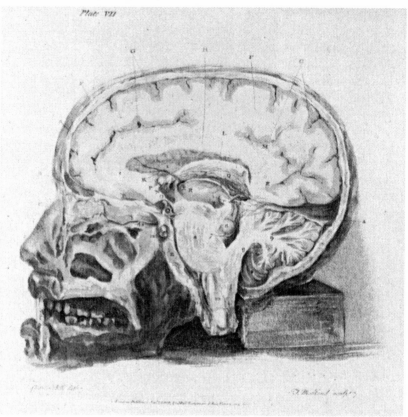

3 Bell, *Anatomy*, plate VII (sagittal view).

Even Darwin and Cabanis, widely considered materialists at the time, were vitalists of a sort, Darwin going so far as to attribute a measure of "sensorial power" to plants.[58] (How plants managed this without a brain or nervous system was a problem that Darwin blithely ignored, as Thomas Brown was quick to point out.)[59] Bell was a vitalist of the best sort, however – the author of a Bridgewater treatise on the design of the hand (one of a series devoted to demonstrating the "Power, Wisdom, and Goodness of God") and a devout Anglican. He contributed toward the development of a brain-based psychology without appearing to slight the soul, constructed telling adaptationist arguments as proofs of God's design rather than results of a blind natural process, and portrayed the mind, brain, and body as a single system without courting charges of materialism. "They would have it that I am in search of the seat of the soul," he complained of some of the "friends" who attended his lectures; "I wish only to investigate the structure of the brain, as we examine the structure of the eye and ear."[60] Thanks to Bell's high standing in the medical community and his unassailable religious views, for once such a disclaimer was taken at face value. For Bell, reductionism could be avoided without resort to a unified, conscious, transcendent subject; the soul could be preserved without minimizing the claims of the body. The same could be said of much Romantic-era poetry as well.

Bell begins the *Idea of a New Anatomy of the Brain*, his startling pamphlet of 1811, by dismissing the "prevailing doctrine" that the "whole brain is a common sensorium," a dated and misleading notion that new insight into the "divisions and subdivisions of the brain, the circuitous course of nerves, their intricate connections, their separation and re-union" should already have put to rest (3). Although no friend to the phrenology movement, Bell proposes that the "portions of the brain are distinct organs with different functions" and he advances a modular view of perception and cognition that seems to build on and clarify the analogous discussion in *Zoonomia*. Bell can dispense with Darwin's baroque notion of a "sensorial" power transmogrifying into various functional states as it pulses along the nerves, however, because he views the nerves themselves, as well as the brain, as more complex than had been suspected. Not only do the "parts of the cerebrum have different functions," but the "nerves which we trace in the body are not single nerves possessing various powers, but bundles of different nerves, whose filaments are united for convenience of distribution, but which are distinct in office, as they are in origin from the brain" (5).[61] The fundamental example of this distinction, the one for which Bell is best remembered, is that between the sensory and motor nerves, rendering the schema of "irritative" and "sensory" powers or motions within single nerves obsolete. But the dense network of distinct nerves and corresponding brain "organs" also explains why information from the various senses does not become confused and indistinct in a common sensorium, resulting in the "chaos" of perceptions and ideas Coleridge saw as an inevitable consequence of Hartley's theory.[62]

As Darwin had emphasized at the beginning of *Zoonomia*, percepts are formed by the sensory organs rather than merely transmitted through them, retaining the character of their specific sensory channel as they are further processed (into ideas) by the brain. In Bell's terms, sensory ideas "are generated by the organs of the senses, and not by anything received and conveyed by them to the sensorium" (*AP* 78). Bell makes the relation of sensorium to brain more clear than does Darwin, however, placing more emphasis on the cerebrum, the "grand organ by which the mind is united to the body" (27). As so often in Bell, the phrasing is carefully dualistic, though the theory it expresses effectively renders the mind–body distinction irrelevant, at least throughout the period of mortal life. The "operations of mind are seated in the great mass of the cerebrum, while the parts of the brain to which the nerves of sense tend, strictly form the seat of sensation, being the internal organs of sense" (13). Sensation "depends on" the relevant sensory and brain organs, not on the impressions from the external world: we can see colored lights by pressing [gently!] the side of the eye-ball, and a needle pressed on neighboring "papillae" of the tongue will produce only a tactile sense of sharpness in one spot, only a metallic taste in another. Indeed a good "blow on the head" should be enough to teach us both the distinctness of various sensory modalities and the ultimate location of sensation in the brain: "the ears will ring, and the eye flashes light, while there is neither light nor sound present" (11). Phantom limb pains show that this creative activity takes place ultimately in the brain rather than in the "external organ of sense"; if more proof is required, Bell evinces (under cover of Latin) the "*exquisitissima*" sensation still remaining at the imagined head of the penis in cases when it has been virtually consumed by cancer ("*ulcus*"). "All ideas originate in the brain" (34).

The brain's active construction of the perceived world does not imply idealism, however, any more than it does for Darwin, because Bell too envisions the mind, brain, body, and physical environment as integrated within an ecological "system," with the senses adaptively designed (when "this whole was created") to convey reasonably accurate information regarding the external world. "The mind was placed in a body not merely suited to its residence, but in circumstances to be moved by the materials around it; and the capacities of the mind, and the powers of the organs, which are as a medium betwixt the mind and the external world, have an original constitution framed in relation to the qualities of things" (8). Here again Bell finds common ground with his Romantic contemporaries:

> How exquisitely the individual Mind
> (And the progressive powers perhaps no less
> Of the whole species) to the external World
> Is fitted: – and how exquisitely, too –
> Theme this but little heard of among men –

> The external World is fitted to the Mind;
> And the creation (by no lower name
> Can it be called) which they with blended might
> Accomplish.[63]

"It may have been a seldom-heard doctrine," as Frederick Burwick comments, "but Bell repeated it often."[64] Wordsworth does not insist here, as Bell does, on the brain and body in and through which the ongoing creation of the perceived world is effected; by comparison, Bell quite literally fleshes out the Mind's relation to the world. But Wordsworth's psychological poetry frequently does root mental growth in embodied experience, most notably in *The Prelude*. Bell, for his part, sometimes evokes comparison with Wordsworth or even Blake in his insistence on the active, creative mind: "The operations of mind are confined not by the limited nature of things created, but by the limited number of our organs of sense" (12). If the doors of perception were cleansed . . .

Bell's holistic sense of the mind, brain, body, and natural environment has several significant entailments, all of which overlap with the theories of Gall and Cabanis. One concerns the pervasive role of "instinctive motions" in mental life and behavior. Bell points out that many bodily "operations" are as "nice and curious, and as perfectly regulated" before the age of reason as after. "Instinctive motions are the operations of the same organs, the brain and nerves and muscles, which minister to reason and volition in our mature years." We begin as creatures of instinct, growing less spontaneous and more consciously directed by "imperceptible degrees." But any number of functions and operations remain unconscious, and subjective awareness has only a limited role in mental life. The entire nervous system maintains bodily integrity and the brain presides, but in a largely "secret" fashion, over bodily functioning. "The frame of the body is endowed with the characters of life, and the vital parts held together as one system through the operation of the brain and nerves; and the secret operations of the vital organs suffer the controul of the brain, though we are unconscious of the thousand delicate operations which are every instant going on in the body" (14–15). Nerves of "peculiar sensibility, having their seat in the body or viscera" convey internal sensations in an obscure manner to the brain, where the "organs of certain powers that seem resident in the body" are most likely to be found (29–30).

Bell's treatise on *The Anatomy and Philosophy of Expression, As Connected With the Fine Arts*, published first in 1806 and in revised and expanded editions throughout his career, explores facial expression as that site where the union of mind, brain, and body announces itself most clearly. In fact, Bell claims that his neurological discoveries were inspired by what initially seemed a problem for esthetics, the human ability to accurately represent and interpret the bodily expression of feeling. "I saw that the whole frame is affected sympathetically with expression in the countenance, and it was in trying to explain that sympathy, that I was led to ascertain, that there exists in the body a distinct system of nerves, the office of which is to influence the muscles in Respiration, in Speech, and in Expression" (*AP* 193). Cognition and emotion, communication (linguistic and nonverbal) and muscular action, the brains, lung, and heart all interact in complex but specific, often predictable, ways. Philosophers have neglected to their cost the interrelations between "mental operations and the condition of the bodily frame," ignoring the "fundamental law of our nature that the mind shall have its powers developed through the influence of the body" (*AP* 76–7). Anatomy provides the "grammar" of a universal language for the visual arts; "expressions, attitudes, and movements of the human figure are the characters of this language," which exerts a "secret," "unconscious," but "constant influence on our opinions" and esthetic judgments (*AP* 2, 37–38). The language of expression is innate, seen in its purest form in infants, enabling the mind to register and categorize emotion by the experience of its effects on and through the body. Perhaps "without the cooperation of these organs of the frame the mind would remain a blank"; at the very least, the mind owes an incalculable debt to "its connection with an operation of the features which precedes its own conscious activity" and is "unerring" from the beginning (*AP* 179–80). Bell is careful to leave room for an immortal "spirit," but in this "material world" the spirit can only relate to the world through an "organised body, without which it could neither feel nor react" (*AP* 76). Mind develops in and through embodied experience, learning from the body's innately driven behaviors, and even the spirit is not so much housed in as realized through a material body.

ROMANTIC NEUROSCIENCE, NEURAL ROMANTICISM

If Romanticism involves promoting feeling and emotion at the expense of "mere" reason, preferring organic to mechanistic theories of nature (including human nature) and art, advancing the claims of the body, reassessing the significance of the natural environment, emphasizing sensation and sensibility, prizing development and growth, and postulating an active and creative mind, then the innovative brain science of the late eighteenth and early nineteenth centuries can usefully be thought of as Romantic. Historians of neuroscience, at any rate, have not hesitated to give a key role to Romantic conceptions and ideals. Edwin Clarke and L.S. Jacyna, in their 1987 study *The Nineteenth-Century Origins of Neuroscientific Concepts*, show in detail how the "foundations of modern neuroscience" were established in the early nineteenth century by new models of the "function and structure of the nervous system" stimulated by "romantic biology" and the "romantic philosophy of nature." They indicate how Gall in particular drew on Herder's "dynamic and vitalistic" view of nature, his conception of the "unity of structure and function" in the organic world, and his comparative approach to anatomy.[65] Gall also profited from the "genetic method" of Romantic biology and the stress on development and "becoming" as well as the affirmation of the "basic affinity" between "human and other living beings" found throughout German Romantic thinking.[66] Gall's significant discoveries in neuroanatomy – he distinguished the white and grey matter of the brain, helped establish the importance of the cerebral cortex for perception and cognition, proposed the conductive nature of the white (axonal) matter, mapped out the principle "pathways in the central nervous system," and described "postembryonic myelinization" – have been seen as enabled by these Romantic presuppositions.[67] His revelatory brain-dissection techniques were themselves inspired by a Romantic approach to neuroanatomy, also anticipated by Herder.[68] Rejecting the crude "ham-slicing" technique of earlier anatomists, Gall traced the brain up from the spinal cord, rather than down from the crown, like a "fruit" emerging from the stalk of the spine, or, as Herder envisioned it, a "flower" (*Observations* 81–2).[69] A "Romantic psychology expressed in positivistic language," Gall's work features distinctively Romantic preoccupations with individual uniqueness, "internal striving," the active, creative brain-mind, the salient role of "unconscious, irrational forces," and the divided self.[70]

Although Gall is the most obviously "Romantic" figure among the brain scientists of his era, Bell's theories have evoked comparison with the Lake poets and Cabanis' *Rapports* has been described as an important link between "Enlightenment ideals of science and universalism" and the "indecipherable, concrete self of the Romantics."[71] Robert Darnton, in his study of mesmerism and the end of the Enlightenment, similarly relates the emergence of Romanticism to thinkers who, like Mesmer, Cabanis, and Gall, attempted in eclectic fashion to "reconstruct general theories from the debris of the Enlightenment," taking the "irrational" more centrally into account.[72] Yet the Romantic character of the era's speculation on the brain often involves much more than a vague eclecticism, postclassical system-building, and respect for irrationality, and historians of science have described a distinctly "Romantic neurology" as well as a Romantic biology and philosophy of nature.[73] It is largely their common predilection for a number of presuppositions and ideals that have long been considered "Romantic," from the unity of nature to the creative activity of mind, that links so otherwise disparate a group as Darwin, Cabanis, Gall, Bell, and Lawrence to one another as well as to contemporary literary developments. Although literary Romanticism has most often been associated with idealistic and transcendental conceptions of mind, the many points of contact between scientific and literary representations of the embodied psyche helps remind us of an antidualistic, materialist register within Romantic writing that has, until recently, been badly ignored.

That does not mean, of course, that the writers conventionally termed "Romantic" were engaged in a common project with contemporaries like Gall and Bell or that they drew uncritically on the neuroscience of the day. Simon Schaffer has argued that Romantic writers eventually recoiled at the "corporeality of mind" posed in the brain science of the era (often, as with Coleridge, after an initial period of enthusiasm) to assert instead "more direct and dynamic relationships between external nature and the powers of mind."[74] There was as much antagonism as common ground between literary Romanticism and the new biology of mind. But with however much ambivalence, Romantic-era writers did engage much more extensively and, in many cases, more directly than has generally been recognized with contemporary brain science. Coleridge was deeply interested in phrenology as well as in mesmerism, acknowledged the importance of Gall and Spurzheim's "Anatomical Discoveries as to the structure of the Brain," and sparred with Lawrence's views in his unpublished "Theory of Life."[75] Henry Crabb Robinson, the friend of both Coleridge and Wordsworth, had met Gall in 1805 and produced one of the first major expositions of Gall's thought in English, *Some Account of Dr. Gall's New Theory of Physiognomy, Founded upon the Anatomy and Physiology of the Brain* in 1807; although it received little notice at the time, it was transcribed almost wholesale into the 1807 edition of Rees's *Cyclopaedia*, where it reached a large audience.[76] Blake designed plates for Erasmus Darwin's scientific poems and has been compared to Darwin in his antidualistic approach to body and soul and his conception of vital energy.[77] According to G. S. Rousseau and Roy

Porter, "early Romantic thinkers" on the Continent as well as in England "derived much of their sense of mind and body from Darwin's materialist biology," and Desmond King-Hele has devoted a career to demonstrating the many links between Darwin and his Romantic contemporaries.[78] Mary Shelley famously cites both Galvani's and Darwin's experiments with animal electricity in the "Introduction" to *Frankenstein*, a work that, according to Butler, responds quite directly to Lawrence's "radical science."[79] Percy Shelley served an intellectual apprenticeship with the works of Darwin and Cabanis and flirted with a materialist view of mind, probably before his period of association with Lawrence.[80] Reed goes so far as to argue that both Shelleys picked up where Darwin and Lawrence left off, promoting a "materialist psychology" in *Queen Mab* and *Frankenstein* that in the wake of Lawrence's humiliation could be advocated only in the guise of poetry and fiction.[81] Keats, as recent criticism by Donald Goellnicht, Hermione de Almeida, and others has detailed, studied the latest developments in brain science as part of his medical training, with profound consequences for his mature poetry and thought.[82] Women poets, despite their unequal education, were by no means insulated from the scientific culture of the era: Anna Seward, for example, was Darwin's protégé and the author of his *Memoirs*. Joanna Baillie was the niece of no less a physiologist than John Hunter and grew up in the house of his brother, the celebrated anatomist and surgeon William Hunter. Her *Plays on the Passions* have been seen as bearing significant affinities to the work of her own brother, the physician and anatomist Matthew Baillie, on neuropathology, and her dramatic theory shares her brother's prescient interest in the physiology of expression.[83]

Such specific points of contact and intellectual debts (on both sides) bear witness to a more pervasive set of intersecting concerns, theories, readings, and key terms common to the scientists and literary artists mutually engaged in rethinking the relations of mind, body, and environment in Romantic-era Britain. Not least important among these is a novel sense of the social environment, both as constrained in its effects on individual development by innate or instinctive factors, but also as arising out of permanent and universal aspects of human nature. Darwin, Gall, Cabanis, and Bell all held that human beings were social creatures by nature, with common tendencies toward bonding, imitation, and empathetic response arising from the specific character of embodied human experience. Human beings also (for all four thinkers) share a universal language of gesture and facial expression that precedes and enables the development of verbal language and suggests a basis for communication across different linguistic groups. Certain artistic phenomena like poetic rhythm and rhyme also are seen as universal. These ideas have a remarkable resonance in the anthropological, linguistic, and esthetic theories of the time and help clarify aspects of a poetic theory such as Wordsworth's that might otherwise seem obscure or simply odd. A related set of ideas concerning the innate or instinctive determinants of character (always seen as conditioning but not entirely determining subjectivity) can help elicit neglected aspects of characterization and subject-formation in the novel of the time, even in an author who, like Austen, has been seen as fundamentally Lockean in her ideas on character and education. These do not, of course, simply constitute "reflections" in literature of scientific ideas but rather represent significant literary contributions to an evolving set of closely related discourses for expressing and analyzing human subjectivity. Graham Richards, in his authoritative history of "psychological ideas," has stressed the contribution of early nineteenth-century novels toward delineating the "new individuality" associated with contemporary developments in physiological psychology. He similarly credits Romantic poetry for helping to revitalize psychological language and creating "new forms for articulating, evolving, and evaluating subjective experience."[84]

Ironically enough, one of the most important aspects of the new individuality, for Romantic fiction and Romantic psychology alike, could be considered "subjective experience" only in a special sense. An unprecedented emphasis on the large areas of mental life that remained, or readily became, unconscious marks both the avant-garde literature and the new biological psychologies of the Romantic era. The connections between the new literary and scientific discourses of the unconscious are particularly rich and fraught with tension. Perhaps no writer exemplifies this ambivalence better than Coleridge, whose fascination with unconscious mental processes repeatedly brings him up against the conflicts between his holistic sense of the embodied mind and his demand for a transcendent, free subjectivity, his speculations on the "organic" character of the psyche and his fear of a "lawless" mental chaos driven by bodily desires and random associations. These tensions come to a crisis in one of Coleridge's most remarkable and most haunting poems, "Kubla Khan," which makes the subject of the next chapter.

CHAPTER TWO

Coleridge and the new unconscious

Given Coleridge's influential defense of a unitary, transcendentalist conception of mind, it seems ironic that "Kubla Khan" is becoming a standard example within cognitivist accounts of a modular and material brain-mind. The pioneering cognitive psychologist Allan Paivio, for one, cites Coleridge's narrative of the poem's composition for its intuitive glimpse into the fundamental "duality" that empirical research would later establish between the visual and verbal systems, supporting two distinct "modes of thought."[1] Steven Pinker, in his popular book *The Language Instinct*, also cites Coleridge's description of poetic "composition in which all the images rose up before him as *things*, with a parallel production of the correspondent expressions," in discussing his conception of "mentalese," a preverbal and unconscious representational system probably closer to computing languages than to any human dialect.[2] The Artificial Intelligence researcher Margaret Boden, for her part, takes issue with Coleridge's "romantic" account of spontaneous composition in her study of cognition and creativity, noticing the introduction to "Kubla Khan" only to dismiss it. Yet Boden also finds in Coleridge's scattered remarks and poetic practice the outlines of a computational approach to unconscious mental composition, recuperating his revisionist account of associationist theory as an inspired premonition of neural network models of creative cognition.[3] What, one wonders, would Coleridge himself make of all this?

The question, it turns out, isn't quite as idle as it might sound. For had Coleridge happened to look into the July 1831 issue of *The Quarterly Review*, he would have found a much earlier citation of "Kubla Khan" in support of a brain-based conception of mind. In the course of a wide-ranging response to John Abercrombie's *Inquiries Concerning the Intellectual Powers* – with the running head "Connexion of the Intellectual Operations with Organic Action" – the reviewer (Sir David Brewster) takes up the novel dream theory advanced by, among others, Cabanis,

called here the theory of "mental excitation." In contrast to the notion
(held by most "metaphysicians") that dreams are provoked only by external causes (like street noise) or simple bodily discomfort (a cricked neck
or dyspeptic stomach), the revisionist theory advanced by Cabanis holds
that the "mind never sleeps," that cognition can proceed without conscious awareness, that the "operations carried on by the mind during the
sleep of the body" can produce coherent and even novel ideas despite
the suspension of the will and the temporary dissolution of the conscious
subject. Brewster lists anecdotal evidence concerning such notables as
Benjamin Franklin and Henry Mackenzie, Condorcet and – Coleridge.
"When Coleridge composed that exquisitely melodious piece of versifi-
cation, which he calls 'a psychological curiosity,' – it is not easy to admit
that operations so purely intellectual had their origin in abdominal or
external uneasiness."[4]

With his lifelong interest in medical matters, all the more as they
touched on mental phenomena, Coleridge may well have discovered in
1831 how readily his publication of "Kubla Khan" as a "psychological
curiosity" would be enlisted in the service of brain-based psychologies.[5]
Might he, in fact, have worried that his visionary poem, with the brief
composition history he attached to it, would be put to just such a use?
This question too is far from idle. For if Coleridge did fear that his dream
poem, allegedly composed under the influence of a narcotic in the
absence of waking consciousness, might become a textbook example of
unconscious, involuntary, or automatic artistic creation, his well-
founded anxiety might go far towards resolving a longstanding mystery
concerning the publication history of "Kubla Khan." Why did
Coleridge hold back one of his most powerful poems for nearly twenty
years? Why, in contrast to "Christabel" or "The Pains of Sleep," other
poems that long remained in manuscript, did he fail to transcribe or even
mention it in a letter, to discuss it in his notebooks, to read it aloud to
more than a select few auditors (almost exclusively poets he trusted and
admired)?[6] Did Coleridge's reticence surrounding this "vision in a
dream" stem, at least in part, from his ambivalence regarding unconscious cognition and the fragmented, naturalistic model of mind it had
come to exemplify?

Coleridge had participated in the 1790s vogue for what he called the
"corporeality of *thought*," going so far as to describe himself (in another
1794 letter to Southey) as an "Advocate for the Automatism of Man"
(*STCL* 1: 137, 147).[7] Yet Coleridge no sooner makes such pronouncements than he begins to distance himself from them. His remarks on

Hartley and the corporeal mind are immediately followed, for example, by a joking, pseudo-materialist account of the violence inflicted on the "thinking corporealities" of a "certain Uncouth Automaton" upon his being heartily thrashed at school (*STCL* 1: 137).[8] The 1800 letter to Godwin outlining a "simply organic" approach to language and consciousness ends with a decidedly less playful qualification: "all the nonsense of the vibrations etc you would of course dismiss" (*STCL* 1: 626). Priestley, Darwin, and others had advanced "corporeal" accounts of thought that were also dismissive of Hartley's vibrations, but Coleridge here might be taken instead as casting physiological models of mind into doubt altogether, while at the same time appealing to connections among language, thought, and the "organic" approach to mind being forged in contemporary brain science.[9] Materialist, naturalistic, and embodied notions of the psyche would continue to play an ambiguous role in Coleridge's thinking throughout his career, particularly in regard to his speculation on the emotions and on the unconscious.

Coleridge's ambivalent attitude toward Spurzheim makes for an especially striking example of the mingled repugnance and fascination with which he regarded contemporary work on the brain. As Trevor Levere has argued, Coleridge found both phrenology and mesmerism intriguing for their antidualistic and organicist tendencies, while at the same time rejecting phrenological theory for its associations with materialism and, more tellingly, for its "fragmented" model of the mind.[10] In 1816, Coleridge approvingly cites Spurzheim's "Anatomical Demonstrations of the Brain" as an authoritative exposition of comparative neuroanatomy (*SW* 1: 540), and in a notebook entry a year later he laments the attacks on Spurzheim in the *Edinburgh Review* and acknowledges the "undoubted splendor and originality of his & Gall's Anatomical Discoveries as to the structure of the Brain" (*CN* 3: 4355).[11] Yet he is also recorded in the *Table Talk* calling Spurzheim a "dense" and "ignorant" German and taking particular umbrage at the conception of a functionally divided mind. "You know, every act, however you may distinguish it by name, is truly the act of the entire man; the notion of distinct organs in the brain itself is absurd."[12] Coleridge is no less ambivalent in his estimation of Erasmus Darwin. In a letter of 1796, for example, Coleridge credits Darwin, "the most inventive of philosophical men," with "perhaps, a greater range of knowledge than any other man in Europe," but goes on to mock him for his atheism and his breezy approach to such a question as "whether we be the outcasts of a blind idiot called Nature, or the children of an all-wise and infinitely

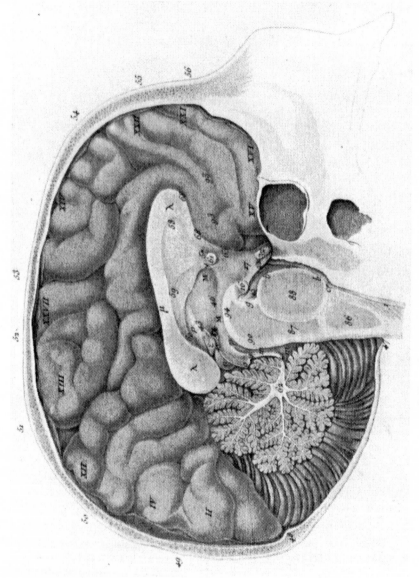

4 Gall and Spurzheim, *Atlas*, plate XI (median section).

good God" (*STCL* 1: 177).[13] And yet, as John Beer has convincingly argued, Coleridge was drawing on his reading of *Zoonomia* during the same period for crucial hints toward an active conception of mind, paying particular attention to Darwin's discussion of "ocular spectra."[14]

As late as 1828, in his fascinating manuscript essay "On the Passions," Coleridge is lamenting the post-Cartesian "separation of Psychology from Physiology, depriving the former of all root and objective truth, and reducing the latter to a mere enumeration of facts & phaenomena without Copula or living form" (*SW* 2: 1421). He also remained intensely interested in phenomena that, like Darwin's ocular spectra, eluded the boundary between psychology and physiology, another source of his wary fascination with Mesmerism or "Zoomagnetism." In an 1821 fragment on the latter, Coleridge refers to the "known sympathy of the Stomach and Bowels with the Skin," and notes that if "imagination" accounts for mesmeric effects, it could be more generally "extended to the Power, by which a Patient's Mind produces changes in his own body, without any intentional act of the Will – as a Blush, for instance, contagious Yawning, Night-Mair, Fever Phantoms, Palpitation of the Heart <from Fear>, in short what not?" (*SW* 2: 912–13). (Darwin's examples of mind–body interaction listed early in *Zoonomia* similarly include heart palpitation from fear and the "glow of skin in those who are ashamed" [*Z* 1: 39]). Here, as in some of his speculations on dreams, one finds Coleridge at his nearest approach to physiological accounts of mind, accounts that advance the claims of the body at the expense of conscious volition. It should come as no surprise that Coleridge coined the term "neuropathology."[15]

Coleridge has also been credited with first using the term "psychosomatic," a coinage that gives some insight into his eventual strategy for overcoming mind–body dualism without verging back towards a materialistic or "corporeal" account of mind. In late works written for his friend J.H. Green, a surgeon and medical lecturer, including the essay "On the Passions," Coleridge works toward a physiological psychology that gives primacy to mind and makes the body its expression. "What is the Body," as he had written in a letter many years earlier, "but the fixture of the mind" (*BL* 1: 151). Working eclectically and brilliantly with ideas developed (and sometimes borrowed wholesale) from his readings in German idealism, *natürphilosophie*, Davy's chemistry, Galvani and Volta's work on electricity and magnetism, German physiology, Christian theology, and neo-Platonic philosophy, Coleridge's "Platonico-Christo-

Kantism" gave him an active conception of mind that countered the passivity he saw in Newton, Locke, and Hartley while skirting the brain-based, potentially materialistic models of Darwin, Priestley, and Gall.[16] If Gall had proposed "specific organs" of the brain to carry out mental functions (*SW* 1: 591), Coleridge could counter with "organs of spirit" that pre-exist the body and guarantee the mind's transcendent nature (*BL* 1: 242)

This primacy of mind, exerted by means of the "Vital Power" that shapes and informs it (*SW* 2: 1442), marks the fundamental difference between human beings and the rest of the "Animal world" (*SW* 2: 1390–1). That is, where contemporary brain scientists like Darwin and Cabanis were eager to stress the continuity between humans and other animals, Coleridge's resolution of the mind–body question demanded an absolute distinction. "In the different species of the Ape I find nothing in the Physiognomy that forbids me to imagine that the mind of the creature has its mold in the body – but in man's I see at once that the Body must have received the impress from a mind" (*SW* 2: 1410). Animal "instincts" and "appetites" become sublimated into "Passions" in man (*SW* 2: 1390–1); unlike animals, men can have had no "*natural state*" (*SW* 2: 1414). Since, in human beings, the vital power, *vis vitae*, or "subject of sensation, volition, and thought" *precedes* and conditions embodiment, the "notorious" facts of mind–body reciprocity can be accounted for without the "degrading and demoralizing Materialism" which would otherwise seem unavoidable (*SW* 2: 1437). Coleridge's 1825 lecture "On the Prometheus of Aeschylus" helps flesh out and clarify his resolution of the mind–body question. As Coleridge reads the Prometheus myth, the equation of "nous" (mind or spirit) with "stolen fire" implies that mind "was no mere evolution of the animal basis" but rather underscores its "difference in *kind*, from the faculties which are in common to man and the nobler animals." Nous can only be bestowed upon "Man" by a God, to "mark the pre-existence, in order of thought, of the Nous, as spiritual, both to the objects of sense, and to their products, formed, as it were, by the precipitation, or, if I may dare adopt the bold Language of Leibnitz, by the coagulation of spirit" (*SW* 2: 1268). That which is uniquely human in the human mind proceeds from above, Promethean fire from heaven. Spiritual "coagulation" predates bodily incorporation, directing psychic development and lending the mind its godlike ("I AM") qualities of "reason, free-will, self-consciousness," the essential and "contra-distinguishing attributes of man" (*SW* 2: 1266).

THE DREAMING BODY

Before its resolution in the 1820s, however, Coleridge's grappling with the mind–body relation was marked by a good deal of anxiety and vacillation. His ambivalence grows most evident in discussions of dreams and other manifestations of unconscious mental life, as David Miall has demonstrated in an important series of essays on Coleridge, dreams, creativity, and emotion.[17] Darwin, Cabanis, and Gall had all discussed dreams in terms that implied a split or fragmented subject, cognition in the absence of conscious volition or supervision, and the subtle and pervasive influence of bodily processes – not least those related to sexuality – on psychic life.[18] Darwin notes the "ceaseless flow of our ideas in dreams," unhampered by the interference of conscious volition and free to jump from association to association. In the absence of external stimulation, "internal stimuli" are given freer reign and take on a "great vivacity," including the brain's stock of remembered sensations, the ideas variously associated with them, and the "internal senses" of "hunger, thirst, and lust," all making part of the "farrago of our dreams" (Z 1: 199, 201, 209, 213). For Cabanis, the brain is in "continuous activity" and sleep, rather than constituting a suspension of neural activity, is in fact "produced" by the brain, a startlingly modern formulation.[19] In dreams the "internal impressions" from what we would now call the hormonal and visceral nervous systems are unusually intense, as can be seen with sexual dreams and nocturnal emission (R 1: 136, 138–9). But the sleeping brain is capable of learned behaviors and even rational activity as well, as seen in the somnambulist's unerring performance of various acts and in the mind's ability to "continue its research in dreams," waking with the solution to an intellectual problem at hand (R 2: 626). Gall, envisioning the brain as an "assemblage of particular organs" enjoying a certain degree of autonomy, holds that the "sensations and ideas which constitute dreams" arise when some cerebral organs are active while others are "suspended" (*FB* 1: 185). The "plurality of organs" also accounts for the "energy" (vivacity) of dreams: "The whole vital strength is concentrated in a single organ or a small number of organs whilst the others sleep; hence their action must of necessity be more energetic." The dreaming brain does not merely recycle and rearrange waking ideas and perceptions, but may "invent" new material as well, since the "internal sources" that give rise to "sentiments and ideas" are as available in sleep as in wakefulness (*FB* 2: 321). All of these theories presuppose an active brain, the continuity of neural activity during sleep, and unconscious cognitive processes liable (but not limited) to expressing the claims of the body. Perhaps most crucially for a discussion of Coleridge, they also entail the suspension of volition: as Darwin writes in *The Botanic Garden*, "The WILL presides not in the bower of SLEEP."[20] They contribute as well to a materialist, neurological approach to mind that goes back at least to Diderot's *Le rêve d'Alembert*, at once a philosophical examination and a fictional representation of the large role of unconscious activity in mental life. Taken together, these neurophilosophical theories of dreaming represent an important (though rarely examined) context for what has been seen as the "discovery of the unconscious" within literary Romanticism.[21]

Coleridge, whose speculations on dreams owe much to Darwin, also relates dreams to the body, to blind or involuntary psychic processes, and to an internally divided and unstable subject. Writing of the "Origin of moral Evil from the *streamy* Nature of Association" in an 1803 notebook entry, Coleridge continues: "which Thinking=Reason, curbs & rudders/how this comes to be so difficult/Do not the bad Passions in Dreams throw light & shew of proof upon this Hypothesis?" (*CN* 1: 1770). With the conscious subject in temporary abeyance, the psyche follows from one idea to the next, motivated (if at all) by bodily desires. That for Coleridge dreaming entails a "suspension of the voluntary . . . power" is clear from his 1818 lecture notes on *The Tempest*, a notion that has been traced to Coleridge's reading of *Zoonomia*.[22] "Fancy and Sleep *stream on*," he writes in an anguished entry of 1805 on libidinous "Impulses from within"; "and (instead of outward Forms and Sounds, the Sanctifiers, the Strengtheners!) they connect with them motions of the blood and nerves" (*CN* 2: 2542).[23] Here Coleridge's speculations on dreaming seem most obviously indebted to contemporary brain science, particularly to Darwin, who had written in *Zoonomia* that in dreams the "power of volition is suspended" and "motions" from "internal senses" are enhanced due to the absence of external stimuli [Z 204, 209]. In both accounts, with the external senses asleep and the conscious will and reason off duty, impulses from within the body drive the production of images in dreams, "even as a Flight of Starlings in a Wind."[24] In a provocative 1818 entry on the "Language of Dreams" (a "language of Images and Sensations"), Coleridge refers to contemporary "physiologic Ideas" and speculates on the divisions between the cerebral, ganglionic, and "sympathic" systems, noting the "paramouncy of the Ganglionic over the Cerebral in Sleep," another formulation reminiscent of Cabanis, who speaks of the ganglionic system as a "partial MOI" with a certain degree of autonomy (*R* 2:

551). Coleridge proceeds to discuss the body's effect, through the internal organs and nervous system, on the dreaming mind. "Liver – &c. The passions of the Day as often originate in the Dream, as the Images of the Dream in the Day. Guilt, Falsehood, traced to the Gastric Life. See my *Pains* of Sleep" (*CN* 3: 4410). The passage taken as a whole reads like a moralized, confessional variation on the new biological theory of dreams being developed by Darwin, Cabanis, and other early neuroscientists.[25] Coleridge's enduring interests in medicine, physiology, and mind–body relations contributed in no small part to his profound (though mostly unpublished) speculative work on emotional and nonconscious aspects of mental life and artistic creativity, as Miall has demonstrated.[26] Coleridge was also a close student of phenomena suggesting mind–body interaction, both in others (particularly his infant children) and in himself. In letters to Thomas Poole, Coleridge reports going through a program of psychophysiological self-analysis, reminiscent of Darwin's accounts in *Zoonomia* of his own experiments and of others going back to Newton (who famously produced the illusion of sparks by pressing on his eyeball). "In the course of these studies," Coleridge writes in 1801, "I tried a multitude of little experiments on my own sensations, & on my senses – and some of these (too often repeated) I have reason to believe did injury to my nervous system" (*STCL* 2: 731). A few months earlier he confides that Wordsworth had begged him to stop his "multitude of minute experiments with Light & Figure" because of the "nervous & feverish" state they left him in (*STCL* 2: 707). Coleridge's anxiety was more than merely "nervous," however; his private research program held metaphysical dangers no less than physical ones. When placed in the context of the new biological approach to mind represented by Darwin, Gall, Spurzheim, and Cabanis, an approach that constitutes the principal contemporary challenge to the position staked out in the central chapters of the *Biographia*, Coleridge's long and productive fascination with physiological psychology seems continually to skirt the abyss of materialism, to force a renewed engagement with the "corporeality of *thought*." In this context, Coleridge's suppression of "Kubla Khan" for nearly two decades, along with the remarkable story of its composition, appears not mysterious but predictable.

For, after all, what Coleridge describes in the introductory notice to "Kubla Khan" might be seen as the most spectacular psychophysiological experiment of his career, though an unplanned one; a "psychological curiosity" of the highest moment. And when read against the background of Coleridge's fraught relation to contemporary biological accounts of mind, the introductory note becomes a still more remarkable document than before. It raises no fewer than three issues crucial to contemporary debates on the mind and brain: the splitting or fragmenting of the psyche, the status of conscious volition within mental life, and the relationship between mental events and the organic body. Moreover, it raises these issues in ways that seem, from an orthodox or transcendentalist perspective, to give aid and comfort to the materialist adversary. Perhaps even worse, it seems designed to court an "abnormal" reading of the poem it accompanies, like J. M. Robertson's notorious characterization of "Kubla Khan" as one of the "chance brain-blooms of a season of physiological ecstasy."[27] The publication of the introductory note with the poem in 1816 all but guaranteed that "Kubla Khan" would become an object lesson for the biological study of psychology and an irresistible subject for the psychological study of literature.

POETRY AND THE UNWILLING SUSPENSION OF CONSCIOUSNESS

Coleridge's objections to Spurzheim stem from the same deep concerns informing his critique of Hartley in the *Biographia*, his demand for a holistic and unified account of mind. Like most contemporary critics of Gall and Spurzheim, Coleridge opposes both the division of mind into discrete, semi-autonomous faculties and the anatomical analog of this division in the "polyorganism of the Brain" (*SW* 1: 410). A holistic approach to mind recurs throughout Coleridge's mature writings, perhaps most famously in his description of poetic creation. "The poet, described in *ideal* perfection, brings the whole soul of man into activity, with the subordination of its faculties to each other, according to their relative worth and dignity. He diffuses a tone, and spirit of unity, that blends, and (as it were) *fuses*, each into each, by that synthetic and magical power, to which we have exclusively appropriated the name of imagination" (*BL* 2: 15–16). Coleridge's "faculties" are not discrete modules but various functions of a unified and unifying soul, "affections or acts of a single general power" as George Combe writes in distinguishing organology from the faculties posited by "metaphysicians."[28] Although Kenneth Burke considered "Kubla Khan" the "kind of poem that Coleridge's own aesthetic theories were not much abreast of," it has seldom been remarked that the introductory notice to that poem implies a view of poetic creation very much at odds with the holistic account of imaginative creation in the *Biographia*.[29] Coleridge's alleged composition of the poem in a "profound sleep, at least of the external senses" does little to convey that the "whole soul of man" has been active. Rather, as Brewster would note in the *Quarterly Review* of 1831, it implies exertion of thought in the absence of a conscious thinker, the unconscious workings of a brain-mind compatible with the psychophysiological models of Darwin, Cabanis, and their ilk. The details of Coleridge's description, as Paivio would argue many years later, imply another level of psychic fragmentation into discrete visual and linguistic modules: "if that indeed can be called composition in which all the images rose up before him as *things*, with a parallel production of the correspondent expressions, without any sensation or consciousness of effort." It is difficult to square this account with Coleridge's insistence, contra Spurzheim, that "every" mental act must be the "act of the entire man." Even if one ignores Coleridge's own qualification ("if that indeed can be called composition") and charitably interprets the parallel imagistic and linguistic production as "faculties" in the "metaphysical" sense, working together – though hardly "fusing" – in poetic production, there remains the embarrassing lack of a conscious, voluntary subject directing or even bearing witness to the process.

Coleridge's celebrated account of the poetic imagination, after all, goes on to specify just such volitional activity: "This power, first put into action by the will and understanding, and retained under their irremissive, though gentle and unnoticed, controul (*laxis effertur habenis*) reveals itself in the balance or reconciliation of opposite or discordant qualities" (*BL* 2: 16). These faculties, moreover, remain engaged in an explicitly conscious manner, with "judgement ever awake and steady self-possession" (*BL* 2: 17). According to the introduction to "Kubla Khan," however, the reins are not so much held loosely as either dropped altogether or never taken up. More than one critic has remarked on the imagination's "peculiar independence from . . . conscious control" in "Kubla Khan," an independence already evident in the account of spontaneous, unconscious composition in the introductory note.[30] Of course, the will and understanding can, perhaps must, work in the absence of full consciousness. Elsewhere, Coleridge (closely following Schelling) defines "unconscious activity" as the "Genius in the man of Genius" and describes the work of art as one in which the "*Conscious* is so impressed on the *Unconscious*, as to appear *in* it" (*LL* 2: 221–22). But here conscious activity seems missing altogether; rather than a joint production of conscious and unconscious activity – an "interpenetration," as Coleridge puts it in the *Biographia*, of "*spontaneous* impulse and of *voluntary* purpose" (*BL* 2: 65) – the poem is depicted as having sprung from a "deep" unconscious state with no contribution from the purposeful subject of volition in evidence. Indeed, "*voluntary* purpose" seems, in this signal case, incompatible with poetic production; once the poet's transcription of the lines is interrupted, the rest of the poem is forever unrecoverable. Coleridge, once a proponent of the "automatism" of man, takes pains to argue in the *Biographia* that Shakespeare was "no automaton of genius" but a deliberate, self-conscious artist (*BL* 2: 26). What, though, to say of the artist who composed "Kubla Khan"?

The presence of a psychoactive drug or "anodyne" further vexes the problematic status of the will in the prose introduction. A note in Coleridge's hand added to the Crewe manuscript of "Kubla Khan" specifies "two grains of Opium," the standard anodyne of the time. And opium was notorious for its capacity to suspend or counteract, even to destroy the will. Coleridge himself calls it a "*free-agency-annihilating* Poison" in his agonized letters of 1814 (*STCL* 3: 490), explaining how an extended course of opium abuse had produced "a derangement, an utter impotence of the *Volition*," though leaving the "intellectual Faculties" intact (*STCL* 3: 477). "By the long Habit of the accursed Poison my Volition (by which I mean the faculty *instrumental* to the Will, and by which alone the Will can realize itself – it's Hands, Legs, & Feet, as it were) was compleatly deranged, at times frenzied" (*STCL* 3: 926). This view of opiates would have been familiar to fellow readers of *Zoonomia*. Darwin had theorized that opium worked by increasing "irritative motions from internal stimulus [*sic*]" and augmenting the amount of "sensorial power" accorded to sensation from within the body at the expense both of "voluntary power" and "irritation from the stimulus of external objects" (Z 1: 242). As in Darwin's theory of dreams, that is, opium precipitates a shift in the psychic economy from conscious volition and external perception to impulses from the body's interior, with their freight of "*natural* or *connate*" desires (Z 1: 136). No wonder opium, dreaming, and reverie held together in the Romantic literary mind. With prolonged use of opium, Darwin warns, the "faculty of volition is gradually impaired" and is "at length totally suspended" (Z 1: 248). Ironically, at least in retrospect, this danger did not keep Darwin from prescribing "very large doses of opium" for one ailment after another (Z 1: 223). It has even been suggested (however fancifully) that Darwin may indirectly have contributed to Coleridge's opium abuse in the 1790s, by prescribing "a grain of opium taken every night for many months" to Coleridge's friend and (soon after) fellow addict, Tom Wedgwood.[31]

It is certain, at any rate, that opium was also widely associated with naturalistic and materialist conceptions of mind. Early on in *Zoonomia*, for example, Darwin refers to several cures he effected with opium that together suggested how "one kind of delirium is a convulsion of the organs of sense, and that our ideas are the motions of those organs" (*Z* 1: 26). Consider again Coleridge's provocative statement of December, 1794, some months after Darwin's words were published: "I go farther than Hartley and believe the corporeality of *thought* – namely, that it is motion – " (*STCL* 1: 137). Opium features in arguments for the corporeality of thought from La Mettrie ("opium even changes the will") to Gall: "A few drops of blood extravasated in the cavaties of the brain, a few grains of opium, are enough to demonstrate to us, that, in this life, volition and thought are inseparable from cerebral organisation" (*FB* 2: 45).[32] Not only does opium, a material substance, act on the will; but by acting on the will, it suggests that mental faculties are affected by material changes in the body. Why, then, should mental events not be reducible to a series of physiological dispositions, to "motions"? The longer one looks at it in the context of Romantic brain science, the more the introductory note to "Kubla Khan" begins to read like an anecdotal report expressly designed for the use of Darwin, Gall, or Cabanis. It implies a mind divided into discrete powers and organs, a subject fractured into conscious and unconscious entities, the persistence of cognitive activity in the absence of conscious judgment and volition, the mind's susceptibility to and perhaps ultimate dependence on material changes in the body. As a case history, it is a brain scientist's dream.

Indeed, one critic has cannily described the introductory note as reading like "straightforward clinical description, rather in the manner of an early scientist reporting an experiment that he performed on himself."[33] All the more reason, then, to recall that Coleridge had written a brief report in this very genre, not too long after the year (1797) he claims to have experienced the opium dream or "reverie" that gave rise to "Kubla Khan." In the fall of 1799, Coleridge took part in what has been called the "first controlled scientific exploration of a consciousness-altering drug," Humphry Davy's experiments with nitrous oxide in Thomas Beddoes' notorious Pneumatic Institution in Bristol.[34] Coleridge's fellow test subjects included Dr. Beddoes, Anna Edgeworth Beddoes, Southey, R. L. Edgeworth, Tom Wedgwood, and Davy himself. Their reports were carefully taken down and published by Davy in his *Researches, Chemical and Philosophical: Chiefly Concerning Nitrous Oxide* (1800). The experiments, like the drug, were quite a success. Edgeworth

"capered about the room"; Wedgwood experienced a "very strong incli-
nation to make antic motions" with his hands and feet; Mrs. Beddoes
confessed that she "frequently seemed to be ascending like a balloon."[35]
Davy found himself proclaiming in a fit of elation, "*Nothing exists but
thoughts!*"[36] Coleridge made brief reports on four separate trials of the
drug, carefully registering its physiological and psychological effects: a
"highly pleasurable sensation of warmth" and an urge to laugh on the
first trial, a dimming of the visual sense on the second. "The third time,"
he writes, "I was more violently acted upon than in the two former.
Towards the last, I could not avoid, nor indeed felt any wish to avoid,
beating the ground with my feet; and after the mouth-piece was
removed, I remained for a few seconds motionless, in great extacy." The
fourth session was even more gratifying: "my heart did not beat so violently; my sensations were highly pleasurable, not so intense or apparently local, but of more unmingled pleasure than I had ever before
experienced" (*SW* I: 103–4).

Given the materialist tenor of 1790s radical science, it is not surprising
to learn that despite his idealist outburst while under the influence, Davy
interpreted these experiments as further evidence for the material nature
of mind. As Golinski points out, Davy's notebooks interpret the effects of
nitrous oxide in terms of a "clear demonstration of the material basis of
human actions, emotions, and perceptions"; issues he had explored in his
"Essay to Prove that the Thinking Powers Depend on the Organization
of the Body," which he prudently left unpublished.[37] Presciently as well,
since Davy (like Coleridge) would later seek to develop a new vitalism calculated to "underwrite the existing social order" that the work with
nitrous oxide seemed more likely to undermine.[38] Coleridge himself
proved eager to leave the experiments, and their materialist implications,
behind. Suzanne Hoover has discussed Coleridge's lifelong "reticence"
concerning his experiences with nitrous oxide, comparing it to his
"defensiveness" concerning his use of opium. It is remarkable, she concludes, that Coleridge's interests in consciousness, sensation, and
mind–body relations did not inspire a more thorough exploration of his
first-hand experience with "consciousness-altering" drugs.[39] Schaffer,
who notes that "galvanism, pneumatics, and mesmerism" were all
deployed by materialists to "efface distinctions between mind and body,"
explains the circumspect character of Davy's published report and the
Romantic reaction typified by Coleridge along ideological lines: "The
unspeakable relationship between the evidence of the imagination and
the power of a material gas proved too vulnerable a resource at a time of

fierce conservative reaction."[40] Given their contemporary ideological implications, the nitrous oxide experiments could only have increased Coleridge's anxieties regarding the possible uses of his own psychophar- macological experiment, one that has not lost any notoriety for having been undertaken by accident and in a lonely farmhouse rather than in the controlled (if hilarious) atmosphere of the Pneumatic Institution. If the drug trials carried out with Davy helped to inspire the "clinical" style of Coleridge's note to "Kubla Khan," they may also help to explain why Coleridge kept the experience quiet for so long.

At least one prominent exponent of the biological approach to mind, George Combe, made the connection between opium, nitrous oxide, and materialist psychology explicit in his open *Letter* to Francis Jeffrey (1826), a pamphlet responding to the series of attacks on Gall and Spurzheim in the *Edinburgh Review*. Combe cites "the well-known effects of wine, opium, and nitrous oxide gas, on the mental manifestations," and pointedly asks how "an immaterial principle can be excited to activ- ity, hurried away in an ungovernable ecstasy, or laid low in a state of sus- pension and debasement, by means of such material substances."[41] This is a question we know Coleridge to have asked himself, at least in regard to opium. "Need we wonder," he asks in a notebook entry in 1808, "at Plato's opinions concerning the Body, at least, need that man wonder whom a *pernicious Drug* shall make capable of conceiving & bringing forth Thoughts, hidden in him before, which shall call forth the deepest feel- ings of his best, greatest, & sanest Contemporaries? and this proved to him by actual experience?" In the context of contemporary brain science, and given the role of narcotics in materialist speculation on the mind going back to the mid-eighteenth century, such striking and imme- diate evidence of the effect of a psychoactive drug upon latent or "hidden" thoughts seems to demand a neurological explanation. "But can subtle strings set in greater tension do this?" As the entry continues, one can see both the explicitly neuroscientific element in Coleridge's anxious speculation, and also the strategy he will use in the *Biographia* for downplaying the threat of materialist accounts of mind by reverting to a dated model of vibrating strings, as though Hartley's model had not been superseded by the work of Priestley, Galvani, Darwin, Davy, and others. Then he moves to an alternate explanation that looks forward to his resolution of the mind–body question in the 1820s. "Or is it not that the dire poison for a delusive time has made the body, <i.e., the *organiza- tion*, not the articulation (or instruments of motion)> the unknown some- what, a fitter Instrument for the all-powerful Soul" (*CN* 3: 3320).

Was Coleridge thinking of "Kubla Khan" in this entry? His reference to "Thoughts," like his allusion to Plato, remains obscure. Coleridge appears, however, to be working at an analysis of the cognitive effects of opium that, if plausibly developed, would enable him to publish "Kubla Khan" without fear of its enlistment in the cause of biological psychology, or of its subjection to the psychopharmacological readings that have met the poem beginning with Robertson's critique ("an abnormal product of an abnormal nature under abnormal conditions") a century ago.[12] The analysis was never fully worked out, "Kubla Khan" remained in manuscript for almost another decade, and when published, it was accompanied by a statement that constitutes an apology rather than a defense.

All this is assuming, of course, that Coleridge is telling something like the truth in his story of the poem's composition, a story that has more than once been assailed, most notably by Elisabeth Schneider and Norman Fruman. Both critics pointedly dismiss the "lonely farm house," dispute the 1797 date (by a year or two, anyway), make much of the discrepancy between a "profound sleep, at least of the external senses" in the published introduction and "a sort of Reverie" in the Crewe manuscript notation, and absolve the gentleman from Porlock of any and all crimes against British poetry in the unlikely case that he existed at all. Both dispute the dream origin of the poem and disrupt the critical consensus – "that 'Kubla Khan' is an 'abnormal product' everybody from Coleridge on admits" – once taken for granted by John Livingston Lowes.[13] Or do they? Schneider rather grudgingly concedes that "Coleridge may have been in a sort of 'reverie' . . . No doubt he had been taking opium"; Fruman similarly owns that, though Coleridge certainly revised the poem, it does seem to embody "themes and images not logically related by the waking consciousness," most likely linked together in a "state of reverie brought on by opium."[14] No more than this is needed to account for Coleridge's reticence on "Kubla Khan", behavior considered "peculiarly out of key" for an exceedingly voluble poet.[15] It is difficult for skeptics like Schneider and Fruman to convincingly address an equally curious problem, why Coleridge should have elected to "write a preface at all."[16] For against what little Coleridge had to gain as a poet in the way of "disarming criticism" must be set all that he had to lose as a "metaphysician" and polemicist in the way of providing an incomparable example of unconscious, involuntary composition, of the spontaneous "brain-blooms" of a fragmented subject, of the creative imagination under the sway of a "material substance."[17]

If, as John Beer suggests, the "facts surrounding its composition act as a comment upon the very powers which he was investigating," Coleridge's presentation of these "facts" entails a far different commentary on the imagination, memory, volition, and like powers of mind than the theories worked out in the *Biographia* and in the manuscript essays of the 1820s.[48] The picture of the mind suggested by the introductory notice is one much more in tune with the tradition of radical brain science running from the 1790s to the very "London Materialists" whom Coleridge, late in his career, would decry for viewing "individuality, intellect, and moral agency" as "properties or functions of organized matter." Coleridge scorns their leader, John Elliotson, for holding, in terms borrowed from Lawrence – who borrows them from Cabanis – that "Mind is secreted by the Brain" (*SW* 2: 904), although this is a view close to that once held by Coleridge himself and eminently compatible with the famous narrative of his composition of "Kubla Khan."[49] Far from considering the introduction to "Kubla Khan" as a sort of "confidence-trick" set to trap the unwary, one could place it instead among Coleridge's most brutally honest and genuinely disinterested confessions.[50]

Reading the introductory note more as confession than confabulation gains impetus from the context of its initial publication in the 1816 volume *Christabel: Kubla Khan, A Vision; The Pains of Sleep.* For "Christabel" and "The Pains of Sleep" both deal overtly, if not blatantly, with dreams and bodily desires, impulsive behaviors and irrational thoughts, suspended volition, and subconsciously produced words and images. Each poem ends, moreover, on a confessional note. "Christabel" features a symbolic dream (with rival interpretations), knowledge that cannot be articulated but must be performed in a trance-like display (Christabel's mimetic hissing), sleeping with "open eyes" and other borderline states of consciousness, involuntary acts (Geraldine's disrobing) and dream-like "perplexity of mind." The poem (begun in 1798) also hints at brain-based notions of cognition – "But thro' her brain of weal and woe / So many thoughts mov'd to and fro" – and creativity: "Carv'd with figures strange and sweet, / All made out of the carver's brain." The use of "brain" to connote mind is rare in English poetry before the 1790s and only adds to the avant-garde feel of a volume that challenged and perplexed its early readers.[51]

Still more intriguing in connection with "Kubla Khan" and its introduction, however, is the strange "conclusion" to "Part the Second."

Rather than concluding anything (the poem remains, like "Kubla Khan," a fragment), this famously enigmatic coda seems to veer away from the body of the poem. It is usually read as an autobiographical aside, triggered by the poet's reaction to his own lines on the Baron's paternal "rage" against Christabel. Speaking now of a father's intense pleasure in his "fairy" child (an image associated with little Hartley), the poet admits that, however unaccountably, his "love's excess" has given vent in "words of unmeant bitterness." What inspires this "wild," unintended, irrationally hurtful language? Coleridge seems momentarily plunged back into his youthful adherence to Hartley's namesake, giving an neo-associationist account of unconscious, affect-laden, embodied cognition:

> And what, if in a world of sin
> (O sorrow and shame should this be true!)
> Such giddiness of heart and brain
> Come seldom save from rage and pain,
> So talks as it's most used to do.

The "I AM" here becomes an "it," the coherent, unified subject yielding to a neural network of emotionally charged associations: not a conscious, controlling ego but a blind, automatic process does the talking. The corporeality of thought and the automatism of man haunt the strangely inconclusive conclusion to "Christabel," giving intimations of "sorrow and shame" should the mind indeed prove a function of the body.

The third poem in the slim volume, "The Pains of Sleep," is the one Coleridge specifically cites for its treatment of the connections among dreams, "passions," guilt, falsehood, and the "Gastric" economy of internal impressions and desires. It too speaks with "shame" of the nonconscious, involuntary production of "shapes and thoughts," fueled by "fantastic passions" and desire "strangely mixed" with loathing. Again the unified subject or agent of volition becomes self-divided and unaccountable: "Which all confused I could not know, / Whether I suffered, or I did." The poet's shameful avowal of his "powerless will" links this poem not only to the two others printed with it but to Coleridge's self-lacerating letters on his addiction to a "*free-agency-annihilating*" substance as well. Bringing the 1816 volume to an anguished close, "The Pains of Sleep" underscores the book's confessional nature, and reiterates its concern with issues of volition, desire, the unconscious, and thought that slips the reins of the sovereign subject.

XANADU AND THE NEW UNCONSCIOUS

Up to now I have been concerned with placing the introduction to "Kubla Khan" in the context of Romantic-era speculation on the relations of mind, body, brain, and nerves, while keeping the poem itself out of consideration. It is tempting to leave things there. "Kubla Khan" has garnered more than its share of allegorical interpretations and I have no interest in developing yet another. Nevertheless, there is a long and rather august tradition of considering the poem in relation to the "psychological" issues so tantalizingly raised in the introductory note and reading it as an "aesthetic representation" of Coleridge's philosophy of art or a meditation upon *"creative inspiration."*[52] Beer interprets "Kubla Khan" as a poem more specifically "about poetry – in some respects even a poem about itself" and Burke views it as "in effect a poeticized *psychology*, detailing not what the reader is to *see* but what *mental states* he is thus empathically and sympathetically *imitating* as he reads."[53] In light of the poem's reception history, it seems appropriate to consider at least briefly whether Coleridge's concerns with mind–body interaction, unconscious cognition, and volition – and the contemporary scientific, medical, and polemical discourses that help shape them – seep into the text of "Kubla Khan." The result would be not another interpretation of the poem, but rather a supplement to the work of contextualization exemplified by Lowes' monumental study *The Road to Xanadu*, with an eye to traces not of early travel writing, exploration accounts, ethnographies, and literary exoticism, but rather of the emergent neuroscientific discourse that haunts Coleridge's career and provides so telling a background for the introductory note.

One might well begin with the common observation that the landscape of "Kubla Khan" presents at once a "mental topography" or map of the human psyche and a representation (however fragmented or overdetermined) of the human body.[54] This conjunction, generally taken for granted in the criticism, suggests the sort of mind one encounters in the biological psychologies of the time: an embodied mind, a mind that perhaps most blatantly manifests its embodied nature in dreams. Here it may be useful to return to the largely unprecedented emphasis on unconscious mental life found in the brain science of Coleridge's era. Literary Romanticism is frequently credited for anticipating various notions of the unconscious, particularly the unconscious of Freud, but Romantic poets and critics were by no means operating in a cultural vacuum. Peretz Lavie and Allan Hobson have called attention to a "rich

pre-Freudian tradition" of scientific work, particularly in eighteenth-
and nineteenth-century Britain, on dreams and the unconscious, a tradition that grounds the mind securely in the brain and body and that
looks forward to recent work in cognitive psychology and neuroscience
rather than to psychoanalysis.[55] Jonathan Miller has more recently
sketched out a line from Mesmer, not to Freud (and what Miller characterizes as Freud's "custodial" conception of the unconscious) but to the
"alternative, non-Freudian Unconscious" of cognitive science. In contrast to the "almost exclusively withholding function" he attributes to the
unconscious of psychoanalytic theory, Miller describes the cognitive
unconscious as "altogether productive," enabling the processes "integral
to memory, perception, and behavior."[56] These mental activities remain
largely inaccessible to conscious introspection not because of any presumed threat to the conscious ego, but rather because a range of mental
functions can be performed more quickly and expeditiously in the
absence of conscious control and supervision. In Miller's telling, this
"new" understanding of the unconscious had been adumbrated by a
group of British psychologists in the mid-nineteenth century who in turn
drew on earlier formulations in the Mesmeric literature, the phrenological school of Gall and Spurzheim, the French materialist tradition, and
the German Romantics with their interest in comparative neuroanatomy and physiology. Herder, to cite one key example, had made a naturalistic argument for the adaptive value of unconscious mental
processing more than a century and a half before such a conception
became standard in cognitive science. "Our poor thinking organ would
certainly not be able to seize every stimulus, the seed of every sensation,
in its ultimate elements . . . without shuddering with anxiety and . . .
letting the rudder go from its hands. So mother nature took away from
it whatever could not be faced by its clear consciousness, weighed every
impression that it might receive, and carefully organized every channel
leading into it."[57]

Post-Freudian accounts of the "discovery of the unconscious" suggest
how those Romantic-era formulations of unconscious mental processes
that most closely anticipate psychoanalysis and other "depth" psychologies form only one subset of a larger discursive field. As Coleridge's scattered remarks on dreaming suggest, writers now associated with literary
Romanticism were aware of the "alternate" unconscious outlined by
Miller, more productive than repressive, working to a large extent independently of the conscious subject, rendering the mind a theater of
instinct, emotion, and desires as well as of reason, perception, and ideas.

Diderot had already suggested in *Le rêve d'Alembert* how a materialist reduction of the self to "mere sensitivity, memory, and organic functions," not so much a bundle of perceptions as a "bundle of fibers," entailed a mind made subject to unconscious motivation by its embodiment, by its nature as a brain-mind functioning integrally within a bodily system.[58] Herder also outlines an embodied, nervous sensibility that can outrun and even "oppose" the conscious reason, adding that the "greater part of our vital functions are performed without any volition or consciousness of the mind" (*Outlines* 100, 112). This line of thought was significantly extended by Cabanis, who places much weight on the impressions received not through the external senses but the "internal organs, notably those of the lower abdomen." Helping to account for a variety of states and behaviors, from the sucking and rooting reflexes seen in newborns, to innate desires and inclinations, to the profound mental changes brought on by puberty or childbearing, to the effects of alcohol and narcotics, finally to those "vague states" of well- or ill-being we experience daily, stemming from "disturbances of the internal organs and of the internal parts of the nervous system," these messages from the interior of the body bypass consciousness, to reach awareness only in an "obscure manner" (*R* 1: 93, 96, 98). Gall similarly emphasizes the importance of "interior sensations" and the "instinctive tendencies" they support in the brain, enhancing survival by equiping the newborn with a set of innate behaviors and the adult with rapid reactions to various threats to the body, "involuntary and without consciousness" (*FB* 1: 102, 111).

De Quincey, in arguing that feelings may crucially convey what "consciousness has not seen"; or Hazlitt, in rooting both genius and "common sense" in an explicitly physiological conception of "unconscious impressions" manifested in bodily "feeling"; or Godwin, in enumerating a surprisingly large range of human activities performed in an irrational state of "reverie" or "human vegetation" – all bear witness to how the "alternative unconscious" of brain science impinges on Romantic writing.[59] In these essays, the material body manifests through "feeling" or "sensibility" an unconscious knowledge of its own, residing in the brain and nervous system and located at once within the body and below conscious awareness. Given his psychosomatic approach to mind–body relations, retaining the traditional primacy of psyche over soma while recognizing their extensive commerce, Coleridge characteristically describes their exchange as running in the opposite direction: "What I keep out of my mind or rather *keep down* in a state of under-consciousness, is sure to act meanwhile with it's whole power of poison on my body" (*STCL* 3: 310).

But scattered among the notebook entries, particularly those concerning dreams, lie those other passages suggesting that the body may have a mind of its own, that dream images may arise from the "Ganglionic" system or that spontaneous emotions and even speech-acts – guilt and falsehood – may be traced to the "Gastric Life."

The conjunction of dreams and the unconscious, the embodied mind and the "Gastric Life" takes us back to the poem allegedly composed "in a sort of Reverie brought on by two grains of Opium, taken to check a dysentery." The dreamscape of "Kubla Khan," at once detailed and indefinite, has been aptly described as a sexualized, amoral version of the conventional *paysage moralisé*, a psychologized landscape that also suggests a dispersed, erotically charged body.[60] There is a fair amount of agreement among critics that the poem's scenery lends itself to such a reading, though somewhat less about what body part goes where and how precisely to locate gender in an obviously sexualized landscape. Where some oppose the patriarch's "walls of culture – his 'stately pleasure dome'" – to a feminine, maternal landscape – the "primal female caverns and 'fertile ground,'" other critics have (notoriously) seen the pleasure dome instead as a representation of the mother's breast or even an image of the "Mons Veneris."[61] The fountain, though issuing from a "female landscape of caverns and chasms," is often read in terms of a "phallic" or "ejaculatory" force.[62] Yet others note instead a mimesis of "childbirth" in the "'fast thick pants'" with which the fountain bursts forth, possibly connected to the "sunless sea" allegorized as "womb-heaven of the amniotic fluid."[63] One Freudian analyst detects a "fantasy of anal birth" at work in this section of the poem, while another, struck by the bewildering "mixing of sexual symbols," can only compare them to the "bi-sexual" imagery he encountered in the course of his psychiatric work with marijuana "addicts."[64] At the same time, and by the same critics, the landscape with its caverns and chasm is linked with the "subconscious" sources of inspiration, "anti-rational forces associated with nature," the Freudian "id," the guilt-ridden deeps of the "poet's unconscious."[65] These irrational forces and depths are in turn connected with somatic "natural periodicity," "choric pulsions," the involuntary and "mysterious processes that go on inside the body."[65]

Reuven Tsur, in his innovative study of the reception and poetic structure of "Kubla Khan," has trenchantly pointed out that psychological analyses of the poem implicitly grant the relevance of twentieth-century conceptions of the unconscious to a late eighteenth-century poem.[67] Burke develops his psychological reading along "transcendental" lines suggested by Coleridge's own writings and finds his students' Freudian readings unduly "*erotic*" by comparison.[68] One could go a long way toward meeting charges of irrelevance or anachronism, however, by recovering a wider sense of the psychological discourse of Coleridge's era, taking better account of the brain-based approaches to mind that Coleridge flirted with at the beginning and then grappled with until the end of his intellectual career. Connections between unconscious mental activity, a dynamic conception of nature ("fertile ground"), internal bodily processes, spontaneous or unwilled thoughts and behaviors, and sexual life in particular are pervasive, as detailed above, in the pioneering neuroscience of the time. Coleridge often broaches such connections in his unpublished writings, sometimes in the very language of Romantic brain science. To read "Kubla Khan" in terms of a biology of mind – one that pays special attention to instinctive, unconscious, or involuntary aspects of psychic life – need not entail abandoning Coleridge's discursive context in favor of later psychological theories. Rather, such a reading can underscore the links between Romantic psychologies and the revival of psychodynamic theories later in the nineteenth century.[69]

Even at a more detailed level, such as symbolically equating the pleasure dome with both esthetic culture and the maternal breast, or the stock ejaculatory reading of the "obviously scandalous" fountain, interpretations inspired by psychoanalysis and related depth psychologies could find warrant in the psychological discourses of Coleridge's own era.[70] Darwin had written in *Zoonomia* that the infant's repeated association between pleasure and the dome-shaped "form of the mother's breast" provides a lasting psychological template for beauteous forms (*Z* 145), a notion he would later versify in *The Temple of Nature*:

> Warm from its cell the tender infant born
> Feels the cold chill of Life's aerial morn;
> Seeks with spread hands the bosom's velvet orbs,
> With closing lips the milky fount absorbs;
> And, as compress'd the dulcet streams distil,
> Drinks warmth and fragrance from the living rill;
> Eyes with mute rapture every waving line,
> Prints with adoring kiss the Paphian shrine,
> And learns erelong, the perfect form confess'd
> IDEAL BEAUTY from its Mother's breast.[71]

The milk of Paradise indeed. And the incorrigible fountain? Erotic dreaming accompanied by ejaculation made a prime example for

French physiological psychologies of the close links between bodily desires, unconscious mental activity, and spontaneous behaviors, from Diderot (who includes a wickedly amusing scene of nocturnal emission in *Le Rêve d'Alembert*) to Cabanis, who cites "nocturnal emissions" in his discussion of the brain's activity and its enhanced susceptibility to "internal impressions" during sleep (*R* 1:136–39).[72] Coleridge's anxious notebook jottings regarding the "bad Passions in Dreams" place him surprisingly close to this tradition. The suggestions of polymorphous or ambiguous sexuality that some psychoanalytic critics have located in Coleridge's revision of the Edenic myth also find resonance in Darwin, who postulates an "original single sex" in *Zoonomia* that accounts, among other things, for the human male's possession of seemingly useless nipples.[73] And readers who would relate the "milk of paradise" to Coleridge's experiences with "laudanum and the whole tribe of stimulants," suggesting an Edenic return to the full pleasures of infancy, might profit from the connections between narcotic states and "connate" desires posed by Darwin and others.[74] Coleridge himself poses associations between opium and an embodied mind, a "sort of stomach sensation attached to all my thoughts."[75] He also describes the "divine" effects of opium as "a spot of enchantment, a green spot of fountain and flowers and trees in the very heart of a waste of sands" (*STCL* 1: 394), another example of the contemporary fascination with mind-altering drugs that found such ecstatic expression in the laboratory reports collected by Davy. Rather than calling psychodynamic interpretations of "Kubla Khan" altogether into question on historical grounds, we can draw support for their general drift and even for some of their more outlandish hermeneutical claims by redirecting the historicist gaze to a different, less familiar section of the archive. Readings of Coleridge's dream poem that emphasize the interrelations among body, mind, and natural world, that link spontaneous acts to unconscious and libidinal forces, that posit a fragmented psyche and reject classical notions of the subject, are as much in the spirit of the emergent biological psychologies of the Romantic era as they are of later "depth" psychologies, though by an accident of literary history such readings became widespread only in the wake of Freud.

Finding a significant area of convergence, however rough, between readings inspired by psychoanalytic criticism and writings from the "pre-Freudian" psychological tradition championed by Miller, Hobson, and others in the neuroscientific camp may come as a surprise. Even those seeking to bridge the gap between the psychoanalytical Unconscious and the unconscious of cognitive neuroscience – which turns out, on Miller's reading, to be at once pre- and post-Freudian, the "new" unconscious but also a reassertion of the old one – tend to find more opposition than common ground. Frequently the opposition is figuratively conveyed in terms of temperature: the Freudian unconscious is hot, seething, a "boiling pot," while the neural unconscious by contrast seems efficient and logical, cool as a computer.[76] But if the parallels that Miller and others have traced between the cognitive unconscious and the embodied unconscious of Romantic-era brain science are more than superficial, then one should expect to find a steamier, sexier side to the "new" unconscious than may have been evident during the early phase of the cognitive revolution, with its pronounced bias toward computational metaphors and its vision of intelligence as "software" relatively autonomous of the brain's "hardware." Recent work in cognitive neuroscience has indeed come to integrate the emotive, instinctive and irrational into its picture of unconscious mental life, often with a respectful nod toward Freud, and has returned to the embodied conception of mind – neither hardware nor software but "wetware" – more characteristic of neuroscience in the period of its Romantic beginnings.[77]

Some of the most persuasive readings of "Kubla Khan" to date have gestured, though without explicit attention to the brain science of the era, toward an understanding of Romanticism as a cultural movement throwing notions of conscious volition and the integral self into crisis and acknowledging the irrational, bodily, and instinctual elements of mental life in unprecedented ways. Burke, who ties his reading of the River Alph as a "stream of consciousness" fed from "*below*" to Coleridge's own musings on the "streamy" nature of association and subconscious inspiration, sees a "'problematical' element implicit" in the "romantically spontaneous waywardness" that drives the poem.[78] Sandra Gilbert and Susan Gubar, more ambitiously, argue that "when the chasm of romanticism opened culture to the revolutionary and anti-rational forces associated with nature, with imagination, with unconsciousness, and with spontaneity – that is, to all the terms that had been repressed" by patriarchal culture, male poets like Coleridge felt "threatened" by the irruption of "the feminine" within themselves.[79] For Tsur this threatening sensation is felt instead by the poem's readers and critics, who deploy a whole range of "cognitive strategies" for dealing with the "irruption of the irrational into our ordered world."[80] Bringing the neuroscientific context to bear on British Romanticism only intensifies the widespread sense of its "problematical" aspects, its anxious subversion of traditional valuations of mind over body, spirit over matter, reason over passion, conscious judgment over unconscious spontaneity. This is a problematic that marks Coleridge's intellectual career and that marks "Kubla Khan" and its confessional introduction as well. Whatever else the poem signifies – and both its amazingly wide range of reference and the seemingly inexhaustible resonance of its imagery have been amply attested to by Lowes and many since – it touches squarely and inescapably on issues that were no less central for Romantic brain science than for Romantic poetry.

Before leaving "Kubla Khan" it is worth at least noting how issues of volition and the counter-will of the body, of the affective and the irrational, also make themselves felt in analyses of its syntactic, formal, and prosodic elements. David Perkins, for example, has noted how the "subjunctive" mood of the verbs at its close ("conditional" is probably a more accurate term) mirrors the vexed status of the will in the prose introduction.[81] The poem that begins with recounting a "decree" and ends in an exclamatory and imperative voice troubles its series of authoritative speech-acts and declarative statements with a mazy construction of conditional phrases ("Could I . . . 'twould . . . I would . . . And all should") that blocks the poet's access to visionary power. The introductory note underscores the poet's "*failure*" to fully engage in the visionary creative activity idealized in its final section, and the structural links that critics have traced between the prose introduction and verse "epilog" only intensify the sense of frustrated or suspended volition as the poem ends.[82] If the prose introduction is read as an integral part of the poem, it becomes difficult to distinguish the wild-eyed poet at the close from the "drugged dreamer" of the introduction: each has beheld a vision inspired by the milk of paradise, and each has seen this vision irretrievably vanish.[83]

Tsur's thoughtful discussion of the poem's meter, one that somehow manages to strike readers as both skillfully nuanced and hypnotically rhythmic, brings out still another dimension of the "irrational and primordial" appeal he too locates in "Kubla Khan." Noting the unusually robust convergence in many lines of linguistic stress and "strong" metrical position, further underscored by deft alliteration, Tsur discusses the "bodily appeal" of the poem's "vigorous rhythms," rooted in certain "fundamental *involuntary* physiological processes" common to humans as well as to other species.[84] These effects contribute in no small part to the poem's uniquely "ecstatic" effect, helping to account for the powerfully emotive aura that many readers have attributed to the poem. I find Tsur's reading compelling not only because of the dexterity with which he develops it, but also for the support it brings at the level of form to Burke's contention that the reader of "Kubla Khan" empathically re-enacts its "poeticized psychology." Tsur's analysis would suggest that some of the same neuroscientific issues broached by Coleridge in the introduction – the embodied nature of the mind, the crisis of conscious volition, the insistence of irrational and unconscious elements in psychic life, the interrelation between cognition and the internal organs – might recur in a given reader's performance of the poem as well. Such considerations depart wildly from Coleridge's own poetic theory, with its mentalistic and transcendental bias and its occasional hostility toward linguistic and cultural primitivism. They do not seem so distant, however, from the poetic theory of Wordsworth, who is quite interested in the bodily effects of meter and whose notions of the "best" part of poetic language, according to Coleridge, might better fit the "languages of uncivilized tribes" (*BL* 2: 53–54). Exploring the relation between Wordsworth's poetics and embodied theories of mind demands a chapter to itself.

CHAPTER THREE

A beating mind: Wordsworth's poetics and the "science of feelings"

In 1799 one T. O. Churchill completed his translation of Herder's *Outlines of a Philosophy of the History of Man*, published in London the next year.[1] Among many remarkable passages, it includes this one on the infant's creation of an object world through passionate interaction with its mother:

The suckling at the mother's breast reposes on her heart: the fruit of her womb is the pupil of her embrace. His finest senses, the eye and ear, first awake, and are led forward by sound and figure: happy for him, if they be fortunately led! His sense of seeing gradually unfolds itself, and attentively watches the eyes of those around, as his ear is attentive to their language, and by their help he learns to distinguish his first ideas. (91)

An English poet also writing in 1799 captured the same developmental process in closely analogous, but more memorable, terms:

>   – blest the babe
> Nursed in his mother's arms, the babe who sleeps
> Upon his mother's breast, who, when his soul
> Claims manifest kindred with an earthly soul,
> Doth gather passion from his mother's eye.
> Such feelings pass into his torpid life
> Like an awakening breeze, and hence his mind,
> Even in the first trial of its powers,
> Is prompt and watchful, eager to combine
> In one appearance all the elements
> And parts of the same object, else detached
> And loath to coalesce.   (*Prelude* 1799 2: 269–80)

Though the poet, Wordsworth, had just spent a year in Germany (where he originally intended to study "natural science",[2] and though his friend Coleridge, also fresh from Germany, was urgently requesting the German original of Herder's *Outlines* in November of 1799 (*STCL* 1: 535), I would not wish to suggest that Wordsworth is directly indebted to

Herder for his great lines on the "infant babe."[3] Nor, however, would I dismiss the parallel as a mere accident of cultural history.

Instead, I think that Herder, in his *Ideen zur Philosophie der Geschichte der Menschheit* (1784) and Wordsworth, in his poetry and poetic theory of the late 1790s and early 1800s, are engaged in overlapping projects, each drawing eclectically on Lockean sensationalist psychology, Enlightenment anthropology, the vein of French radical thought running back to Diderot, and the new naturalistic and biological approach to mind then prominent in scientific and radical circles. In the passages just quoted, both Herder and Wordsworth are attempting to frame naturalistic accounts of infant development that balance the empiricist stress on sensation with the infant's active participation in shaping the objects of that sensation. Each depicts a process of cognitive unfolding that confounds distinctions between reason and emotion and that places the infant in a world of passionate social interaction from the moment of birth. This new approach to psychological development is a remarkable departure from the more passive, mechanistic accounts of Locke, Hartley, and Condillac; it looks as much forward to recent cognitive neuroscience as backward to analytic philosophy. It places Wordsworth, at least for a few crucial years, in the midst of one of the most daring intellectual ventures of his era – the reinvention, along naturalistic, physiological, and ecological lines, of the study of human nature.[4]

My claim for a Wordsworth attuned to the new biology and biological psychology of his time is not unprecedented but builds on the work of other scholars going back to H. W. Piper. In *The Active Universe*, Piper found an unexpected convergence between the poetry of Wordsworth and the physiological psychology of Cabanis that he attributed to a common grounding in the "new 'materialism'" of the late eighteenth century, a "pantheistic materialism" current within the French revolutionary and English Jacobin circles that Wordsworth frequented during his "radical years" in France and London.[5] Erasmus Darwin, whose *Zoonomia* provided Wordsworth with material for *Lyrical Ballads*, was one of the most important theorists of the "new" materialist psychology, working (like Wordsworth) from a grounding in Hartley, the first physiological psychologist.[6] Priestley's *Disquisitions Relating to Matter and Spirit* (1777), which Wordsworth probably read, argues against dualism on scientific, philosophical, and religious grounds, redefining the *"mental"* powers of sensation, perception, and thought as properties of the *"nervous system."* The physiological effects of emotion present Priestley with further evidence that the "mind" and the "body and brain" properly designate "no other than *one and the same thing*."[7] Wordsworth had direct personal links as well to the new, biological materialism. John Thelwall, a onetime student of anatomy and physiology whose lecture adducing the "phenomena of mind" from "principles *purely physical*" had got him expelled from Guy's Hospital Physical Society earlier in the decade, was friendly with Wordsworth in the late 1790s.[8] Another acquaintance of Wordsworth's was James Tobin, Humphry Davy's assistant at Thomas Beddoes' clinic, then a hot-bed of "materialist pneumatics" and the scene of Davy's psychopharmacological experiments with laughing gas, with Southey and Coleridge among Davy's test subjects.[9] And there was Coleridge himself, no longer the "Advocate for the Automatism of Man" he claimed to be in 1794, but still steeped in the intellectual atmosphere that had made the "corporeality of *thought*" another of his slogans of that year.

Speculation on Wordsworth's early intellectual history is always, of course, just that. Unlike Coleridge, Wordsworth did not leave an elaborate paper trail for future scholars documenting his reading and opinions in letters, marginalia, literary autobiography, notebooks, and table talk. Reconstructions of Wordsworth's intellectual atmosphere typically rely on such hedges as "probably," "must certainly have," "could not but have been aware of," and the like. Though Wordsworth has been called the "associationist poet" he cannot be shown conclusively even to have read Hartley, and though his associationist language was "likely to have been" modified by his reading of Darwin, he is known to have had possession of *Zoonomia* for only a few weeks in 1798, though – undoubtedly – he had read it "previously" and "knew precisely what he wanted" when he begged to have it sent "*by the first carrier.*"[10] At a pinch Coleridge, whom scholars can show to have read nearly anything, and who was not known for keeping his impressions to himself, can always be brought in as a link to this or that writer or idea. Coleridge read it all and, as John Jones comments, "No doubt Coleridge said it all."[11] The critical license unleashed by such an indirect approach has meant, however, that a disarmingly wide range of philosophical positions and theoretical "influences" have been attached to Wordsworth over the years. Looking only at the *Lyrical Ballads* period, for example, we find Wordsworth's philosophical views characterized in terms of idealism, empiricism, mysticism, humanism, and Platonism; his poetry described as crucially indebted to Hartleyan psychology, "natural science," Enlightenment anthropology, and Evangelical religion; his political ideals evincing Burkean conservatism or defining a "new radicalism."[12]

This list of viewpoints and influences, moreover, has been chosen (from among still others) not just for the contradictions among various scholarly constructions but also for their plausibility taken singly. Each can be cogently defended, none has yet been definitively dismissed. In part this reflects the relative freedom that Wordsworth's reticence affords his interpreters. But in part too it stems from the flexibility and adventurousness of Wordsworth's thought in the 1790s, a decade of unusually dramatic and changeable intellectual weather. It is not only more cautious but more accurate to speak of Wordsworth's philosophical interests in terms of tendencies rather than firm positions. Wordsworth, as Jones remarks, "though no fool, was no philosopher."[13] He seems not to have craved the consistency that impelled Coleridge to continually redefine his own changing, but carefully delineated, positions. In what follows, then, I wish to bring out a materialist tendency in Wordsworth's thinking and elicit a biological register in his writing rather than refashion him as a 1790s materialist. Even as a tendency, Wordsworth's materialism must be qualified, in Jones' terms, as "more than materialism," a phrase applying equally well to Darwin, Cabanis, Bell, or Gall.[14] As Piper notes, materialist and vitalist notions were "not in fact very different" in this period, helping to explain why John Hunter's legacy could be seized by both parties in the materialist–vitalist controversy of the 1810s (and why historians resort to awkward terms like "material vitalists" in describing the early biological thought of the time).[15] A naturalistic, physiological, ecological approach to psychology and anthropology was fully compatible with the belief in a "motion and a spirit" coursing through the body (and its mind) and, it might be, through every other particle of the universe as well.[16] Whether that indwelling power was itself material (perhaps a superfine "fluid" related to electricity and magnetism) or altogether unworldly was a question that could be left open, though the lack of a firm spiritualist commitment made writers like Darwin notoriously vulnerable to orthodox attack. "*God and the brain! nothing but God and the brain*" Gall would desperately proclaim, after repeated charges of atheistic materialism (*FB* 6: 292). It did not keep him from being excommunicated, or his books from being placed on the Papal *Index*.

ORGANIC SENSIBILITY

What, though, is gained by placing Wordsworth with the "material vitalists" of his time, given that he cannot be numbered simply or decisively among them? Primarily, it can help to make sense of certain longstanding cruxes in Wordsworth's linguistic and poetic theory concerning the continuity between poetry and prose, the status of meter and other extrasemantic features of poetry, and the relation of the "best part of language" to rustic life. It can also show that in simultaneously building upon and resisting key aspects of Enlightenment thought on language and culture, Wordsworth was by no means singular.[17] Rather, his writing in the late 1790s bears strong affinities with the physiological psychologies of Herder, Darwin, Cabanis, Gall, and Bell, not because (with the exception of Darwin and perhaps Herder) he was then familiar with their ideas, but on account of a network of shared pretexts, ideals, and aims. Finally, it can help give substance to certain key terms that have recently returned to Romantic criticism, such as "sensibility," "universal," and "organic," without sufficient attention to their valence in Romantic-era discourse.

In the *Poetics of Sensibility*, for example, McGann rightly stresses the importance of "organic sensibility" in Wordsworth's Preface to *Lyrical Ballads*.[18] McGann neglects, though, to specify what "organic" might convey in 1800, some years before its adaptation by Coleridge (from German *natürphilosophie*) as a specialized term freighted with metaphysical import. Heard with its post-Coleridgean resonance, "organic" tends now (at least for Romanticists) to include "holistic" or "systematic" among its connotations. Yet as late as 1807 Henry Crabb Robinson, in his pamphlet helping to introduce Gall's brain-based psychology to England, speaks of "Dr. Gall's Organic Theory," a decidedly fragmented approach ("the brain is not *one* organ of the soul . . . but a receptacle for distinct organs") that Coleridge would later criticize on that very basis.[19] Similarly, in translating Herder's *Outlines* Churchill employs "organic" in contrasting the mind's embodiment in the brain *through* which it acts with the irreducibly *"psychological"* laws *by* which it acts: "organic it is true, yet acting of itself, and according to spiritual laws" (*Outlines*, 118).[20] Although Coleridge's later writing might lead literary scholars to expect the reverse, "organic" here attaches not to the transcendent psyche but to the body and its material organization. These are the sensory and cognitive "organs" celebrated in the 1799 *Prelude*:

> Thus day by day
> Subjected to the discipline of love,
> His organs and recipient faculties
> Are quickened, are more vigorous; his mind spreads,
> Tenacious of the forms which it receives.   (2.280–84)

The phrase "organic sensibility," in the context of the late 1790s, over-laps significantly with related terms like Darwin's "*sensorium*" and Cabanis' "*sensibilité*." It implies a mind shaped by and realized in bodily organs, though not entirely defined by them. The poet of superior organic sensibility is not necessarily the one with the most susceptible sensory organs; Wordsworth, after all, had "*no sense of smell*" (and there-fore, one assumes, little sense of taste).[21] But sensations felt (or rather, produced) by internal as well as external "organs" provide the material out of which mind is constructed, an active sensibility stimulated or "quickened" by emotion and contributing an affective tone to cognition: "all my thoughts / Were steeped in feeling" (*Prelude*, 2.447–48). A genuine poetic sensibility, for Wordsworth, is one that continues to reg-ister the permeation of thought with feeling and remains in touch with the sensational, bodily, and emotive origins of mind, the "lovely forms / And sweet sensations" and the "passions" that "build up our human soul" (*Prelude*, 1.134, 461–62).

The 1799 *Prelude* is only one among several key texts from this period that suggest Wordsworth's interest in a naturalistic, biological approach to mind. In the fragmentary "Essay on Morals" (*c.* 1798) Wordsworth laments the absence of a moral philosophy "with sufficient power to melt into our affections, to incorporate itself with the blood & vital juices of our minds" and thus help transform our moral "habits," a revision of Hartley in the language of the new physiology altogether reminiscent of Darwin's *Zoonomia* (*WP* I: 103). A like conception inheres in a startling metaphor from the (*c.* 1799) preface to *The Borderers*, the "milk of human reason" (*WP* I: 77). This metaphor, a play on the "milk of human kind-ness" in *Macbeth*, also underscores how the conventionally gendered opposition between (masculine) transcendent reason and (feminine) embodied emotion begins to erode within Romantic-era physiological theories of mind. Soon after, in the sonnet "1801," Wordsworth will enjoin the virtuous "Governor" to "temper with the sternness of the brain / Thoughts motherly, and meek as womanhood." The "nursing mother's heart," celebrated in the 1799 *Prelude* for its "awakening" role in subject formation, will recur in later versions as the model for "feeling intellect," a masculine no less than feminine ideal (*Prelude*, *1805* 13.205–7).[22]

The *Lyrical Ballads* of 1798, as Richard Matlak has shown, owe their rich and innovative "inner-body imagery" – "Felt in the blood, and felt along the heart" – to Darwin's "bio-medical" understanding of a "phys-iologically-based mental system" in *Zoonomia*.[23] In addition, that is, to the psychophysiological case study (Z2: 369) that famously gave Wordsworth the germ for "Goody Blake and Harry Gill", Wordsworth found in *Zoonomia* a theory of active perception and a conception of ideas grounded in charged physical sensations.

> 'The eye it cannot choose but see,
> 'We cannot bid the ear be still;
> 'Our bodies feel, where'er they be,
> 'Against, or with our will.

("Expostulation and Reply")

Our bodies do not require, can in fact override, conscious awareness in actively gathering the sensations necessary to building up and maintaining a human mind. Wordsworth also profits from Darwin's "symbiotic" model for the interrelations among mind, body, and natural environment[24]: "To her fair works did nature link / The human soul that through me ran" ("Lines written in Early Spring"). *Lyrical Ballads* responds as well to the brain-based approach to mental illness popularized by *Zoonomia* and embraced by contemporary "radical" scientists like Beddoes, whose *Hygëia* classes mania and melancholia along with epilepsy under "nervous disorders" and understands insanity as a "disorganization of the brain."[25] "A fire was in my brain" might be read as conventional mad diction for Wordsworth's "Mad Mother," but the fragility of an embodied mind is also broached by the sane (if superstitious) narrator of "The Thorn" – "Sad case for such a brain to hold" (144) – and by the "Female Vagrant," who attributes her past fits of madness to a "weak" and "dizzy" brain (196–200).

The 1799 *Prelude*, however, proves an even richer source for images that fuse the mental and the corporeal, as it explores the "growth of mental power" and models how the "mind of man is fashioned and built up" (1.67, 257). The mind is active and emotive from the beginning, "infantine desire" (2.24) impelling the growth and organization of mental life through impassioned interaction with the natural and social world, guided by the "innate activity" of the developing mind itself.[26] The infant's first "object" (2.249), linking perception from the outset both to affective human bonds and to a nourishing connection to the natural world, is the mother's breast, the archetype in *Zoonomia* for pleasure and esthetic form (Z 1: 145), the stimulus in the 1799 *Prelude* for the "first / Poetic spirit of our human life" (305–6). The poet who recognizes a "grandeur in the beatings of the heart" and celebrates the "hallowed and pure motions of the sense" acknowledges throughout the role

played by the body and its organs in the formation and continual refor-
mation of an active subject of perception, "creator and receiver both"
(1.383, 141; 2.303). The developing subject's "intercourse" with the
natural world can be "unconscious" as well as consciously directed,
another idea in harmony with the embodied psychologies of the time (1:
394). "Drinking in / A pure organic pleasure" from natural forms (1:
395–96), the growing child maintains the active, emotive, bodily relation
to the object world inaugurated in its "first trial" at the mother's breast.
Together, these images of organic growth and interaction convey a thoroughly and often deliciously embodied sensibility, in a phrase, a "beating
mind" (2: 16).[27]

The dependence of mental life on the brain is now taken so much for
granted that one could well miss a related feature of the 1799 *Prelude*, the
use of the term "brain" where an earlier poet (or where the later
Wordsworth) would prefer "mind." At a time when Gall was devoting
much of his energy to arguing, against established opinion, for the
mind's location in the brain, phrases like Wordsworth's "for days my
brain / Worked with a dim and undetermined sense / Of unknown
modes of being" (1: 120–22) participate in a distinctively novel psychological discourse. Natural scenes providing the backdrop for intense
emotional experiences "Remained, in their substantial lineaments /
Depicted on the brain, and to the eye / Were visible" (1: 430–2), a new-
fangled, bio-associationist account that would have irked the confirmed
dualist Thomas Reid, who had tried, in 1785, to demonstrate the impossibility of storing or representing images in the brain.[28] Also reminiscent
of Darwin's revision of Hartley is the bodily, emotive, and organic tenor
of Wordsworth's new associationism in the early *Prelude*. As a boy he
experiences "giddy bliss / Which like a tempest works along the blood"
and sparks the unconscious retention of images in the brain, implying
connections among emotion, physiology, brain, and mind recently delineated in *Zoonomia*. Unconscious, embodied, emotive cognition is also
experienced in "thoughtless hours" when "from excess / Of happiness,
my blood appeared to flow / With its own pleasure, and I breathed with
joy" (2: 225–7). The interconnectedness assumed here among the lungs,
brain, and circulatory system will form the cornerstone of Bell's physiologically based esthetic in *The Anatomy and Philosophy of Expression* a few
years later.[29] Bell will also develop an adaptive, nativist, environmental
approach to cognitive development along the lines of Wordsworth's
"first-born affinities that fit / Our new existence to existing things" (1:
387–88). The convergence, here and there in Wordsworth's writing of

the late 1790s, of the physiological, the psychological, and the esthetic may have been avant-garde but it was by no means eccentric.

FROM LOCKE TO SWEETSER

Psychology, esthetics, and the new physiology also become intertwined in Wordsworth's poetic and linguistic theory of the *Lyrical Ballads* period, though not in any systematic manner. Recovering Wordsworth's embodied approach to language is the more difficult owing to the recent emphasis on the role of arbitrariness and relativity in his linguistic thought, placing Wordsworth squarely in a line running from Locke to Saussure.[30] As some of the best work on Romanticism and linguistic theory has shown, however, Wordsworth's various pronouncements in this area manifest a characteristically Romantic ambivalence, at times lamenting the arbitrariness and "incompetence of human speech" (*Prelude*, 1850, 6:593) yet also maintaining the ideal of a "natural language" guaranteeing enduring connections among words, objects, and feelings.[31] In one of the *Peter Bell MS. 2* fragments (1799), for example, the poet's naive confidence in achieving a "universal language" is punctured by his later realization that he "scarcely had produced / A monument and arbitrary sign." Yet a related fragment describes the "considerate and laborious" work of poetic creation that "doth impart to speach / Outline and substance, even till it has given / A function kindred to organic power."[32] Natural and "organic" approaches to language have, of course, seen a major revival over the past several decades, along with an interest in the origins of language that is as serious and intense as that of Wordsworth's time. In particular, cognitive linguists like George Lakoff and Eve Sweetser have reopened the question of "*nonarbitrary*" or "motivated" aspects of language, seeing certain linguistic regularities as "natural," rooted in "general human cognitive abilities" and in "human physiology."[33] Placing Wordsworth in a tradition leading from Locke not to Saussure but to cognitive linguistics may help disentangle some of the knottier aspects of his poetic theory. At the same time, reconsidering Wordsworth's poetics along cognitive lines can help bring out their relation to neglected issues in Enlightenment and Romantic linguistic and cultural thought, issues that have again become prominent in recent cognitive theory.

Wordsworth's debt to eighteenth-century speculation on the origins of language is sometimes presented as an uncritical absorption of "cultural primitivism," a charge anticipated by Coleridge.[34] Viewing

Wordsworth as an Enlightenment primitivist, however, underestimates the revisionary impulse in his use of Enlightenment paradigms. Moreover, it conflates the progressive universalism of the earlier part of the century, grounded in a universally shared but unequally developed "Reason," with the embodied universalism emerging later in the century, grounded in human physiology and skeptical with regard to differences between the "savage" and "civilized" mind.[35] The earlier thinkers, for all their differences, tend to bracket off the body (in the manner of Locke) or to minimize its relevance to language and culture. They emphasize instead a widening gap between nature and culture that progressively leads to the attainment of mature reason or reflection, enabling the emergence of an "arbitrarily" produced language with no "natural connection" between words and the ideas they signify.[36] James Harris, in *Hermes*, begins from the postulate of universal "REASON," dividing human beings from the "irrational animals" and enabling thought *"without"* the "medium" of the body. His linguistic theory is predicated on an absolute distinction between (physical) "sound" and (abstract) "meaning," with linguistic symbols attached to ideas in a manner *"quite arbitrary."*[37] Lord Monboddo opposes the *"rational"* mind of civilized humans to the "savage" whose "mind is moved only by impulses from the body"; only the former can master the "exceedingly artificial" faculty of verbal articulation and develop language, an entirely learned rather than "natural" accomplishment.[38]

Even in Monboddo, however, and still more in Condillac, one begins to find a contrasting interest in the "natural cries" that might have provided a springboard to the first proto-language.[39] Condillac distinguishes "natural" from "instituted" or "arbitrary" signs, the latter enabling the development of reason or "reflexion," which constitutes the divide between human beings and animals.[40] Yet Condillac assumes that the first language must have developed out of "natural cries" and gestures suggested *"by instinct alone,"* providing a template or "pattern to frame a new language" that would rely more and more extensively on arbitrary signs.[41] Rousseau, too, points to the natural "accents, cries, lamentations" and gestures from which, prompted by a language "instinct," speech proper gradually arises.[42] Reid, despite his dualistic approach to mind and body, also feels impelled to reground the origins of language in human physiology. "Certain features of the countenance, sounds of the voice, and gestures of the body" make up a language of "natural signs" that we interpret automatically "by the constitution of our nature, by a kind of natural perception similar to the perceptions of sense."[43]

Without the foundation of this "natural language," humankind could "never have invented an artificial one" by reason and ingenuity alone.[44] For Reid, these natural signs are incorporated into rather than replaced by artificial language and contribute to its vitality and force: "Where speech is natural, it will be an exercise, not of the voice and lungs only, but of all the muscles of the body."[45]

In Herder's "Essay on the Origin of Language" the dependence of language on physiology becomes even more pronounced, though Herder still maintains a distinction between "natural" language and the "truly human language" that relies on arbitrary signs.[46] As does Condillac, Herder associates arbitrary language with the rise of "reflection" or reason, the most distinctively human capacity. Yet reason proceeds not from a disembodied mind or spirit but from the "total economy" of our sensuous, cognitive, volitional nature, "associated with a particular organization of the body" (110). Before the full development of reflection and with it language proper, human beings communicate by means of a "language of nature," composed of "wild articulate tones" arising naturally out of the speaker's bodily "machinery" and in turn appealing directly to the "inner nerve structure" of the listener (87–88, 96–97). This "maternal language" (89) is "obviously animal in origin," the "natural law of a mechanism endowed with feelings" (99). The acquisition of artificial language is in its own manner instinctive or innate. "Parents never teach their children language without the latter, by themselves, inventing language along with them" (120).

The overall effect of late Enlightenment speculation on linguistic origins was to weaken the distinction between natural and artificial languages while maintaining that between natural and artificial signs. In place of an older consensus stressing the human uniqueness and divine origins of language (which Hartley, among others, keeps current well into the eighteenth century), Wordsworth's generation inherited a thoroughly naturalistic approach, alive to continuities as well as distinctions between human and "animal," learned and instinctive communication systems, prizing the emotive as well as the rational aspects of language, and increasingly grounding linguistic behavior in human physiology rather than a disembodied mind or "REASON." These tendencies become still more pronounced in the Romantic psychologies of Darwin, Cabanis, Gall, and Bell. Darwin, in *Zoonomia*, follows Reid in assuming the priority of "natural signs" over artificial ones, deriving the former from a "universal language" arising from a common human body plan and neurophysiological organization (Z 1: 147). "Natural signs," as

Darwin explains in *The Temple of Nature*, enable us to read one another's "passions," extrapolating from the effects of emotion on "our own bodies."[47]

> When strong desires or soft sensations move
> The astonished Intellect to rage or love;
> Associate tribes of fibrous motions rise,
> Flush the red cheek, or Light the laughing eyes.
> Whence ever-active Imitation finds
> The ideal trains, that pass in kindred minds;
> Her mimic arts associate thoughts excite
> And the first LANGUAGE enters at the sight.   (3: 335–42)

Cabanis similarly traces the "true universal language" of look and gesture to human "physiognomy" in the *Rapports* (*R* 1: 68–69), while Gall's model of a "natural," "universal," "pathognomic language" significantly overlaps with Darwin's theory despite a different emphasis on the role of discrete brain organs and their instinctive operations (*FB* 5: 295). Bell devotes much of *The Anatomy and Philosophy of Expression* to studying the "expressions, attitudes, and movements of the human figure" as a universal "grammar" for the fine arts (AP 2). Grounded in basic human neurophysiology, it constitutes a "natural language" intertwined with spoken language due to the role of the lungs, face, tongue, throat, and diaphragm in speech production (113). Like Herder, Bell sees artificial language not abandoning natural signs but extensively incorporating them, especially for expressing emotions (85). These ideas were clearly available, at least among an avant-garde group of physicians, radicals, and intellectuals, in 1790s England. Matthew Baillie outlines the links among mind, brain, nerves, body, and "emotions," arguing for a "natural language" ("universally understood" and "not connected with any arbitrary customs of society") arising from them, in his 1794 lectures to the Royal College of Physicians.[48] Joanna Baillie, positing a natural, bodily "language" of expression that conveys the passions in a manner that "every age and nation understand" in her 1798 "Introduction" to *Plays on the Passions*, tacitly relies on the new neurophysiology summarized four years earlier by her brother in the Gulstonian lectures.[49]

Viewed in this context, Wordsworth's speculation on language and poetic theory does not seem anachronistic, exceptional, or particularly odd.[50] In seeking to frame a more "natural" and emotive language for poetry, one making use of extrasemantic as well as semantic resources, widening its appeal by addressing the "primary laws of our nature"

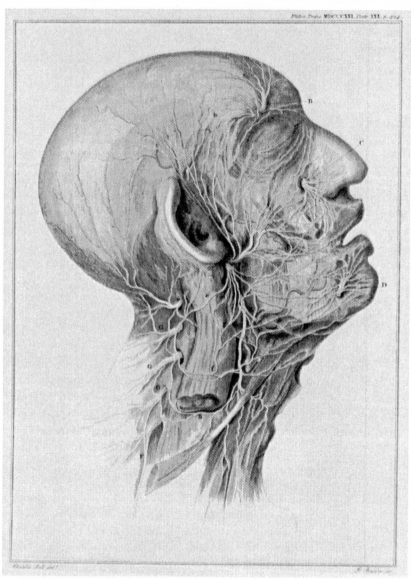

5 Bell, "On the Nerves," *Philosophical Transactions* 111 (1821), plate XXXI (the facial nerves).

(*WP* 1: 122), Wordsworth puts to practical use the emergent post-Enlightenment discourse on language that Herder, Darwin, Cabanis, and others were developing around the same time. Particularly for a poet who, like Wordsworth, composed out loud and performed his verses orally – according to Hazlitt, in a kind of "*chaunt*" – the emphasis on extrasemantic, "natural" features of language in post-Enlightenment linguistic and neuroscientific theory would be instantly appealing (*HW* 17: 118). Rather than feeling "puzzled" by Wordsworth's connection, posed in the preface to *Lyrical Ballads*, between poetic meter, pleasure, sexual "passions," and the "great spring of the activity of our minds" (*WP* 1: 148), one can see how readily these connections might occur, given the intellectual climate, to someone at least fitfully interested in the organic approaches to mind and culture then in vogue.[51] Both Rousseau and Herder, building on hints in Condillac, had emphasized the impassioned character of the "natural language" from which artificial languages arose. Herder calls it a "language of feeling" (88) and Rousseau hypothesizes that sexual desire provided the first incentive for articulate speech (11, 45–6). For all three thinkers, rhythm is a "natural" aspect of early speech, closely related to its highly emotive character.[52] As Rousseau writes, "verse, singing, and speech" are initially undifferentiated and poetic meter remains linked to the "natural cries" of the instinctive proto-language (50). For Herder, this accounts for the universal presence and appeal of "rhythm" in the "poems and songs" of ancient peoples as well as modern "savages," and for the susceptibility of young children and others who "live through their senses" to ballads (92, 97–98). The notion of metrical and musical universals recurs in Darwin (*Z* 1: 250–1), Cabanis (*R* 1: 160–1, 2: 595), and Reid, who describes a man who could make infants alternately cry and "dance for joy" at will by whistling in different tones and tempos.[53] In insisting that the effects of metrical language are universally acknowledged "by the consent of all nations" and arise from the "great and universal passions of man," Wordsworth belongs in this company (*WP* 1: 144).

Whereas Cabanis and Reid both speak of a class of innate or "instinctive" esthetic responses,[54] Darwin constructs a more elaborate neurophysiological theory to account for the pleasure associated with "musical time," "poetic time," rhyme, alliteration, and related devices. All capitalize on the mind's "propensity" to repetition, which is accounted for by Darwin's fluid dynamic model of the "sensorium" or "spirit of animation." Constantly accumulating, the body's store of neural energy must be regularly expended through "some kind of action" by the various sensorial powers. Thanks to the power of association, a repeated action is the mind's readiest and most pleasurable source of relief (Z 1: 250–51). As Darwin summarizes in a note to *The Temple of Nature*, our pleasure in poetic rhythm arises "because the sensorial power of association" is "combined with the sensorial power of irritation."[55] Certain phrases in the preface to *Lyrical Ballads* – the "fluxes and refluxes of the mind," the "pleasure which the mind derives from the perception of similitude in dissimilitude" – recall Darwin's dynamic theory of neural energy and may imply some variation on it. More broadly, however, work such as Darwin's provides a contemporary analog and discursive context for the "complex interplay of the sensuous and intellectual" that Stuart Sperry, in a subtle meditation on the role of rhythm in Wordsworth's poetry and poetics, makes central to Wordsworth's writing in the late 1790s. For Sperry, the "sustaining rhythms of a familiar beat" recur in the mother's heartbeat and in the "rhythmic" activities – skating, rowing – celebrated in the 1799 *Prelude*, connecting these in turn to the "pulsations" of biological existence and the rhythmic verse intended to convey it. The entire pattern yields an "almost physical sense of the community between metrical language and the underlying rhythms of life."[56] Meter allows the rhythmic, passionate character of "natural language" to flow into articulate language and help remedy the "sad incompetence of human speech."

Contemporary notions of "natural language" also come up in Wordsworth's discussion of meter, repetition, and passion in his 1800 note to "The Thorn," one of the more aggressively experimental of the lyrical ballads. Defining poetry both as "passion" in itself and as the "science of feelings," Wordsworth explains that he drew on the resources of meter and of verbal repetition in trying to convey words "impregnated with passions" to the sensibilities of his readers. While he notes our "consciousness of . . . the deficiencies of language" in attempting to "communicate impassioned feelings," he also suggests a recourse in emphasizing the extrasemantic properties of speech – those, according to Herder and others, inherited from the natural "language of feeling" – to counterbalance the poverty of words considered only as arbitrary symbols.[57] Repetition, found in the "impassioned poetry of every nation," is one such device for conveying the "interest which the mind attaches to words, not only as symbols of the passion, but as *things*, active and efficient, which are themselves part of the passion," a holdover from the proto-language of natural cries.[58] This appeal to the extrasemantic aspects of language (closely related to the care Wordsworth brings to matters of prosody) comes up in other quite noticeable ways throughout the *Lyrical Ballads*, in addition to the frequent use of repetition and repetitive devices like alliteration. More directly related to the notion of "natural cries," for example, is the nonsensical but expressive "burr, burr" of the "Idiot Boy," not to mention the many exclamations and sighs, apostrophes and interjections – the *O!*'s, *alas!*'s, *Oh!*'s, and *ah!*'s – that punctuate the volume and contribute so insistently to its overall feel.

The context of "natural" language theory and early neurophysiological speculation on language also helps resolve another apparent problem for Wordsworth's poetics: the tension between his call for a "plainer and more emphatic" language in the 1800 preface and his recourse, in the 1802 "Appendix" on poetic diction, to the "original figurative language of passion" employed by the "earliest poets of all nations" as a standard for modern poetry (*WP* 1: 160–61).[59] For those who, like Horne Tooke, assume that the proto-language of "natural cries" is displaced by the rise of symbolic language – that the "dominion of Speech is erected upon the downfall of Interjections" (61) – it might seem that a plainer language would be *less* emphatic or at least less emotive.[60] But for thinkers who, like Rousseau and Herder, view articulated speech as absorbing the "natural" language of cries, expressions, and imitative gestures, a simpler, "plainer" language would simultaneously be more sensuously concrete and more metaphorical and emotive than the overly abstract and specialized sociolects of urban cultures.[61] Wordsworth's key phrase "the real language of men" goes on, "in a state of vivid sensation"; such language is prized for "forcibly" expressing "elementary feelings" and "passions" (*WP* 1: 118, 124). In all of these ways it evokes the early language described by Rousseau as one of "images, feelings, and figures" (15). For Herder the first language is a "collection of elements of poetry" taken from "interjections of all beings" – imitating their sounds and calls in a symbolic but nonarbitrary fashion. More importantly, the ur-language is "animated by the interjections of human emotion," the presymbolic language of natural cries persisting not as root words but rather as the "sap that enlivens the roots of language" (91, 135).

The same "vital juices," Wordsworth declares in like terms, run through both good poetry and good prose, the "same human blood circulates through the veins of them both" (*WP* 1: 134). Wordsworth's refusal to distinguish between the languages of poetry and prose, at their best, grows out of a decidedly organic understanding of language, one given direct as well as metaphorical expression in the "Preface." "They

both speak by and to the same organs": linguistic exchange is produced
and processed neurophysiologically, not through some ideal transparent
medium, and good prose no less than good poetry will reflect the advantages as well as the limitations of embodied communication. The
"bodies in which both of them are clothed" – the sensuous and extrasemantic aspects of language, akin to the notion of words as "*things*, active
and efficient" in the note to "The Thorn" – "may be said to be of the
same substance, their affections are kindred and almost identical."
Again, language at its most expressive is described as embodied, organic,
and emotive, terms that tie Wordsworth's poetic theory closely to the
post-Enlightenment, naturalistic discourses on language and culture of
the time. But why should the "best" language usage be found most
readily among what Wordsworth terms "rustic" speakers? Given the
interest Wordsworth will show, in the 1802 appendix, in the "language
of passion" developed by the "earliest poets," perhaps some variant of
cultural primitivism is implicated in Wordsworth's poetics after all.

THE BEST PART OF LANGUAGE

Coleridge devotes much of chapter xvii of the *Biographia Literaria* to
attacking Wordsworth's ideas on the relation between poetic language
and rustic life. One of the chapter's subheadings gives a fair idea of what
follows: "The *best* parts of language the product of philosophers, not of
clowns or shepherds" (*BL* 2: 40). Taking issue with Wordsworth's statement that in a rustic existence "men hourly communicate with the best
objects from which the best part of language is originally derived" (*WP*
1: 124), Coleridge compares the notion of a core language concerned
mainly with "bodily conveniences" to the prelinguistic forms of communication found among some animals and to the "languages of uncivilized tribes." For Coleridge, the "best part of human language" is
"derived from reflection on the acts of the mind itself," formed by a "voluntary" (or arbitrary) "appropriation of fixed symbols to internal acts,"
many of which "have no place in the consciousness of uneducated man"
(*BL* 2: 53–54). Like Harris or Monboddo, Coleridge grounds language
"properly so called" in acts of reason and reflection, here minimizing the
body's role in communication and linguistic production. Much as for
Condillac, for Coleridge language grows more refined and useful in
tandem with the progress of civilization; it facilitates the very acts of
"imagination, contemplation, and memory" that help to improve it (*BL*
2: 58). By contrast with Coleridge's progressive approach to the develop-

ment of human language, Wordsworth's statements on rustic speech seem nostalgic and primitivistic, as Coleridge implies in the *Biographia* and as Abrams and other critics have reiterated since.[62]

There is no doubt that Wordsworth idealizes rustic language in the preface, as he himself seems to acknowledge in noting that he has "purified" it by removing "what appear to be its real defects" (*WP* 1: 124). He also takes, without argument, one local variant of rural speech as representative. Coleridge, in contrast, considers the "language of the shepherd-farmers in the vales of Cumberland and Westmoreland" to be rather idiosyncratic, shaped in part by widespread (though limited) schooling and an immersion in the King James Bible but few other books (*BL* 2: 44). Wordsworth's opposition between the "plainer" speech of "low and rustic life" and the corrupted dialect of cities, aggravated by the "rapid communication of intelligence" (newspapers?), might also be read in terms of his later conservative stance on the politics of mass literacy, though some find a democratic impulse at work in Wordsworth's validation of the "language of conversation" among middle- and lower-class speakers (*WP* 1: 116).[63] There is, too, a distinctly nostalgic strain running through the tradition that sees artificial language gradually emerging out of a more impassioned and affective "natural" language. Rousseau laments that language becomes progressively "duller and colder" even as it becomes more rational and "exact" (16). Herder contrasts the "refined, late-invented metaphysical language" of modern Europe to the "original wild mother of the human race," a language of pure "poetry" (91, 135). Especially when the 1802 appendix is taken into account, it is hard not to see such cultural nostalgia at work in the theoretical apparatus Wordsworth added to *Lyrical Ballads*.

Nevertheless, something more than primitivism motivates Wordsworth's interest in rustic language. Reading Wordsworth's theory of poetic diction too narrowly through the lens of Coleridge's critique, a common enough practice, fails to do justice to its complexity.[64] As an alternative, one might return to Wordsworth's interest (typical of his time) in the nonarbitrary aspects of linguistic communication, discussed above mainly in relation to the extrasemantic features of speech and poetry. Cognitive linguistic theory has also explored the nonarbitrary or "motivated" aspects of semantic meaning, reopening certain avenues of thought earlier broached by the Romantics.[65] It has been argued (following Aarsleff) that for Wordsworth all linguistic signs are arbitrary and notions of "natural" language and nonarbitrary linguistic structures can therefore play no role in his thinking on poetic diction.[66] This view falters, however, if one moves beyond Aarsleff's false dichotomy between "Adamic language doctrine" and Lockean arbitrariness to explore a third alternative; namely, the naturalistic, proto-evolutionary, psycho-physiological theories of language represented by Herder, Darwin, and others in the period.[67] These thinkers underscore the continuities between natural and artificial, animal and human languages as much as the distinctions; they also view basic features of human anatomy and physiology as constraints on the play of linguistic arbitrariness. It is hard to see in any case how there could be a "best part of language" for Wordsworth if he views all linguistic signs as equally arbitrary and language as a system of differences. Wordsworth could reject the older model of a divinely ordained, Adamic language linking words absolutely to objects of nature, without accepting the notion of an entirely arbitrary semantic system, as a comparison to cognitive linguistic theory may help clarify.

Cognitive semantics, a field (like the language theory of Wordsworth's time) at the intersection of linguistics, anthropology, and philosophy of mind, views language as integral to the larger cognitive life of a human being with "a human brain in a human body in a physical environment that it must make intelligible if it is to survive."[68] Language cannot be fully understood at an autonomous level because it reflects everyday human needs and the basic character of human experience, shaped to be sure by different sociocultural environments but also by widely if not universally shared features of life in a human body. "As animals," writes the philosopher Mark Johnson, in terms that hearken back to the Romantic era, "we have bodies connected to the natural world, such that our consciousness and rationality are tied to our bodily orientations and interactions in and with our environment" (xxxviii). For Mark Turner, a pioneer in "cognitive rhetoric," language and literature are properly understood as the acts of an "embodied human mind" employing its "ordinary conceptual capacities"; that is, linguistic meaning is a subtype of human meaning-making in general.[69] The fact of our embodiment, according to Lakoff, entails a system of "*nonarbitrary* links between cognition and experience" that, without determining the conceptual and linguistic categories of a given culture in advance, nevertheless account for certain regularities in the way that those categories are structured and interrelated (154). A key example for Johnson is the widespread human tendency to "understand the mental in terms of the physical, the mind in terms of bodily experience" (53), as when we "see" someone's point or "sense" someone's irritation. These examples manifest the

metaphorical structure of much everyday cognition, while their perva-
siveness across any number of languages suggests that the basic metaphorical schemata behind much cognitive and linguistic activity are
"motivated" by common features of embodied human experience. In
this sense, there is indeed something "natural" about human languages
and the way they develop over time. Instances of linguistic "polysemy"
(multiple meanings of the same word), for example, manifest a predictable movement from physical and concrete meanings to more abstract
ones, in keeping with the primacy of bodily experience within general
cognition (107).

Johnson here is indebted to Sweetser, whose work on semantic change
suggests how "our linguistic system is inextricably interwoven with the
rest of our physical and cognitive selves" and that "not only our language . . . but our cognition operates metaphorically" (6, 8). Noting that
meaning frequently develops from "concrete to abstract" across a
number of different languages, Sweetser concentrates on one particularly intriguing instance, stemming from what she calls the "Mind-as-
Body Metaphor" (25, 28). A common ("if not universal") tendency to
understand the "internal self" in terms of the "bodily external self"
underlies such pervasive metaphors as using "see" to mean "know" ("I
see what you're up to"), "hear" to mean "understand," "grasp" to mean
"comprehend," or "touching" to mean "emotionally affecting." This
tendency grows in part out of common physiological experiences.
"Indo-European words for the emotions," for example, often derive
from "words referring to physical actions or sensations accompanying
the emotions," as in using "hot" to express feeling "angry" (28). But the
larger pattern of "mind-as-body" metaphors suggests an entrenched
cognitive schema, probably "motivated" by such common physiological
experiences but more elaborate, regular, and constrained in its operation
than could be reduced to a simple set of physiological/psychological
correlations. (For example, you cannot simply turn things around and
say "I'm feeling angry" for "I'm hot.") The "equation of the physical self
and the inner self" implicitly and unconsciously invoked when we use
"vision" to mean "mental prospect" or "good taste in" to mean "specialized knowledge of" bears witness to the pervasive working of "large-scale
conceptual metaphors" within cognitive life, shaping the structure and
development of conceptual and hence of linguistic categories (31, 45).

It might seem farfetched to view Wordsworth's notions on the continuity between poetry and prose, the derivation of the "best part of language" from what Coleridge calls "bodily" life, and the intimate relation

between language and human physiology as held together – though in no systematic way – by anything like a cognitive approach to linguistic and poetic issues. Late Enlightenment and emergent Romantic thought on these subjects, however, had generated a set of hypotheses analogous to those informing recent work in cognitive semantics. Reid, for one, observed a basic uniformity in the "structure of all languages" and therefore assumed a comparable uniformity in the core "notions upon which the structure of language is grounded," anticipating the "cognitive wager" posed by linguists like Lakoff and Sweetser. Not only, for Reid, do linguistic universals reflect cognitive universals, but the "greatest part of every language" is metaphorical as well. More particularly, Reid identifies a universal and "natural" human propensity to "conceive of the mind as having some similitude to body in its operations," though, as a committed dualist, he regrets this basic metaphorical tendency as a barrier to accurate thinking on the subject.[70] Adam Smith held that languages developed historically by adding increasingly abstract senses to an original set of physical and concrete terms, while Darwin assumed that as language became more "abstracted" it became less densely metaphorical.[71] For Herder, "every family of words is a tangled underbrush" around the "sensuous central idea" that roots it, giving a vestigial "sensuous" character to modern languages (134–35). All languages are animated by this indwelling "spirit of metaphors," though the metaphorical interrelations helping to structure different languages vary along with "national character" and grow more faint as a language becomes more "polished" (147–50).

It is this emphasis on the productive force of metaphor that distinguishes Herder's theory of word families growing around a "sensuous central idea" from the superficially similar Lockean notion of words deriving from ideas that in turn derive from sense experience. For Locke, ideas arise from "Sensation and Reflection" and are attached "arbitrarily" to words, which can readily drift from the optimally clear and distinct ideas they are meant to convey (105, 405–8). Metaphorical language is suspect as a prime source of linguistic corruption: rhetoric and "figurative" speech belong to the "Arts of Fallacy" (508). Condillac's model is more complicated, as it postulates an original language that combines signs derived from "natural" cries and gestures with arbitrary symbols, giving it an initially poetic and "picturesque" character (227). But as language is progressively improved by growing powers of reflection, poetic language becomes deviant and fit only for "amusement" (232–33).[72] However, abstract words are created, within the Lockean tradition, by a process that resembles metaphor: words are based, Locke writes, on "obvious sensible ideas" and then "transferred" to "more abstruse significations." Thus the word "imagine" is ultimately based on the more concrete notion of eyesight, and "Spirit, in its primary signification, is Breath" (403). This sounds like an early formulation of the "Mind-as-Body" metaphorical schema discussed by Sweetser. But within the Lockean tradition, hostility toward the "Arts of Fallacy" entailed that, rather than metaphor being prized as a creative engine for linguistic production, abstract terms are rendered suspect by their remove from "sensible ideas." The most extreme example is Horne Tooke's reductive etymological method, assailing the "metaphysical jargon" of conventional discourse by insisting that "words are the *signs* of *things*," and demeaning "rhetorick and poetry" in favor of the "useful arts or sciences" (18–19, 63). Tooke's corrosive etymologies appealed to certain radical materialists, who saw them as ammunition for attacking political and religious orthodoxies. William Lawrence, for example, contends that "the Latin *spiritus*, or original of our spirit, from *spiro*, 'to breathe,' means merely 'breath' . . . this is the original sensible object, out of which all the abstractions and fancies, all the verbal sophistry and metaphysical puzzles, about spirit, have proceeded" (*LPZ* 53). Etymological analysis could become another way to challenge the split between mind and body, by reducing the former to the latter.

Wordsworth's references to "plainer" speech and "best objects" have been viewed as placing him within this reductive tradition. If so, there is indeed a contradiction between his championing of the "real language" of men in the 1800 preface and his yearning for the "daring and figurative" language of early poets in the 1802 appendix. Placing Wordsworth too narrowly within the Lockean orbit, however, ignores the strong bias against poetry and metaphor characteristic of Locke and his followers; Wordsworth, in contrast, is defending his own poetic practice, interjections, figurative language, and all. Herder had suggested that early languages were less abstract yet still highly metaphorical, plainer *and* more emphatic, incorporating the passionate energy of interjections as well. More importantly, Herder insists that modern languages retain the "metaphors in the roots of words," though in a less overt manner than in "unpolished" languages (149). Wordsworth's approach to language in the apparatus to *Lyrical Ballads* taken altogether seems closer to Herder than to the Lockean tradition, particularly given Wordsworth's standard of passionate expression rather than logic and precision.

Wordsworth also evinces an organic and environmental understanding of human language, closer to Herder's than to Locke's, in stressing that the best part of language derives not merely from the perception of the "best objects" of nature but from interaction with them. To return to the key sentence in question, rustic speakers "*hourly communicate* with the best objects from which the best part of language is originally derived"; the "passions of men are *incorporated* with the beautiful and permanent forms of nature" (*WP* 1: 124, my emphases). The human mind brings its own innate structure and qualities to bear on what is presented as a richly interactive process: "certain inherent and indestructible qualities of the human mind, and likewise of certain powers in the great and permanent objects that act upon it which are equally inherent and indestructible" (*WP* 1: 130). In appealing to inherent mental qualities, Wordsworth means something much more robust than the Lockean faculties of sensation and reflection. At one point he goes so far as to cite human characters "belonging rather to nature then to manners, such as exist now and will probably always exist" (*WP* 1: 128), a notion much easier to square with Gall's "organology" and other psychobiological theories of the time than with Locke's *tabula rasa*. Wordsworth adds in 1802 that the true poet considers "man and nature as essentially adapted to each other" (*WP* 1: 140), a statement that would readily be endorsed by Gall, Darwin, or Bell. Whether by evolution (as Darwin would have it) or design (as Bell argued), the human mind is fundamentally patterned for embodied interaction with a social and physical environment that despite "difference of soil and climate" manifests certain predictable features. In turn, "human nature" remains relatively stable ("indestructible") over time (*WP* 1: 141).

Although Wordsworth's presuppositions and aims place him closer to Herder than to the Lockean tradition, his notion of the "best part of language" does not much resemble Herder's onomatopoeic theory of root words. A better analog than either Locke or Herder might be found by looking forward to cognitive semantics, which also begins from a postulate of "universal prelinguistic cognitive structures" shaped by and for interaction with a relatively stable, though variable, "sociophysical" environment.[73] Cognitive linguists speak of a "basic" conceptual and linguistic level that bears certain similarities, both in its relation to "natural kinds" and in its emphasis on human interaction with the sociophysical environment, to Wordsworth's several formulations in the preface to *Lyrical Ballads*. The basic level is another nonarbitrary feature of human conceptual and linguistic systems, though just what natural (and artifactual) objects count as "basic" can vary somewhat from one linguistic community to another.[74] Unlike some philosophical versions of "natural kinds" theory, basic-level structure is not "purely objective." Lakoff instead terms it "species-specific," a matter of correspondence between our cognitive apparatus and the world "as we interact with it: as we perceive it, image it, affect it with our bodies, and gain knowledge about it" (50).[75] Basic-level categories are easier to recognize and remember and are the first categorizations made by young children, the most readily named by adults, and presumably the first names to emerge in the "evolution of languages."[76] They occur at a middle level of relative abstraction, "cat" rather than "animal" or "Persian," "car" rather than "vehicle" or "sedan." Like basic metaphorical schemata, basic-level categories reflect common "perceptual and functional" experience. They conform to visual gestalts ("commonalties in shape" and "overall look") and "sets of common motor movements" performed when using or interacting with them.[77] (You can know you've caught a glimpse of a dog, without being sure of the breed; you use the same motor program in sitting down on a chair, whether it's a kitchen chair or a throne.) Basic terms facilitate the ongoing creation of a "human-sized" environment out of the flux of experience, reducing the "limitless variation of the world to manageable proportions."[78] In tandem with basic metaphors (like "mind-as-body"), they provide much of the groundwork underlying concept formation and hence language.

The cognitive theory of basic-level terms can help make sense of Wordsworth's remarks on the relation between the rustic's "hourly" interaction with natural objects and enduring features of language. "Such a language arising out of repeated experience and regular feelings is a more permanent and a far more philosophical language," he asserts, than the language of "false refinement" preferred by poets alienated from the common experiences and "sympathies of men" (*WP* 1: 124). If we gloss "best objects" as "basic objects," "more philosophical" as something like "more cognitively salient," and provisionally accept the assumption that rustics lead a life more richly involved with basic human tasks, movements, emotions, and natural objects than do urban sophisticates, Wordsworth's equation of "rustic" and "philosophical," so provoking to Coleridge, seems a good deal less odd. In fact, this interpretation is close to that proposed by one of the Preface's most careful readers to date, W. J. B. Owen, who understands Wordsworth to mean "those human passions, habits, occupations, and environments which are sufficiently basic, important, and permanent in human experience to ensure that the corresponding elements of language do (more or less) survive."[79] What a comparison with cognitive theory can add is a better guess at how "basic" features of the environment and "elements of language" might have been linked in Wordsworth's thought, a link that seems to demand some notion of a universal cognitive apparatus, organized according to the "primary laws of our nature" and constituting the "universal intellectual property of man" (*WP* 1: 122, 2: 78). In addition, cognitive semantics provides another example (along with Herder) of a linguistic theory for which language can be grounded in a set of core metaphors while also built up from a vocabulary biased toward the physical and concrete, although critics of Wordsworth's poetics have sometimes assumed that these are incompatible notions.

It would be a mistake, however, to view Wordsworth as somehow "anticipating" cognitive linguistics rather than as sharing some analogous presuppositions, aims, and attitudes. For one thing, Wordsworth's thinking on language is anything but systematic. Even if, as I have suggested, there is more continuity than contradiction between the "Advertisement" of 1798, the "Preface" of 1800, and the additions and "Appendix" of 1802, there are certainly changes in emphasis and in immediate purpose. Although the parallels in Herder, Reid, Darwin, Bell, and other contemporaries suggest that it is not anachronistic to reconstrue Wordsworth's poetic and linguistic thought along neurophysiological lines, positing a cognitive Wordsworth still depends on making tentative links among a number of detached passages scattered throughout the poetry and prose. Moreover, even if a significant area of common ground is granted, Wordsworth's pronouncements on language and poetics diverge quite starkly from a modern cognitivist approach. Although cognitive semantics does establish some distinctions, for example, between the "basic-level" categories of rural and urban speakers, these differences are seen as trivial and value-neutral; there are "basic" parts of language but not "best" ones.[80] Despite some speculation on the more densely "sociophysical" character of early languages, continuity is emphasized over change and there is no sense of linguistic "decline" as one finds in Rousseau, Herder, and Wordsworth's 1802 "Appendix." The cognitive linguist is more concerned with establishing the deeply and pervasively metaphorical character of modern languages, marking even philosophical and scientific discourses. Modern language – and cognition – are seen as no less fundamentally "literary" or "poetic" than what Wordsworth terms the "original figurative language of passion."[81] This emphasis on passion or emotion marks the most significant area of divergence between Wordsworth's thinking on language and the primary concerns of recent cognitive theorists. As David Miall points out in a sympathetic but critical response to Mark Johnson, cognitive linguists tend to overlook the "affective and kinesthetic" aspects of language so important within Romantic theories of poetry.[82] Little attention is given to extrasemantic features of communication like meter and other rhythmic and repetitive devices, nor is much said about the affective component of literary and linguistic response. For Wordsworth, cognition and communication – particularly poetic communication – not only reflect embodied experience but are fundamentally emotive as well. Rustic manners and speech "germinate" not simply from repeated interaction with enduring features of the sociophysical environment but from the "elementary feelings" endemic to rustic life, the "essential passions of the heart" (*WP* 1: 124). The poet of exceptional "organic sensibility" draws on connections between his own "elementary" feelings and those of his subjects and intended audience in representing human nature in its "naked dignity" (*WP* 1: 126, 140). His "passions and thoughts and feelings are the general passions and thoughts and feelings of man," connected with "animal sensations" as well as "moral sentiments," and attuned to such widespread features and conditions of human life as the "operations of the elements," weather and seasonal change, the basic set of human emotions, the consequences of mortality, and common aspects of social exchange (*WP* 1: 142). In granting a primary role to feeling and emotion within an embodied and ecological understanding of mind and culture, Wordsworth is closer to the brain science of his time than to what is sometimes called "cognitivism."

The points of contact, however, deserve emphasis, both for the greater consistency they allow one to see in Wordsworth's views on language and poetry, and in helping to elicit neglected aspects of his writing that place him among the "more than materialists" of his day. In his naturalistic approach to language and culture, his "organic" understanding of mind and sensibility, his conviction of an enduring and universal (though malleable) human mental apparatus, his assumption of nonarbitrary or motivated aspects of language, his appreciation for the "philosophical" consequences of everyday experience, his refusal to divorce poetry from prose or to bracket off linguistic meaning from a larger area of meaningful activity, his belief in an adaptive fit between the mind and its physical environment, his sense of pervasive interrelations among psychological, linguistic, physiological, and social aspects of human life, Wordsworth makes common cause with cognitive linguistics. (This may say as much about the "Romantic" character of certain tendencies in cognitive theory as it does about the "cognitive" side of Wordsworth.)

Wordsworth did not entertain such views exclusively or for very long. They coexist even in the 1799 *Prelude*, particularly the second part, with a countervailing impulse to oppose the "corporeal appetite" and "fleshly" senses to "our purer mind / And intellectual life," a dualism that will find its most notable expression in the "Immortality" ode (*1799* 2: 97, 363–64, 462). His understanding of language, too, remains haunted by a fear that speech may drift free of common experience after all, that words may hold "dominion over thoughts" and language prove a "counter-spirit" to "subvert" and "vitiate" (*WP* 2: 84–85).[83] Yet however unsystematic or tentative, the notions that link Wordsworth to the physiological psychologies of his own time and to the cognitive linguistics of ours leave a lasting mark on his poetic theory. They play a major role in his attempt to understand "in what manner language and the human mind act and react on each other" (*WP* 1: 120), a richly interactive process that depends crucially on an implied third term, the human body.

CHAPTER FOUR

Of heartache and head injury: minds, brains, and the subject of Persuasion

The intellectual attraction of the new, brain-based theories of mind for a poet coming of age around 1798 could only have been heightened by their distinctly avant-garde tinge. The brain science being disseminated throughout the 1790s in the writings, lectures, and laboratories of iconoclasts like Darwin, Beddoes, Thelwall, and the youthful Davy came charged with a Jacobin frisson, redolent of religious dissent and political radicalism, and inspiring accusations of dangerous skepticism at best, godless materialism at worst. Despite a growing climate of reaction, the "radical science" of the mind continues well into the early nineteenth century, reaching a crisis point with the Lawrence controversy in the late 1810s, when it moves "underground" to find oblique expression in the works of a new generation of avant-garde intellectuals typified by the Shelleys.[1] But at the same time, in a subtler but equally significant fashion, key tenets of the new psychology were seeping into the mainstream, helping to transform notions of subjectivity, of culture, and of character. Charles Bell gave the imprimatur of the scientific establishment and the aura of the Established Church to physiological conceptions of mind, esthetics, and human development that overlapped significantly with the ideas of radicals like Darwin and revolutionaries like Cabanis. The relentless critical attention devoted to Gall and Spurzheim in the major reviews guaranteed that at least the basic elements of the new brain-based psychologies were widely known; "no speculations have engaged more attention, or have more frequently afforded a topic for conversation," acidly remarks a reviewer in 1817, "since the time of Joanna Southcote."[2] Medical men in particular were avidly discussing, and selectively embracing, the innovative ideas and challenging findings of Galvani, Bell, and the craniologists.[3] New scholarship on the medical education of John Keats suggests that a number of "radical" scientific developments, including Gall and Spurzheim's new brain anatomy, had become part of the standard London medical curriculum by the time that Lawrence gave his outspoken lectures to the Royal College of Surgeons.[4]

The novel, too, was beginning to take up (and in some ways extend) the brain-based approaches to mind and personality being aired by the materialist–vitalist debates and popularized by the phrenology movement. Jane Austen is often thought of as a novelist working primarily from the empiricist standpoint of an experientially constructed subject, and a succession of critics have paid careful and rewarding attention to the education, socialization, and cultural predicaments of her heroines. In her last novel, *Persuasion*, however, Austen anticipates Victorian novelists in looking to biological and innate aspects of mind and character, in tune with and in some ways ahead of the brain science of her time. Moreover, Austen's famously innovative style for conveying the heroine's impressions in *Persuasion* speaks as much to a new psychological appreciation of unconscious mental life and embodied cognition as to a new esthetic mode for representing the flux of conscious experience.

DUCTILE MINDS, ORGANICAL BRAINS

The shift within Romantic-era discourses on mind and character from environmental to biological approaches to psychological behavior and subject-formation emerges most starkly, perhaps, in the changing views of William Godwin. In the 1790s, Godwin presents a rigorous and influential social constructivist account of mind, one obviously indebted to Locke and Hartley. The "actions and dispositions of mankind," he writes, are the "offspring of circumstances and events, and not of any original determination that they bring into the world"; "innate principles" and "original differences" of physiological "structure" have no role in shaping mind or character. Education in particular, and the effects of social and political life – institutions and ideologies – in general, become all-important in shaping and imprinting the mind's initially "ductile and yielding substance" for good or ill.[5] By 1831, however, in *Thoughts on Man*, Godwin has become convinced that "Human creatures are born into the world with various dispositions" most likely rooted in the "subtle network of the brain." Contrary to the claim of Helvétius (and, by implication, his own earlier view) that the human character "depends upon education only, in the largest sense of that word," Godwin now maintains that innate "temper" significantly shapes psychological development. "He must have been a very inattentive observer of the indications of temper in an infant in the first months of his existence, who does not confess that there are various peculiarities in that respect which the child brings into the world with him."[6]

Godwin's conversion to a psychology of individual differences, human "peculiarities," and innate predispositions reflects the considerable influence of the new brain-based theories of mind, particularly Gall's "organology." A later essay in *Thoughts* is devoted to the "extraordinary vogue" for phrenology, dismissing its precise division of the mind into "twenty-seven compartments" but accepting some of its basic premises: that the "thinking principle" is located in the brain, the "great ligament which binds together" body and mind; that the sensory "nerves all lead up to the brain" and that acts of volition initiate "in the brain itself"; and that the brain is modular, with "one structure of the brain better adapted" for a given discrete "intellectual purpose" than another. Although craniology has not discovered it, a method for identifying these structures is probably an attainable science, one that will help discriminate those "attributes and propensities" that "a human creature may bring into the world with him" from those others that are the "pure growth of the arbitrary institutions of society."[7]

As Godwin's early reliance on Hartleyan associationism attests, Hartley's pioneering physiological psychology was thoroughly compatible with a sensationalist, "blank slate" conception of mind. But as biological approaches to physiology came to displace mechanistic ones, brain-based models of mind began to feature, in Herder's phrase, the "innate, organical, genetic" aspects of mind (*Outlines* 179). Herder takes for granted that "diseases and features, nay that tempers and dispositions, are hereditary," a fact known "to all the world" (*Outlines* 183). Darwin, despite his strong associationist bias, writes of hereditary temperaments in *Zoonomia*, defining temperament in psychopathological terms as "a permanent predisposition to certain classes of diseases" (Z 1: 354). Cabanis sets out to update Galen's theory of temperaments, arguing that the innate organization of each brain and nervous system profoundly shapes experience, and that "congenital" inclinations cannot be effaced though they can be modified by education (R 1: 267, 306, 2: 259). Gall similarly argues that innate dispositions can be modified, though neither destroyed nor produced, by education, holding that mental characters are "transmitted from family to family" by means of neural "organization" and explicitly condemning, with Cabanis, "tabula rasa" accounts of mental development such as Locke's and Hartley's (*FB* 1: 135, 185). In thus emphasizing the innate and hereditary aspects of character, the new biological psychologies were reasserting a dominant medical and philosophical view of "temperament" as old as the Greeks, while giving scientific credibility to a common folk view of the time.[8]

The novel of the Romantic era made its own contribution to this profound discursive shift regarding character, individuality, and temperament. The radical or "Jacobin" novel of the 1790s offers a fleshed-out version of the Lockean constructivist approach, showing in vivid detail how, as Mary Hays writes in *Emma Courtney*, "We are all the creatures of education."[9] In place of the anecdotal childhood episode or two, revealing innate bias of character, supplied by earlier eighteenth-century novelists such as Fielding, detailed accounts of childhood and early education became the norm. Novelists learned to elaborate basic fairy-tale plots to set off the "advantages of education" by contrasting the fortunes of one of three daughters (or cousins) in Cinderella fashion (as in Austen's *Mansfield Park*), or one of two sisters (or friends) in the tradition of the "Kind and Unkind" tale type (as in *Sense and Sensibility*). Needless to add, the heroine with the best education – the one who has most thoroughly internalized moral principles and developed habits of self-regulation – wins out.[10]

As the example of Susan Ferrier's *Marriage* (1818) shows, however, notions of innate bias, if they ever disappeared entirely, were returning to at least complicate fictional representations of character by the time of the Lawrence controversy. Anticipating the later use of twin studies to explore issues of nature and nurture, Ferrier invents twin sisters, Mary and Adelaide, raised in different families according to markedly different principles. Mary, the sister whose more careful education has produced a "well-regulated mind," ends up (predictably enough) rising from her Cinderella status to marry happily and well, while her vacuous twin Adelaide (like Maria in *Mansfield Park*) marries a wealthy "fool" before ruining her reputation with an adulterous elopement. Complicating an otherwise schematic plot, however, is the twins' cousin, Emily, who is raised in the same fashion and environment as Adelaide, but whose native intelligence and generosity assert themselves in a "noble" though "wild" character, lacking Mary's exemplary self-control, to be sure, but also remarkably free of Adelaide's meretriciousness and short-sighted egotism.[11] Within another decade, novelists begin to take innate biases of character explicitly into account, using them to balance or at least qualify environmental influences on development. As Mary Shelley puts it in *The Last Man* (1826): "We are born; we choose neither our parents, nor our station; we are educated by others, or by the world's circumstances, and this cultivation, *mingling with our innate disposition*, is the soil in which our desires, passions, and motives grow."[12] Whether or not *Frankenstein* represents the extreme expression of a socially constructed mind, Shelley's later work anticipates the growing influence of phreno-logical and other physiological theories of personality informing the novels of Charlotte Brontë and later Victorian writers.[13]

NERVOUS SENSIBILITY IN AUSTEN'S LATE STYLE

Austen's portrayal of character in relation to experience has been seen as thoroughly Lockean in spirit, though unusually deft in execution.[14] Her novels include some of the most inventive and subtle reworkings of traditional tale-types to display the effects of contrasting upbringings and the habits of self-scrutiny and discipline they instill – or fail to instill, as Sir Thomas finds to his grief in contrasting Fanny to her favored but miseducated elder cousins at the end of *Mansfield Park*. In *Persuasion* (1818), Austen's last novel, a Cinderella plot is again deployed to set off the virtues of an undervalued sister, Anne Elliot, to the detriment of her spoiled siblings, the status-conscious, superficial Elizabeth and the plain-tive, self-involved Mary. Austen varies this traditional plot by making Anne the middle, rather than youngest, sister, as well as by introducing still another folk character type, the "false heroine," in the person of Louisa Musgrove. As in many a folktale, the false heroine in *Persuasion* functions to delay the eventual union of the true heroine with her "object" (Frederick Wentworth) by temporarily displacing Anne and claiming Frederick for herself.[15] As in many a domestic novel, Anne and Louisa are contrasted in terms of the quality of their upbringing and the degree of their self-discipline. Louisa is more "fashionable" and adept at superficial "accomplishments" while Anne is "more elegant and culti-vated," showing modesty and self-restraint where Louisa appears willful and flirtatious, a combination that proves nearly fatal at the novel's crisis point.[16]

That crisis – Louisa's mistimed leap towards Frederick's arms and her headfirst fall onto the paving stones of a massive sea-wall – introduces a further and more startling contrast, this time one without precedent. For while Anne's character has been shaped over her twenty-seven years of often painful experience, most notably her mother's death (when Anne is fourteen) and her youthful break with Frederick (five years later), Louisa's character is "altered," remarkably and apparently for life, by a single incident, a severe knock on the head (223). Once "happy, and merry" and rather giddy (67), Louisa is, as a consequence of head injury,

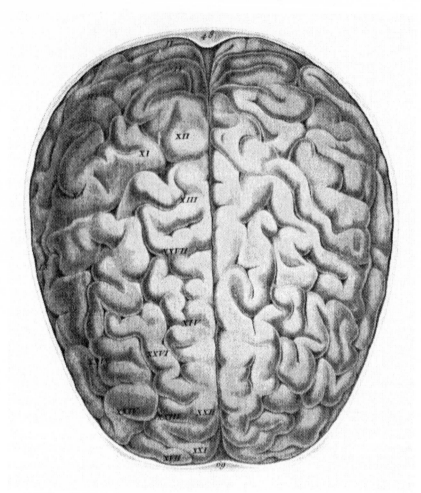

6 Gall and Spurzheim, *Atlas*, plate IX (superior surface – Keats's "globed brain").

"turned into a person of literary taste, and sentimental reflection," sed-
entary and neurasthenic. "The day at Lyme, the fall from the Cobb,
might influence her health, her nerves, her courage, her character to the
end of her life, as thoroughly as it appeared to have influenced her fate"
(178).

Critics of *Persuasion* have not known quite what to make of the connection Austen poses here between nerves and character, head trauma
and mental alteration, and sometimes they have simply made fun of it.
"True, she has fallen on her head," writes one, "but it had never been a

good one, and the blow seems to have cleared it."[17] To read what another calls the "zany incident at Lyme" as slapstick, however, fails to do justice to what has been aptly described as the "most sensational moment of physical violence in Austen's work."[18] It also fails to bring out the truly remarkable implications of Louisa's character change. At the very least, the fall and its consequences serve, in John Wiltshire's phrase, as a "graphic reminder that human beings are bodies as well as minds."[19] In the context of Romantic-era speculation on the brain and nerves, however, it also suggests that the relation between bodies and minds is of more consequence, at least in *Persuasion*, than critics of Austen have wanted to acknowledge.

Wiltshire offers his account of the body's salience in *Persuasion* to counterbalance readings that he worries may have exaggerated its "historicist dimension."[20] But Austen's portrayal of an embodied mind – most remarkably in relation to Louisa's fall but in quieter ways throughout the novel – has an important historicist dimension of its own. Head injury, strange as it may seem in retrospect, was a politically loaded topic at the very time Austen was writing *Persuasion*. From Hartley to Lawrence, proponents of physiological accounts of mind cite the effects of "Blows upon the Head" among other reasons to locate the mind in the brain – a notion that was still considered unproven, unorthodox, and ideologically subversive in Austen's time.[21] Concussions serve, along with visual illusions, somnambulism, and intoxication, as favorite examples of what might be called in retrospect the neuropathology of everyday life. Particularly loaded are instances in which (as Andrew Combe writes) the "temper and moral sentiments have . . . been entirely changed, in consequence of certain injuries to the brain, while the intellect remained unimpaired," suggesting that not only cognition but character is physiologically based.[22] Some of these instances are evocative of Louisa's transformation, including Hartley's claim that "concussions" have sometimes resulted in a "Melancholy" temperament, or Gall's "lady of fine talents" who falls, striking the "back part of her head against the mantel-piece," and comes to lose "all of her brilliant qualities" as a result (*FB* 2: 119).[23] Gall mentions more exotic cases as well. A split brain subject "continually heard insults against him" on his left side only, causing him to turn "his eyes that way, although, with the right side, he distinctly perceived, that these sounds came from no other source than a derangement in the left side of his head" (*FB* 2: 164). A man who suffered a fall could no longer remember proper names, though otherwise intact; another, after a similar accident, "lost the memory of nouns"

(*FB* 2: 285–86). Still another case reads like a Romantic-era version of
Phineas Gage (whose reconstructed head injury forms one of the central
illustrations for Damasio's *Descartes' Error*).[21] After having his skull
"broken in by a blow from a stone," a man once known as a "peaceful
citizen" becomes "quarrelsome" and contentious: "people saw with surprise that his character was wholly changed." Gall managed to procure
the cranium for his collection, which plainly showed "by mere inspec-
tion, how much the brain had suffered" (*FB* 2: 119–20).

The ideological threat that such accounts represented is clear from the
response they generated in establishment journals, conservative and
liberal alike. A few months before Austen began work on *Persuasion* (in
August 1815), in fact, the *Edinburgh Review* had devoted a long article to
countering the implications of an essay on localized brain injury published the year before in the Royal Society's *Philosophical Transactions*. The
author, Sir Everard Home, was not the ready object of ridicule presented by the phrenologists and most of their allies, but rather something
of a medical icon: Fellow of the Royal Society, sergeant-surgeon to the
king, professor at the College of Surgeons, protégé and executor of John
Hunter, and baronet. In his "Observations on the Function of the
Brain" Home avoids "general deductions," instead cataloguing all of the
cases he has encountered of brain injury to help "procure accurate information respecting the functions that belong to individual portions of the
human brain."[25] Nevertheless, the implications of Home's attempt to
connect "still more closely the pursuits of anatomy with those of philosophy" were hard to miss: an intimate relation (if not identity) between
mind and brain, a physiological account of mental function, and a
brain-based, modular conception of mental behavior distinctly related
to Gall's organology, if far more scientifically respectable.

Rather than attack Home directly, the reviewer in the *Edinburgh*
instead compiles an imposing list of counter-examples, intended to
prove that brain injury need not disrupt mental functioning and, ultimately, that mental life can go on in the entire absence of a brain. Some
of the examples approach surrealism in the nonchalance with which
they treat head wounds and other neural insults. "VESLINGIUS found
the end of a stilletto in the brain of a woman, who had been wounded
by it five years before, but who had complained of nothing in the mean
while but occasional head-ach; and . . . LACUTUS mentions a case, in
which the half of a knife remained in the brain of a man for eight years,
without his being at all incommoded."[26] Five pages of such examples are
given not as evidence of neural plasticity (which Cabanis discusses from

a neuropsychological perspective [*R* 1: 140]), but rather to dismiss altogether any necessary connection between the mental act of "Sensation" and "*particular*" parts of the brain (445). The reviewer then goes on to produce examples in which "the *whole* brain has been destroyed without loss of sensibility" (446) though, as one might imagine, these are not very satisfying. ("We have found indeed, several instances of children born without a brain who lived for a short time; but the state of the sensibility in these, is not quite unequivocally ascertained" [447–48].) Nevertheless, the essay concludes that, despite the cases evidenced by a "person of SIR EVERARD HOME's reputation," there are "very strong grounds for believing, that the brain is not at all concerned in the changes which precede Sensation" (448), and if not in sensation, than not, "*mutatis mutandis*," in the "phenomena of Thought and Volition" (440).

Home's paper on brain function and the response in the *Edinburgh Review* are worth noting in this context not, of course, as possible "sources" for *Persuasion*. They are valuable, rather, for underscoring the tense co-existence, in Austen's day, of two diametrically opposed yet equally credible notions of mind–body relations, one unabashedly dualistic and in line with orthodox notions of the soul, the other aligning mental acts with discrete brain functions and open to a materialist interpretation. These rival conceptions seem initially to correspond, in an odd way, to the contrasting subjectivities of the rival heroines of *Persuasion*: one shaped by mental and emotional experience, able to transcend bodily discomfort, and exemplifying Frederick's ideal of a "strong mind" (87), the other "altered" by an insult to the brain and even before that deficient (again according to Frederick) "in a point no less essential than mind" (192). One living with the pangs of a broken heart, the other with the lasting effects of a cracked head. Though the episode on the Cobb is not meant to elicit laughter, these rival systems for representing subjectivity do collide comically later in the novel. When Anne, overwhelmed with emotion, struggles to compose herself after reading a passionate letter from Frederick, Louisa's mother, apparently converted to a brain-based psychology, needs reassurance that "there had been no fall in the case; that Anne had not, at any time lately, slipped down, and got a blow on her head; that she was perfectly convinced of having had no fall" (241). But Anne's very confusion, here and elsewhere in the novel, suggests that the comic disparity in this passage between mind and brain, heart and head, is something of a red herring. For the characterization of Anne touches, in its own way, on the embodied notion of mind, the fragmentation of the subject, and the greater appreciation of unconscious mental life all characteristic of the new Romantic psychologies.

Mrs. Musgrove's comic mistake reasserts the contrast between Anne and Louisa while also emphasizing that this is a moment when, as Wiltshire puts it, Anne's "body takes over."[27] Not that Anne becomes even remotely comatose at such times; rather, her periods of dislocation mark the collision of conscious awareness with unconscious thoughts and feelings and the intense physiological sensations that accompany them. Anne may be prized for her "rational" demeanor, yet she also proves highly susceptible to influxes of feeling from sources not always consciously present to Anne herself, registered instead in the body, in ways that at times become so pressing as to overwhelm the conscious subject.[28] "The absolute necessity of seeming like herself produced then an immediate struggle; but after a while she could do no more. She began not to understand a word they said" (240–41). The "struggle" between rational control and passionate feeling, conscious volition and the physiological rush of intense inner emotions, manifests not a split between mind and body but the impossibility of ever teasing them apart. The illusory unity of the conscious subject is punctured by the actions of an embodied mind that often finds unconscious action and expression more expedient, working in despite of the conscious subject if need be. "Mary talked, but [Anne] could not attend . . . she began to reason with herself, and try to be feeling less . . . Alas! with all her reasonings, she found, that to retentive feelings eight years may be little more than nothing" (85).

Underlying such passages is a view of mind as sensibility, less reminiscent of Locke than of Herder – "It's vibrating fibres, it's sympathizing nerves, need not the call of Reason: they run before her, they often disobediently and forcibly oppose her" (*Outlines* 100) – or of Darwin, Gall, or Cabanis. Austen grants the "inward" senses (never discussed by Locke) the central role given them by brain-based Romantic psychologies, necessarily acknowledging the subject's fragmentation in the process. "For a few minutes she saw nothing before her. It was all confusion. She was lost; and when she had scolded back her senses, she found the others still waiting for the carriage." The intimation of a divided subject ("scolded back her senses") builds to the acknowledgment of a fundamental split between a superintending conscious self and a potentially unruly, desiring, unconscious other: "Why was she to suspect herself of another motive? . . . One half of her should not always be so much wiser than the other half" (185). In related passages, equally in keeping with the emphasis on unconscious mental life found throughout Romantic brain science, Anne performs complex behaviors in an explicitly "unconscious" manner, playing at the keyboard (a prominent example of non-conscious cognition in Darwin's *Zoonomia* [1: 190–94]) and even conversing "unconsciously" (96, 113). Anne can make music and make conversational sense equally well without the benefit of conscious awareness, though her unconscious life emerges more spectacularly in those moments when she seems, for a time, altogether senseless.

Anne's periods of "confusion," episodes lasting up to "several minutes" when internal sensations crowd out external ones, rendering her unseeing and inattentive, bear an uncanny resemblance (seen from the outside) to Louisa's deeper passage into unconsciousness after her fall. Louisa's head injury serves to call attention, in sensational fashion, to the mind's embodiment, a condition that is shown in more subtle ways to be shared by the characters around her. The chapter that recounts the accident is generally seen as the novel's dramatic hinge, limning the contrast between the two rivals by juxtaposing Louisa's "heedlessness" with Anne's display of the "resolution of a collected mind" (244). Yet the scene at the Cobb also serves to soften that very contrast, as one character after another succumbs to emotional and cognitive overload, lapsing into various mental states that appear not so very different from Louisa's; even Anne acts as much from blind instinct as from conscious reason. The indirect cause of the accident is Louisa's love of "sensation" – "In all their walks, he had to jump her from the stiles; the sensation was delightful to her" – a richly complex feeling that confounds the temporary disorientation of an inner sense (proprioception) with the heightening of an external one (touch), connected in turn with the sexual thrill of a kind of robust physical contact ordinarily forbidden to genteel unmarried couples. No wonder Louisa, after being "jumped" once down to the lower level of the Cobb, wants to do it again. The second, more precipitate jump, ironically, leaves her insensible: though by no means farcical, or (given the real horror of the accident) quite so "zany" as sometimes described, the episode is written throughout with a tactful, but in its own way rather remorseless, wit. The immediate reactions of those around her bring the other characters into physiological and even cognitive conditions reflecting back the "corpse-like figure" of Louisa. Frederick looks at her "with a face as pallid as her own"; Charles is rendered "immoveable"; Henrietta, "sinking under the conviction, lost her senses too, and would have fallen on the steps" (129–30). Overcome with genuine shock and horror, one character after another becomes, like Louisa, a prone or otherwise inert body.

Austen underscores the parallel in various ways as the episode continues to unfold. When Anne proposes to send Benwick for a doctor, "Every one capable of thinking felt the advantage of the idea," a formula that groups the fainting Henrietta and the "hysterical" Mary with the unconscious Louisa. Harville's arrival is described in terms that in context weirdly reduce him to a physiological specimen: "Shocked as Captain Harville was, he brought senses and nerves that could be instantly useful" (130–31). Even the "thinking" characters, that is, are portrayed as organic assemblages of nerves and senses under duress. Frederick, though remaining sentient, becomes automaton-like, responding as mechanically as any Hartleyan association network when Anne mentions a surgeon: "He caught the word; it seemed to rouse him at once, and saying only, 'True, true, a surgeon this instant,'" he begins rushing away when Anne reminds him that only Benwick "knows where a surgeon is to be found." Even Anne, foremost among the minority who remain "rational," preserves the situation through the "strength and zeal, and thought, which instinct supplied" (130). Appearing just at this point in the episode, Austen's choice of "instinct" does not seem casual. At a time when writers like Coleridge adamantly distinguish between the "instinct" of beasts and the "higher" intuitions of human beings (*SW* 2: 1390), countering "materialists" like Darwin who view instinctive human responses as a crucial animal inheritance and a key manifestation of the adaptive "inner" senses, "instinct" is a loaded term, one that early brain scientists like Cabanis and Gall had only recently reasserted in the teeth of Locke's dismissal. In this context, Anne's most heroically "rational" episode could be placed on a continuum with, rather than directly opposed to, her automatic, non-rational, but quite natural responses elsewhere in the novel at times of heightened emotion.

Marked by a "strong sensibility" from her adolescence, Anne is represented not as some eviscerated or denervated rational agent, but as an emotive, embodied subject, uncommonly reasonable and also uncommonly sensitive (165). She can become "speechless" from "nervous" sensations or "fixed" by powerful emotions (103–4, 111) and, at her most intense, feels things "in a nervous thrill all over her" (235). But in a novel that asks women to be treated as "rational creature" not "fine ladies" (94), Anne's exquisite sensorium does nothing to diminish or otherwise qualify her exemplary strength of mind. The continuity suggested throughout between reason and emotion, "instinct" and judgment, conscious and nonconscious mental activity sets *Persuasion* apart both from the eighteenth-century "sentimental" novel, which aligns enhanced powers of feeling and empathy with the irrational and the effeminate, and from Austen's earlier novels as well.[29] Although *Sense and Sensibility* (1811), to cite the inevitable example, does not oppose feeling and reason quite so schematically as its title might suggest, it does pointedly contrast Elinor's "coolness of judgment" with Marianne's "excessive sensibility" (42). Marianne's unbridled sensibility, moreover, erupts in an extended "nervous complaint" that equates sensitive feelings, the female body, and illness (234). In *Persuasion*, "senses and nerves" become positively revalued along lines remarkably consonant with the new biological psychologies, integrated within a neurocognitive system that does not always require conscious awareness to function rapidly and effectively, although it remains vulnerable (like the rest of the body) and subject to breakdown as well.

Anne's blend of superior rationality and heightened sensibility, her susceptibility to surges of emotion with their marked cognitive and physiological effects, and the mental splitting or fragmenting she regularly manifests, together find voice in the stylistic innovation critics have noted in *Persuasion*. A. Walton Litz first called attention to Austen's "move away from the Johnsonian norm" in her last novel, with its "rapid and nervous syntax designed to imitate the bombardment of impressions upon the mind."[30] Marilyn Butler similarly describes Austen's "experiment with a new kind of subjective writing," marked by a "high-wrought nervous tension" in conveying a particular consciousness (Anne's) for which "the senses have a distinct advantage over reason and fact."[31] It is appropriate that both critics use the term "nervous" to evoke the quality of Anne's subjectivity and the prose that conveys it, for in this novel mind cannot be disentangled from the central nervous system that enacts it. Austen's new subjective style is all the more innovative for prominently including the gaps and disruptions in the represented flux of consciousness, what Wiltshire calls "invasions of feeling."[32] Unconscious mental events are shown in a complex and frequently adversarial relation with conscious ones, and feeling is often known through its mark on the body before it can be registered in conscious awareness. "No, it was not regret which made Anne's heart beat in spite of itself, and brought the color into her cheeks when she thought of Captain Wentworth unshackled and free. She had some feelings which she was ashamed to investigate" (178). Anne's shame here reminds us that the domestic novel, considered as an extension of the literature of female conduct, implicitly enjoins such inner splitting by insisting that "proper" young women feel desire for their future husbands – marry for love – *without* acknowledging such desire too soon, even to themselves.[33] Yet the deft interplay in passages like this between thought and feeling, physiological expression and conscious introspection, signals not just another elaboration on the modest blush but a new, "Romantic" sense of mind–body relations.

Terms like "flow of consciousness" or "interior monologue" cannot entirely do this new style justice.[34] Even if they allow for some shading from unconscious impulses or bodily intrusions upon introspective awareness, they tend to evoke a conscious, integral Cartesian subject, the central self that oversees the conscious flow or articulates the internal monologue. As represented through the "nervous" sentences of *Persuasion*, however, subjectivity seems corporate rather than monologic, unconscious feelings and ideas become as important as conscious ones, and the division between interior and exterior is regularly breached. "Shudder," for example, should be read as a simultaneously physical and psychological reaction in the passage that describes Anne's semi-conscious acknowledgment of her temporary interest in her wealthy cousin, William Walter Elliot: "Anne could just acknowledge within herself such a possibility of having been induced to marry him, as made her shudder at the idea of the misery which must have followed" (216). It is left suggestively unclear whether "within herself" refers to Anne's conscious or unconscious mind, or even whether the "shudder" represents Anne's act of acknowledgment rather than her reaction to it, such that she discovers the nature of her feelings partly through reading their bodily manifestations. The plot owes much of its tension, in fact, to the ongoing threat that feelings which can only be read indirectly can always be misread: Frederick will continue to overvalue his feelings for Louisa, Anne will be "induced" to display feelings for Mr. Elliot, neither Frederick nor Anne will correctly gauge their renewed feelings for one another. Frederick makes this dilemma explicit in an acknowledgment of his own: "Thus much indeed he was obliged to acknowledge – that he had been constant unconsciously, nay, unintentionally; that he had meant to forget her, and believed it to be done" (244). In a novel of the 1790s generation, the claim to have been constant "unintentionally" would be transparently absurd, the statement of a cad; the sort of thing that Darnford, in Mary Wollstonecraft's *Maria*, might be expected to come up with. In *Persuasion*, however, the claim, self-serving as it obviously is, can nevertheless be considered sincere. Unconscious motives can contradict and even come to outweigh conscious ones, feelings that are "believed" to be forgotten can have been present, in retrospect, all along. A "Romantic" novel indeed: one that takes up and extends, in its innovatory syntax, characterization, and narrative style, the embodied approach to human subjectivity being worked out concurrently by Romantic poets like Coleridge and Keats and Romantic brain scientists like Gall and Bell.[35]

Persuasion also bears comparison to Romantic brain science in its emphasis on extrasemantic, bodily communication, unexpected though this may be in a novel that depends on a hastily written letter for its resolution. Characters frequently communicate by non-verbal expression alone ("a look between him and his wife decided what was to be done" [131]) – or reveal by expression what their words are intended to conceal.[36] "There was a momentary expression in Captain Wentworth's face at this speech, a certain glance of his bright eye, and curl of his handsome mouth, which convinced Anne, that instead of sharing in Mrs Musgrove's kind wishes, as to her son, he had probably been at some pains to get rid of him" (92). Some of the novel's most impassioned moments are wordless, as when Anne, having read Frederick's letter, conveys her response with her eyes and is answered by Frederick's flushing skin. "He joined them; but, as if irresolute whether to join or to pass on, said nothing – only looked. Anne could command herself enough to receive that look, and not repulsively. The cheeks which had been pale now glowed, and the movements which had hesitated were decided" (242). (Frederick, no less than Anne, is capable of looking "quite red" [185]; neither has quite "outlived the age of blushing" [75]). In the canceled chapter that records Austen's first attempt at resolving the plot, Anne and Frederick come to an understanding through a "silent but a very powerful dialogue" conducted entirely through "expression" (259). If subjectivity cannot be disentangled from physiology in this novel, neither can communication.

TEMPERAMENTAL SUBJECTS

The concurrence between Austen's late style and emergent biological notions of the subject would not, of course, necessarily commit her to viewing character or temperament as even partly shaped by heredity. Even if one believes that a significant change in brain physiology (such as the neurological effects of a particularly severe head injury) could bring about a change in temperament, one need not agree with Gall or Cabanis that certain patterns of neurophysiological organization associated with specific temperaments or character traits can be passed

down within families like a snub nose or a predisposition to hemo-
philia.[37] Physiological psychology and a renewed interest in the hereditary transmission of character traits do, however, generally go together
in Romantic-era brain science and it is significant that, in *Persuasion*,
Austen seems to pose a similar connection.[38] Again, the most overt
example in the book concerns a relatively minor female character who
functions as yet another foil to Anne, her former school-friend Mrs.
Smith. Smith's experience has been much harsher still than Anne's: marriage to a spendthrift husband, early widowhood, relative poverty
("unable even to afford herself the comfort of a servant"), and illness
(165). Yet, as Anne wonderingly observes, "in spite of all this . . . she had
moments only of langour and depression, to hours of occupation and
enjoyment. How could it be?" (167) How could temperament so thoroughly belie the effects of experience? Mrs. Smith exemplifies, Anne
decides, that "elasticity of mind, that disposition to be comforted, that
power of turning readily from evil to good, and of finding employment
which carried her out of herself, which was from Nature alone" (167).
Here, at least, is one character not altogether shaped by experience, but
with a pronounced (and, one could add, adaptive) native "disposition."

Anne herself initially seems another case altogether. Psychoanalytical
critics of *Persuasion* argue that Anne's particular temperament is precisely
what one would expect of a girl effectively abandoned by her mother at
14, a traumatic and formative experience that makes a history of heart-
break and melancholy seem to follow as a matter of course. As Anita
Sokolsky writes, "Anne's tendency to melancholy emerges in reaction to
the death of a mother whose attachment to her home and daughters
had, terribly, made it 'no small matter of indifference to her to leave this
life'".[39] Austen, however, does suggest that Anne's temperament may
owe as much to a biological as to a psychological relation to the mother.
Later in the same chapter in which Anne speculates on Mrs. Smith's
elastic "disposition" (a key term for Gall and his adherents), Lady Russell
remarks that Anne is "her mother's self in countenance and disposition"
– that she has inherited her mother's temperament along with her physical features (172). Lady Russell's judgment is evidently one of long
standing: in the novel's first chapter, her early preference for Anne
reflects her sense that "it was only in Anne that she could fancy the
mother to revive again" (37). A paragraph above, Sir Walter's contrary
preference for his eldest daughter, Elizabeth, is similarly explained on
the basis of physical and temperamental resemblance to a parent:
"being very handsome, and very like himself, her influence had always

been great." Few readers would disagree with Sir Walter's assessment; throughout the novel, Elizabeth reacts and behaves in a manner all too like her father's. Physiology may not be destiny in *Persuasion*, but it seems to play no small role in character formation.

The links implied here between character and physique, heredity and fate, raise the issue of how sexual differences are perceived to shape differences in mind – an issue that Austen will raise herself toward the end of the book (237). In a novel that, in various ways, "upsets conventional conjunctions of ideas about gender," it might seem that appeals to embodied notions of mind and hereditary notions of "disposition" could only serve to reassert those same conjunctions.[40] Both Janet Oppenheim and Sally Shuttleworth have demonstrated how, in the Victorian era, the new biological psychologies were invoked to "bear witness against women's brains" and to reassert conventional oppositions between male self-control and female helplessness, male rationality and female sensibility.[41] As John Elliotson (a radical materialist and early proponent of phrenology) puts it in *Human Physiology* (1835), the "male is formed for corporeal and intellectual power; the female for gentleness, affections, and delicacy of feeling."[42] These tendencies, though much exaggerated over the course of the nineteenth century, are certainly present already in the work of pioneers like Cabanis and Gall. Cabanis holds that women have "softer" brains than men, and remain, in some respects, "children all their lives" (*R* 1: 183, 227); Gall illustrates the power of instinct by observing that the "little girl reaches out her hand for the doll, as the boy, for a drum or sword." "The whole physical constitution of woman," he continues, "combines with her moral and intellectual character, to prove that she is destined, more particularly than man, to take care of children" (*FB* 3: 272). For Lawrence the mind is "male or female, according to the sex of the body" (*LPZ* 94).

Yet as readily the new physiological discourse on the mind lent itself to supporting the received dichotomies of the gender system, it could also serve to unsettle those same oppositions and, at least in principle, to destabilize the traditional system of evaluations. Hazlitt, in a critique of phrenology, complains that Gall's organology weakens the distinction between men and women by localizing it, limiting it to relative differences between only several among the numerous brain "organs." "Women in general," Hazlitt counters, "have more softness and flexibility both of mind and body than men – they have not the same strength and perseverance, but they take their revenge in tact and *delicacy*: Shall we suppose this marked and universal difference which runs through the whole frame and through every thought and action of life, to proceed from a particular bump or excrescence of the skull, and not to be inherent in the principle (whatever that may be) which feels, and thinks, at all times, and in all circumstances?" (*HW* 20: 253). By fragmenting the mind and disrupting the continuity of the thinking "principle," the new physiological psychologies not only threaten orthodox notions of the soul but throw the system of absolute gender differences into question.[13] If sex-specific mental differences can be localized, moreover, those local differences can be further eroded by the effects of accident and experience. Men, for example, come equipped with the same mental predisposition (and accompanying brain organ) for child-rearing as women, but in a much less pronounced manner; through exercise, however, that organ can be developed and the original difference can be "repressed" (*FB* 3: 263, 275). A thoroughly "domestic" man like Captain Harville would fit readily into Gall's system, but would seem aberrant within Hazlitt's (120). The propensity for sexual behavior, on the other hand, is generally stronger in men but by no means always. For Gall, despite his commitment to basic gender differences, there are no absolute or unalterable distinctions.

In terms of their larger implications, the emergent brain-based psychologies of the era threatened to destabilize received notions of gender in more pervasive ways. Discussing the ambivalent relation of women writers to scientific discourse in the Romantic era, Marina Benjamin remarks on the "masculine character of scientific epistemologies" that align the opposition of masculine to feminine with "dichotomies like rational/emotional, deductive/intuitive, objective/ subjective." But the biological psychologies of Darwin, Cabanis, and Gall were engaged in undoing those very dichotomies, at a time when (again quoting Benjamin) the "cognitive role of the passions, imagination, sensation, and individual experience" was being fundamentally rethought.[14] In giving an expanded and often leading role to unconscious cognition, instinctive behaviors, "inward" sensations, emotional reactions, and bodily sensation within mental life, Romantic brain science threw traditional valuations of reason over passion and mind over body into crisis. Moreover, although women were still seen as more emotional and "softer" than men, men were nevertheless fully implicated within a changing vision of the human, one that displaced the rational, disembodied, male-coded ideal subject with an embodied model of human subjectivity, forcing a revaluation of traditionally feminine prerogatives like sensibility and intuition.

Here too one finds unexpected convergence between Austen's experiments with representing character and subjective life in *Persuasion* and the physiological psychologies of her time. Another of the features supporting a "Romantic" reading of the novel (such as Litz's) is its revaluation of rationality and emotion, one that cuts across gender lines. The heroine, after all, is one who, famously, "had been forced into prudence in her youth" and "learned romance as she grew older" (58), while Frederick too must learn to respect the wisdom of his unconscious and even involuntary feelings by the novel's close. The novel's most systematically "rational" characters – Lady Russell and William Walter Elliot – are the very ones who cause the most pain and give the worst counsel (42, 173). Frederick's great advantage over Mr. Elliot, in fact, resides in his characteristic "ardour" (58), a trait that is at once psychological and physical, described elsewhere as "glowing" (86). Indeed, Frederick's "sanguine temper" is said to have contributed to his successful career, "command[ed]" his "proper path" (56, 58). All of the sympathetic naval characters share this quality of "warmth" (120), one singularly lacking in Frederick's rival. "Mr Elliot was rational, discreet, polished, – but he was not open. There was never any burst of feeling, any warmth of indignation or delight" (173). Or, in Mrs. Smith's harsher terms, Elliot is a "cold-blooded being," a "man without heart" (206). This last phrase relies on the most conventional of figures, but in a novel that so insistently reevaluates the claims of the body, metaphors like "heart" ask to be taken quite seriously. In conjunction with terms like "warmth" and "ardour," "heart" functions metaphorically just at the uncertain borders between psyche and soma, where character traits are indistinguishable from the "glowing" physical sensations that make them known – to the self as well as to others. (The very notion of "temperament," a term obviously allied to "temperature," ultimately relies on the same basic metaphorical pattern).[45] Harville is "warm-hearted" not just metaphorically but in the concrete way he experiences his own body, and thus knows his own mind (119). After expressing his love for his wife and children "in a tone of strong feeling," he adds, "'I speak, you know, only of such men as have hearts!' pressing his own with emotion" (238). Men who fail to speak from feeling and to feel from the body are not to be trusted in *Persuasion*.

Not that feelings, sensations, vocal tones, and physiological displays can be trusted in any simple way, either. Austen's turn to an embodied epistemology in *Persuasion* introduces new complications of its own, such as the difficulties both Anne and Frederick encounter first in consciously perceiving, then in fully acknowledging, their "unconscious" desire for one another. Sensations can be misinterpreted and feelings under- or overvalued, as in the case of Benwick, whose broken heart heals sooner than anyone, least of all himself, could reasonably suppose. Mrs. Musgrove, who rekindles feelings for a son's death that she seems not really to have felt at the time, and whose "substantial" physical bulk is said to belie her feelings of "tenderness," functions as an icon of such misprision (92). This is still a Jane Austen novel. It is, however, a Jane Austen novel like no other, and its difference owes a great deal to its affinities with the biological psychologies just then becoming notorious through the debates on phrenology and the materialist-vitalist controversy. Although it has been claimed that Austen "all but erases" the body in her novels – and that a body reconstructed from her lexicon would have no thighs, no "intestines, wombs, or navels," not even fingers or toes – the body is crucial to character, plot, and subjective life in *Persuasion.*[46] The skin that glows or goes pallid, the heart that swells or goes "cold," the "susceptible" nerves and the brain that, once injured, must be "set to rights," all speak of a mind that has no location or meaning apart from the body (144, 181).

In representing an embodied, nervous sensibility, Austen takes brilliant advantage of the novel's capacity to move rapidly among various perspectives (both internal and external to different characters and sometimes hovering in an uncertain middle ground) and to shuttle between passages of description and snatches of indirect discourse in order to convey, not just the flow of consciousness, but its ebbs as well. The phrase recounting Louisa's condition during her extended period of recovery – "intervals of sense and consciousness" (138) – could provide an apt starting point for a characterization of Austen's late style. Consciousness plays only a limited role in defining the heroine's impressions – and conveying her expressions. At times the body speaks eloquently in a language of its own. "Her eyes were bright, her cheeks glowed, but she knew nothing about it" (194). More noteworthy still are those moments during which emotional, cognitive, and physiological impulses engage in a complicated dance of action and reaction, as when Anne learns that Frederick does not love Louisa. "Anne, who, in spite of the agitated voice in which the latter part had been uttered, and in spite of all the various noises of the room, the almost ceaseless slam of the door, and ceaseless buzz of people walking through, had distinguished every word, was struck, gratified, confused, and beginning to breathe

very quick, and feel an hundred things in a moment" (193). The disquisitions of brain scientists like Darwin and Bell can point towards such
deft interaction between mind and body, emotion and cognition, but
cannot portray it nearly so effectively or so evocatively. The closest ana-
logue to this aspect of Austen's style – surprising as it may seem for a
novelist more often compared to Samuel Johnson – may be found in the
poetry of John Keats.

CHAPTER FIVE

Keats and the glories of the brain

On July 12, 1821, Charles Bell read the first of a brilliant series of lectures, "On the Nerves," to the Royal Society, with Humphry Davy (now a respectable baronet) in the President's chair.[1] The lectures, published soon after in the *Philosophical Transactions*, summed up Bell's work to date, with special attention to the facial nerves and their network of connections, via the brain and spinal cord, to the respiratory and circulatory systems – the cornerstone of his thinking on how facial expression, speech, breathing, the heart, and the "emotions and passions of the mind" all functioned holistically through the medium of the brain and nerves (112: 285–6). They also bore witness, Bell announced, to the "new character" that the nervous system had assumed through the "gradually accumulating" discoveries of the metropolitan "schools," thanks to which its "intricacies" had been "unravelled, and the peculiar structure and function of the individual nerves ascertained," replacing the "absolute confusion" of the past with the revelation of its "natural and simple order" (111: 398). Now "even the youngest students" of the London medical schools learn enough about the newly revealed nervous system to understand its basic workings and to "decypher and to read" its hermetic "language" (111: 400).

Bell's claims for the innovative character of "metropolitan" neuroscientific teaching find confirmation in a number of important lecture series that have been preserved, from Matthew Baillie's prescient Gulstonian lectures to the Royal College of Physicians in 1794, through Bell's own lectures on the anatomy of expression to London artists in 1806, to Lawrence's controversial series on anatomy, physiology, and natural history at the Royal College of Surgeons from 1816 to 1819. Some of the most incisive and entertaining were taken down by Frederick Tyrell from the great surgeon and anatomist Sir Astley Cooper, who gave yearly lectures to the students at the United Hospitals, Guy's and St. Thomas's.[2] Lecture notes have survived from some of the

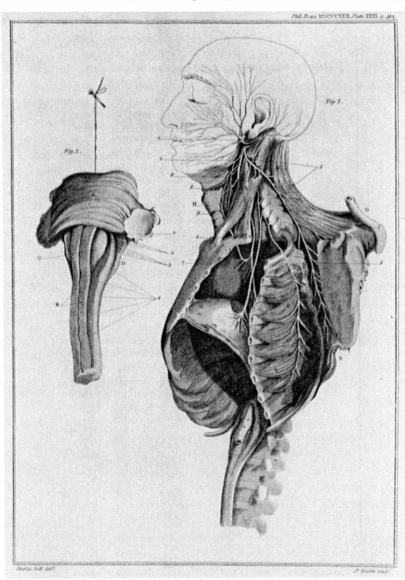

7 Bell, "Of the Nerves which associate the muscles of the Chest, in the actions of breathing, speaking, and expression," *Philosophical Transactions* 112 (1822), plate xxx.

"youngest students" as well, among them the highly intriguing notebook of a protégé of Cooper's who roomed with Tyrell. This well-placed student at Guy's Hospital was none other than John Keats.[3]

Keats's medical training was once used, most infamously in the "Cockney School" series in *Blackwood's*, to denigrate his high poetical pretensions, suggesting that as a would-be apothecary Keats belonged with the "footmen" and "farm-servants" whom Southey would soon categorize as "uneducated poets."[4] "My name with the literary fashionables is vulgar," Keats confided in a letter to his brother; "I am a weaver boy to them" (*JKL* 2: 186). "Z," the anonymous reviewer in *Blackwood's*, put it more cruelly: "It is a better and a wiser thing to be a starving apothecary then a starved poet; so back to the shop Mr John, back to 'plasters, pills, and ointment boxes,' &c."[5] By one of the happier ironic reversals of literary history, however, an emphasis on Keats's training as an apothecary-surgeon, at a time of educational reform, professional consolidation, and unusual intellectual vitality in the London medical world, has returned in support of a new view of Keats, not as "Z"'s "uneducated . . . stripling" but instead as a sophisticated thinker in touch with important developments in the sciences as well as in literature, a "poet-physician" whose medical background left profound marks on his verse. Recent scholarship has amply demonstrated how Keats's training at the United Hospitals, then the "most well-rounded medical school in London," put him abreast of the "most advanced scientific and philosophical lines of inquiry" through teachers like Astley Cooper and J. H. Green (Coleridge's friend and an anatomy demonstrator at Guy's).[6] The most exciting aspect of this story, however, has yet to be told in full: how Keats's exposure to the revolutionary brain science of the time transformed his understanding of the mind and its relation to the body, facilitating an unprecedented poetics of embodied cognition that runs throughout his best and most characteristically daring verse.

The faculty at the United Hospitals rubbed shoulders not only with the leading medical figures of London and beyond, but with the larger scientific and radical intellectual circles that contributed so decisively to the iconoclastic character of Romantic brain science. Keats's teachers at Guy's were linked, professionally, personally, or (most often) both, to a long list of medical and scientific innovators, particularly those who belonged (or, like Davy and Coleridge, had once belonged) to the radical Dissenting network.[7] Priestley and Darwin, Baillie and the Hunters, Beddoes and Lawrence, Bell and Home, all had friends, pupils, or colleagues at Guy's, and their books were in its library, along with works by

Gall and Spurzheim, Herder, Blumenbach, Lamarck, and von Humboldt.[8] Astley Cooper's career neatly demonstrates how rich the affiliations among this group could be: he studied with John Hunter and taught William Lawrence, succeeded Home and preceded Lawrence as lecturer to the College of Surgeons, was included on the distribution list of Bell's privately printed *New Anatomy of the Brain* in 1811, counted himself a "great admirer of Darwin" and, in his radical youth, a political disciple of Thelwall.[9] When Thelwall gave his explosive lecture to Guy's Physical Society on the "Origin of Mental Action explained on the system of Materialism" in 1793, Cooper chaired the meeting.[10] Cooper had crossed the Channel the year before to study French surgical practices – and celebrate the nascent Republic – at first hand.[11] Although his medical career eventually demanded that he lower his political profile, Cooper kept in touch with French medical and scientific developments and maintained an allegiance to the values of comparative anatomy, clinical observation, and experimentation very much in line with the scientific ethos of outspoken radicals like Lawrence (*LPZ* 58). The poet who stated that "axioms in philosophy are not axioms until they are proved upon our pulses" – a doctor's image – was obviously touched by the same ethos (*JKL* 1: 279).[12]

Keats began his hospital training in 1815 with a background well-fitted for the scientific, philosophical, and political atmosphere at Guy's. He had become a star pupil by the time he left Enfield Academy, a fine though unpretentious school steeped (as Nicholas Roe has shown) in the Dissenting culture that had put the great Nonconformist academies like Warrington, where Priestley taught, at the forefront of scientific education in England.[13] Keats's master at Enfield, John Clarke, was personally acquainted with Priestley and other leading Dissenting intellectuals and shared their reformist views on education and politics. The apothecary-surgeon to whom Keats was apprenticed for five years, Thomas Hammond, was himself a former student at Guy's and, as a member of the Corporation of Surgeons, kept up with medical advances. Whether through Hammond's connections at the hospital or, as Roe surmises, on account of the "sceptical and republican" views that Keats brought with him from Enfield, Cooper took a personal interest in this promising new student, who may have reminded him of his younger self.[14] Cooper arranged for Keats to room with his apprentice, Tyrell, and shortly afterwards Keats was awarded the coveted position of surgeon's dresser, placing him among the elite group of medical students. Despite the received image of Keats dreaming his way through medical lectures and demonstrations, his rapid progress (he successfully passed the difficult new Licentiate examination for apothecaries at the youngest possible age) suggests that Keats was a serious and attentive student, especially in relation to the subjects that most interested him.[15] As his *Anatomical and Physiological Note Book* shows, he was particularly intrigued by Cooper's innovative teaching on the brain and nerves.

THE SPECTACULAR BRAIN

The scientific picture of the central nervous system had been revolutionized in the decade preceding Keats's medical training not only by Bell's "new anatomy," but by the controversial yet also influential work of Gall and Spurzheim. Their anatomical discoveries (mainly Gall's, though Spurzheim also was a talented dissector) had become well known in medical circles through the publication of the first volume of their "large work," *Anatomie et physiologie du système nervaux en général, et du Cerveau en particulier*, along with their lavish anatomical *Atlas* of the brain, in 1810.[16] (The main points of this work were popularized in England over the next decade by Spurzheim, both through his lively anatomical "demonstrations" and his publication in English of the widely reviewed *Physiognomical System of Drs. Gall and Spurzheim* in 1815, some months before Keats arrived at Guy's.) The appeal of their dissection technique even for skeptics is already evident in one of the earliest English reviews of the "large work," which dismisses their "craniological" and many of their physiological claims, but affirms the value of their key anatomical "truths" and concedes that "their method of dissection is preferable to every other, whether the object be to acquire a perfect knowledge of the structure of the brain, or that of its functions."[17] Even Hazlitt, a diehard critic of phrenology, wrote of contemplating "with eager curiosity the transverse section of the brain, divided on the new Spurzheim principles. It is here, then, the number of the parts, their distinctions, connections, structures, uses; in short, an entire new set of ideas, which occupies the mind of the student" (*HW* 4: 73). This was a far cry from the "spongy, inorganized, pulpy substance" that the brain had looked like (in Gall's scornful words) to earlier anatomists (*FB* 2: 18). The new vision of neural "distinctions, connections, structures" and functions opened up by the anatomical advances of Bell, Gall, and Spurzheim made possible a similarly complex vision of brain-based psychology, and gave credence to the embodied understanding of mind that had been gaining support in the medical world since the work of Priestley and Darwin in the last century.

Cooper had helped make the United Hospitals into "one of the best anatomy schools in Europe," and Keats would certainly have been exposed to some of the latest advances in neuroanatomy as well as the new physiological accounts of mind that went with them.[18] Not that his medical training would have been his only source of exposure to at least the main ideas of Gall and Spurzheim, which were widely disseminated in the monthly and quarterly reviews, in pamphlets and encyclopedia articles, and in public anatomy demonstrations. Keats's (and Wordsworth's) friend B. R. Haydon, the painter, was one of the many who attended Spurzheim's popular lectures in London in 1815; Henry Crabb Robinson had characterized Spurzheim the season before as the "lion of the day."[19] Haydon, moreover, had attended Bell's 1806 anatomy lectures for artists that became the foundation of his great work on the *Anatomy and Philosophy of Expression*. In fact, Haydon (according to his own account) helped "beat up" the sixteen pupils whose fees underwrote the lectures at a time when Bell was "poor and anxious for reputation."[20] By the time he met Haydon in 1817, however, Keats was already familiar with a number of key elements of the new view of the brain, as one can see in his notes from "Mr C.'s" twelve introductory lectures on anatomy and physiology.

The notes as they have survived are uneven and often sketchy. Keats does not seem to have later made a fair copy, filling them out from memory, as did some other students. As a result, the *Note Book* has proved confusing and some scholars have even voiced doubts regarding which course of Cooper's lectures they reflect. More than sixty years ago, however, William Hale-White argued convincingly, on the basis of evidence from course advertisements, schedules, and student memoirs, that the *Note Book* records the series commonly called the "first twelve lectures" on anatomy and physiology, given by Cooper in the 1815–16 session at the United Hospitals, most likely in 1816.[21] Fortunately, a full set of notes from the same lecture course, given a year later and taken down by an American student named Edward Reynolds and copied fair in a beautiful hand, has survived, though Keats scholars seem to have missed it. Reynolds's note book, *The Twelve first Lectures of Mr Astley Coopers Anatomical Course delivered at St. Thomas' Theatre*, corresponds so closely to Keats's more fragmentary notes that there is no longer reason to doubt which lecture course Keats's notes reflect. Based on similarities in organization and phrasing, moreover, Cooper seems to have altered his lectures on the nervous system very little.[22] Although we cannot be certain what minor changes Cooper might have made from one year to the next, not to mention what Reynolds might have heard that Keats missed, Reynolds's notes provide an extremely helpful supplement to those of Keats, especially in expanding and clarifying passages that are not always obvious in the latter. Transcriptions of related lectures by Cooper, particularly those taken by Keats's roommate Tyrell, provide a further, though less immediately relevant, supplement. It is important to keep in mind, however, that Keats's surviving notes represent the beginning, rather than the whole, of what he would have learned as a medical student regarding the new neurobiology.

First and foremost, Cooper endorsed a brain-based, corporeal approach to mind. His definition of "Sensation," a leading term in Keats's later thought, is transcribed by Keats as follows: "it is an impression made on the Extremities of the Nerves conveyed to the Brain. This is proved," Cooper adds, "by the effects of dividing a Nerve." "Volition" is defined as the "contrary of Sensation it proceeds from the internal to external parts" (*JKNB* 55–6). Self-evident as these definitions may seem now, they were being explicitly denied in the leading journals of the time; the rebuttal of Home in the *Edinburgh Review*, insisting that the "brain is not at all concerned in the changes which precede Sensation" or "Volition," had been published only a few months before (440, 448).[23] Cooper, however, like Home – and like Darwin, Gall, Cabanis, Bell, and Lawrence – bases his reasoning on experiment and first-hand observation, a point he insists upon throughout his lectures. His is what we would now term a "medical-model" view of the mind. Cooper also follows Darwin and other Romantic brain scientists in emphasizing the shaping role of the sensory organs in perception and in allowing for volition without a conscious subject. "The different sensations," Keats reports, "reside in peculiar structures as the toes & fingers which have papillae through which the sense of feeling – the papillae of the Tongue are different from those of the Toes & fingers & are larger – the papillae of the Membrane of the nose are very minute & sensitive" (*JKNB* 55). Sensation is not a uniform, disembodied psychological faculty but a biological process, and the sensory stream is highly differentiated, to begin with, by the bodily organs that help produce it.[24] Volition, as in Darwin and Cabanis, is not the sole prerogative of the conscious subject but can be unconscious and is even, to a degree, dispersed throughout the body: "It does not reside entirely in the Brain but partly in yᵉ spinal Marrow which is seen in the Behaviour of a Frog after having been guilloteened" (*JKNB* 56).

Cooper knew from Bell's work that the sensory and motor nerves were distinct, although this is touched on only tangentially in Keats's notes: "Volition is sometimes present while sensation is destroyed" (*JKNB* 57). More generally, Keats learned that the nerves were not simple cords, certainly not hollow tubes, but bundles of fibers, as Home, Bell, and Gall and Spurzheim had all asserted against received opinion. This is stated both of the brain's white matter (that is, axons) – the "Medullary substance seems to be composed of fibres" – and of the nerves running throughout the body. "Nerves are composed of numerous Cords – this is still the Case with the smallest." (Reynolds notes more precisely: "They are composed of numerous Bundles of chords, which have à free communication together. This you will always find to be their structure" [*C/R* 118]). Keats goes on, "They take a serpentine direction. They arise by numerous branches from the Substance of ye Brain – there is however a contrary opinion extant" (*JKNB* 54). This contrary opinion is that of Gall, who argued on the basis of comparative anatomy that it was more appropriate to conceive of the brain growing out of the nerves, the nervous system growing upwards like a tree. But the notion that the brain's white ("Medullary") matter is fibrous, which Cooper accepts, is also a contribution of Gall's, and a (then) controversial one at that.[25]

Cooper's estimate of Gall has been described as everything from sympathetic to hostile; one student records Cooper's skepticism regarding the craniological part of Gall's system, which seems in character.[26] But Cooper certainly recognized the preeminence of Gall's neuroanatomy. Keats notes that the "Spinal Marrow is composed of 2 Columns – of late it has been said to have been discovered that these at the upper part cross each other," a passage that has been consistently misunderstood (*JKNB* 53).[27] Keats is referring here neither to Bell's work on the sensory and motor nerves nor merely to the basic structure of the spinal column, but to the crossing or decussation of the pyramids in the medulla spinalis, an important anatomical discovery that had recently been restated and definitively demonstrated by Gall.[28] Reynolds's account is unambiguous: "The Medulla Spinalis is composed of two separate columns which are united at their upper part by a decussation of their fibres . . . This structure was first described by Duverney, and lately, it has been pointed out by Gall & Spurzheim" (*C/R* 108–10). Just as unambiguous is Cooper's praise for Gall's anatomical work, inspired by an earlier mention of the same discovery. "Gall has thrown great light on this subject and I am surprised that his opinions should be so little thought of, as they are, viz, as regards simply ye dissection of ye brain. I think that the Brain can only be properly studied properly [*sic*], as recommended by him. Once well dissected in the way he points out is worth a dozen times in ye old way; for by that many important Parts must necessarily be destroyed. He preserves ye idea of ye connection of ye Parts" (*C/R* 107). This echoes Gall and Spurzheim's own defense of their new dissection techniques; in fact, the lecture on brain anatomy corresponds generally to the first chapter of Spurzheim's *Physiognomical System*, which had appeared early in 1815 and may well have been consulted by Cooper in working up the lecture series attended by Keats. Keats later joked about phrenology ("Well! I'm a craniologist," he writes in his comic poem "On Some Skulls in Beauley Abbey"), but it is something of an insider's joke. Gall's basic anatomy was clearly respected at Guy's, whatever the reservations concerning his craniology.[29]

In addition to the basic structure of the brain and nerves, Cooper's lectures covered the new theory of electrical neural transmission that made brain-based accounts of mind more plausible by proposing a sufficiently rapid means of communication throughout the body. Cooper credits John Hunter with first proposing that the "Nerves were conductor [*sic*] of electric fluid," based on his experiments with the "Gymnotus Electricus" (an electric fish); Galvani's further experiments have led, Keats notes, to the "present opinion" that a "fluid, like that of the electric is secreted in ye brain which is thence communicated along the Nerves" (*JKNB* 58). Cooper also stresses the "Involuntary Powers" supported by the nerves – as in the regulation of breathing and the circulation of the blood – further decentering the conscious subject in stressing the holistic character of the nervous system. "*Sympathy*" between various parts of the body is another nonconscious function mediated by the nerves: as in coughing and sneezing ("an instance of complicated sympathy"), stock examples for Bell too of the system linking the stomach, lungs, and head (*JKNB* 56). The corresponding passage in Reynolds defines the sympathetic function of the nerves as a "universal communication between the different parts of ye Body – by which one is made to feel for another" (*C/R* 138). The overall picture conveyed by Cooper – an embodied mind and a nervous, sensible body, with no clear dividing line between – will be familiar to any reader of Keats's poetry.

By now, a succession of critics have shown how key terms from Keats's medical note book reverberate throughout his later writing, their senses not confined by their scientific definitions but clearly anchored by them. "Sensation" is an especially rich term for Keats, one with a range of connotations, and a full accounting of its role in his poetry and letters would

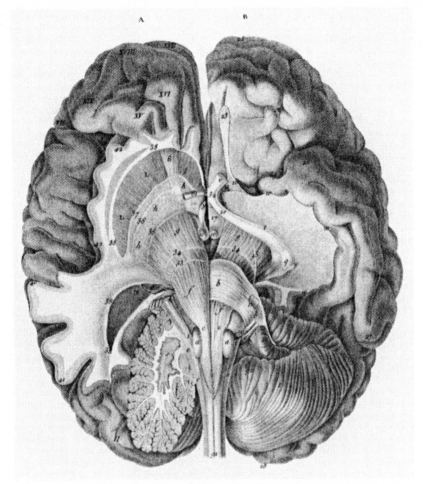

8 Gall and Spurzheim, *Atlas*, plate v (horizontal section, showing convolutions, "arbor vitae," and pyramidal tract).

take a chapter in itself.[30] But understanding a statement like "O for a Life of Sensations rather than of Thoughts" (*JKL* 1: 185) must at least begin with the primary role given to sensation in Keats's lessons from Cooper, its relation to physical experience, its anti-mentalistic tenor, its resonance within a corporeal account of mind. As Donald Goellnicht comments, poetic creativity for Keats is "ultimately rooted in material existence, in sensations perceived from concrete objects," an esthetic thoroughly consonant with the experimentalist ethos of Guy's and with the methodological claims of the period's radical science generally.[31] That such perception is an active and transformative process and not a passive or mechanical registration of an objective world out there – that "Sensations" are the constructs of an embodied mind – constitutes a corollary truth for Romantic brain science, no less than for Romantic poetry. When Keats writes of an "ellectric fire in human nature" (*JKL* 2: 80) the conceit is, once more, as much scientific as poetic, recalling the "electric fluid" attributed to the brain and nerves by Cooper. The image recurs again, resonant with its original context in Romantic brain science, in some of the most striking lines of the *Fall of Hyperion*:

> for the scenes
> Still swooning vivid through my globed brain
> With an electral changing misery
> Thou shalt with those dull mortal eyes behold.   (1: 244–47)

Moneta's "globed brain" also harks back to Keats's anatomy lessons, describing the brain seen from above with its rounded hemispheres.[32] Keats's most elaborate and imaginative reworking of his early knowledge of brain anatomy, however, can be found in the remarkable concluding stanza of the "Ode to Psyche."

EMBODYING PSYCHE

Many of the images that fill out the mental landscape of the "Ode to Psyche" have been traced to specific features of the new brain anatomy as Keats understood it.[33] The "wild-ridged mountains" suggest the convolutions of the cerebral cortex, which had appeared more like intestines to earlier anatomists but had been given new visual definition (as well as unprecedented functional significance) by Gall and Spurzheim.[34] The "dark-cluster'd trees" with their "branched thoughts" evoke the tree-like appearance of some brain structures as revealed by the new dissection techniques (most notably the cerebellum with its "arbor vitae") and echo Keats's note on the nerves arising "by numerous branches from the Substance of ye Brain" (*JKNB* 54). The "streams" and "rosy" sanctuary correspond to the network of blood vessels nourishing the brain and connecting it with the circulatory system; Cooper states in the *Twelve first Lectures* that the blood vessels "distributed to ye nerves are small but very numerous" and that "under Injection their whole surface becomes reddened" (*C/R* 118). Most strikingly, the "wreath'd trellis of a working brain" evokes the fibrous texture of the brain's "medullary" or white matter as described by Gall and Spurzheim. Their description of how the "fibres" of the medullary pyramids "cross or decussate each other," which so impressed Cooper, especially brings trellis work to mind.[35] The mixing of architectural and natural images picks up in a general way on the descriptive language in the brain atlases and dissecting manuals of the time,[36] while the insistence on organic growth ("branched thoughts, new grown with pleasant pain") shares more particularly in the organic tenor of both Gall's and Bell's new anatomies, mutually (though distinctively) influenced by the new, Romantic, emphasis on biology.

In tracing out this pattern of specific links, however, it is important to keep sight of the larger issues involved in Keats's reworking of Romantic brain science. Psyche is the "latest born" of the Olympians; as Keats tellingly writes in the journal letter to George and Georgiana Keats, "Psyche was not embodied as a goddess before the time of Apulieus," after the "Agustan age" (*JKL* 2: 106). The same point is made by Lemprière, whose *Classical Dictionary* Keats pored over at Enfield, and who defines Psyche as a personification of the "*soul.*"[37] Her double significance as belated goddess and "embodied" image of the soul or psyche makes her the ideal muse for the modern poet, whose unique task, as Keats had declared in contrasting Wordsworth and Milton, is to explore the "dark Passages" of the human mind (*JKL* 1: 281).[38] ("I will assay to reach as high a summit in Poetry as the nerve bestowed upon me will suffer," he writes in another letter a few months later [*JKL* 1: 387]). But in its thematic design, the "Ode to Psyche" owes less to Wordsworth than to Coleridge, who in "Kubla Khan" had already depicted a psychologized landscape with vivid erotic overtones, casting its speaker in the role of wild-eyed prophet and broaching issues of unconscious inspiration, involuntary creation, and the body's encroachment upon the life of the mind.[39] As "pale-mouth'd prophet" of Psyche, Keats creates his own vision in a dream ("Surely I dreamt to-day"), yearning for transcendence yet underscoring the inextricability of mind and body – or more pointedly, mind and brain.

The close relation between "Kubla Khan" and the "Ode to Psyche" has not featured in readings of either poem, yet the biographical record, along with the profound thematic links and a number of particular verbal echoes, would seem to make such a comparison inevitable.[40] Keats's sole (and often recounted) meeting with Coleridge took place on April 11, 1819; he describes it in the journal-letter to George and Georgiana on April 16 and within two weeks writes the "Ode to Psyche," which he transcribes into the same long letter. The meeting with Coleridge was facilitated by none other than J. H. Green, "our

Demonstrator at Guy's," as Keats remarks. Green, that is, was Keats's former anatomy demonstrator, one who shared, incidentally, Coleridge's interest in Spurzheim (*JKL* 2: 88).[41] Significantly, Keats's medical training had been on his mind even before the reunion with Green: earlier in the journal-letter he writes that he has been thinking of going to Edinburgh to "study for a physician" (*JKL* 2: 70). He has also been thinking about the brain: in the aftermath of a head injury (a blow on the eye from a cricket ball), he feels delightfully faint, the "fibres of the brain are relaxed in common with the rest of the body"; the same entry refers to the "ellectric fire in human nature" (*JKL* 2: 78–80). The conversation with Coleridge, or rather Coleridge's monologue, circles almost compulsively around issues directly associated with "Kubla Khan," published three years before: "Poetry," "poetical sensation," "Different genera and species of Dreams," a "dream related," "First and second consciousness," the "difference explained between will and Volition" (*JKL* 2: 88–89). Did Keats re-read "Kubla Khan" after this remarkably suggestive meeting? Later in the same entry, after a stray reference to "opium," he transcribes a sonnet ("As Hermes once took to his feathers light") based on a "dream" of his own, one directly inspired – like the dream behind "Kubla Khan" – by reading (*JKL* 2: 91).[42] On April 30 he transcribes the "Ode to Psyche," "wrung / By Sweet enforcement, and remembrance dear," lines that might also describe Coleridge "instantly and eagerly" attempting to record his "recollection" of an earlier dream-vision back in 1797.

The wild-eyed visionary of "Kubla Khan" would "build that dome in air"; the "pale-mouth'd prophet" of Psyche would "build a fane / In some untrodden region" of his mind. Both visions involve "incense," trees, gardens, forests, hills or mountains, flowing water. Coleridge's "pleasure" parallels Keats's "soft delight," "girdled" parallels "wreath'd," "holy and enchanted" chimes with "holy were the haunted," "twice five miles" with "wide quietness," and Kubla's walled asylum recurs as Psyche's "rosy sanctuary." The tantalizing phrase "shadowy thought" in the "Ode to Psyche," in addition to broaching the issues of unconscious cognition that play so large a role in both "Kubla Khan" and its prose introduction, also touches on Coleridge's "shadow of the dome of pleasure" and the "vague and dim recollection" that renders the pleasure-dome so shadowy. The "vision" of the Abyssianian maid "singing" and the poet's attempt to "revive" that song parallels the poet of Psyche invoking the goddess as muse only to "see, and sing, by [his] own eyes inspired." It could be argued that such a list of resemblances could only be expected in a pair of poems that similarly draw on pastoral and romance conventions to update the traditional psychologized landscape, sharing a modern emphasis on the individual imagination, a Romantic concern with unconscious inspiration and thought, and a fascination with mind–body relations shaped by each poet's interest in contemporary medical and scientific speculation. Once that much is conceded, however, it seems almost perverse to ignore the fact that, within two weeks of writing the "Ode to Psyche," Keats had been describing his fascinating recent encounter with Coleridge, in the context of poetry, dreams, consciousness, volition, and even his anatomy lessons at Guy's. Keats's dream or vision (the status remains typically unsettled) revises Coleridge's vision in a dream, Coleridge's superimposition of landscape, psyche, and body neatly contracted by Keats into the compass of the brain, where body and psyche most evidently and crucially meet. The elements of sexuality and passion remain but are softened and refined, even domesticated, by Keats: compare "woman wailing for her demon lover" with Psyche waiting, beneath her open casement, for the nightly visit of Eros.[43]

Of course, the "Ode to Psyche" is not taken up solely with the medical and philosophical issues dating from Keats's period at Guy's and only its final stanza deals primarily with those questions. Even that stanza, the one I am almost exclusively concerned with here, slips the harness of such a reading. The "untrodden" psychic region it maps out not only gives poetic life to the newly complex brain revealed by Gall and Bell, but provides too a fresh canvas for Keats to exercise the imaginative powers he grounds in the embodied psyche. Birds and bees, Dryads and unearthly flowers populate the "wide quietness" of this mental space built from the subtly naturalized images of a "working brain." "Fancy" has its place along with anatomy in a stanza that deftly shuttles between myth and science, conventional poetic topoi (the psychologized landscape, the fanciful bower) and novel images of the brain-mind. Its resonant final images – "A bright torch, and a casement ope at night, / To let the warm Love in" – both touch on neurobiological speculations going back to Keats's *Note Book* and exceed those concerns, not least in their tactful evocation of the darker aspects of the "Eros and Psyche" myth. Yet, in this context, the "bright torch" cannot but also recall the "ellectric fire" of the human mind and the "electric" transmission between the brain and nervous system. Goellnicht's reading of the "casement ope at night" as the "fenestra rotundum" of the inner ear, part of its channel to the brain, is both ingenious and limiting.[44] The wider resonance of the image must include, however, the importance of the brain's commerce with the world (through the ear, eye, and other sensory openings) and its integration with the rest of the body (by means of the larger nervous system), touching on the holistic and ecological character of Romantic accounts of embodied thought. In opening to "let the warm Love in," the casement image also gives primacy to the passionate, affective aspects of mind that play a crucial role throughout the embodied psychologies of the Romantic era, flouting not just the traditional opposition of mind and body, but the corresponding one of cognition and emotion.

THE POETRY OF INTEROCEPTION

Why is Love warm? And why, in particular, is love associated across so many human cultures with a warm heart? Bell, in the second of his lectures to the Royal Society, held that his work on the respiratory nerves and their connections with the brain, the facial nerves, and the circulatory system had answered this very question. "The language and sentiments of every people have pointed to the heart, as the seat of passion, and every individual has felt its truth. For though the heart be not in the proper sense the seat of passion, it is influenced by the conditions of the mind, and from thence its influence is extended through the respiratory organs, so as to mount to the throat, and lips, and cheeks, and account for every movement of passion, which is not explained by the direct influence of the mind" (III: 308). Love is warm because the blood rushing from the heart into the skin of the face and throat feels warm. In *Endymion*, Keats calls Eros the "God of warm pulses" (III. 984).

The spontaneous physiological expression of passion and other "conditions of the mind" had long served, along with head injuries, dreams, sensory illusions, and the effects of psychoactive drugs, as a prime example in anti-dualistic arguments. La Mettrie had pointedly asked why his blood heated up when "lying peacefully" in bed and planning a book or following through a line of reasoning; "why is the fever in my mind transmitted to my veins?"[45] Priestley had argued, in the *Disquisitions Relating to Matter and Spirit*, that "as the mind is affected in consequence of the affections of the body and brain, so the body is liable to be reciprocally affected by the affections of the mind, as is evident in the visible effects of strong passions . . . These are certainly irrefragible arguments that it is properly no other than *one and the same thing* that is subject to these affections."[46] Bell would have demurred at Priestley's materialist conclusion, yet his work on the nerves served to advance corporeal theories of mind by describing a biological system capable of mediating mind–body interaction without appealing to occult qualities like "animal spirits." Bell's psychology, beginning with the *Essays* on anatomy and expression, hews as closely as possible to describing the mind and body as a single system without altogether losing sight of an immaterial principle; it places the body in the mind without confining mind entirely to the body. Much the same could be said of Keats, who can speak of the "hot hand of thought" or write that his "mind is in a tremble" without, at least at moments, closing out the possibility of an immortal and immaterial soul (*JKL* 1: 209, 2: 5, 224).

One might even call Keats the most visceral of the English poets, so long as "visceral" is understood as continuous with, rather than opposed to, intellectual – the sense it had in the brain science of his time. (This is also the sense it has regained in recent neuroscience and cognitive theory, captured in the phrase "hot cognition.")[47] A conviction in the importance of "internal" sensation – as opposed to Locke's exclusive attention to the five external senses – makes one of the key features interconnecting the various theories of mind heuristically grouped together here as "Romantic" psychologies. Darwin includes in his discussion of sensation in *Zoonomia* not only "appetites" associated with the internal organs, like hunger and the "want of fresh Air," but leaves room for "many more senses" associated with the glands as well (*Z* 1: 124–6). Bell draws an analogy between the operation of the "organs of the senses" in producing specific ideas and the means by which "other organs of the body may have a relation existing with the mind, and a control over it, without reference to outward impressions" (*AP* 78). Communication with the brain takes place both through the "secret operations of the vital organs" (like Cabanis, Bell presumes the existence of something like the hormonal system without so much as a guess concerning its specific mechanism) and by the visceral nervous system, "nerves of peculiar sensibility, having their seat in the body or viscera."[48] Spurzheim, popularizing a key idea of Gall's in the *Physiognomical System*, highlights the "influence of the viscera upon the brain, and vice versa" (141). Careful attention is paid throughout Romantic brain science to what would now be called "interoception" and the corresponding ability of the mind to influence the internal organs.

In his provocative study, *Keats and Embarrassment* (1974), Christopher Ricks has shown how pervasively and centrally bodily fluids and their dynamics function in Keats's writing: the rush of blood to the skin in blushing or sexual arousal, the welling up of tears, the operation of sweat

glands. But with a governing interest in the "moral and social" meaning
of these actions, Ricks barely hints at how large a role such mind–body
phenomena play in the medical and scientific thinking of Keats's time,
nor has he much to say about their philosophical and ideological significance.[49] Cooper's interest in such phenomena is clear from the discussion of "involuntary" and "sympathetic" nerve functions that Keats
alludes to in his notes from the introductory lectures on the nervous
system. The notes to a following lecture on the glands show how, once
sensation, thought, and volition were located in the brain, it became
natural to view the mind and body as aspects of an integrated system
rather than as distinct, much less dichotomous, entities. Experimental
data is characteristically cited as evidence that the glands and the nerves
that "contribute" to them form part of a network of interlocking functions, in turn connected with the brain and its cognitive and emotive
activities. "Nerves are supposed to contribute to this operation, which is
proved by the secretion being stopped in those Glands the Nerves going
to which have been divided . . . The passions of ye Mind have great influence on the Secretions, Fear produces increase [of] Bile and Urine,
Sorrow increases Tears" (*JKNB* 64). Cooper's example of the former
effect gives a wonderful sense of his lecture style: "Thus, I have seen a
man when he was going to a Hospital to perform an operation, stop, like
a dog, at almost every corner to make water" (*C/R* 190). Coming from
a celebrated surgeon in the course of a lecture to medical students, this
is a distinctly humanizing as well as funny anecdote. Although this
passage exists only in Reynolds' notes, it suggests how readily Cooper's
sensibility would have appealed to Keats.

Another of Cooper's lectures, this one transcribed by Tyrell, underscores his sense of a unified bodily and psychic economy, as well as providing yet another example of head injury cited in support of a
corporeal account of mind.

If an injury happens to the head, the functions of volition and sensation are
diminished; the stomach is disordered through the medium of the par vagum;
and from the communication between the grand sympathetic nerve, and those
of the brain and spinal marrow, the functions of the heart and of the abdominal viscera become affected. The powers of mind are also diminished; the
memory is lost; the judgement is enfeebled; thus sensation, volition, the involuntary actions, and the powers of mind, are diminished or suspended. (*C/T*
253)

Keats's poetry manifests a comparably rich and complex sense of the
interconnectedness among psychological and physiological functions,

conscious and unconscious mental activity, the head and the heart, the viscera and the "powers of mind." As early as "Calidore" (written in 1816), this keen appreciation for the embodied character of thought and emotion emerges as a signature aspect of Keats's poetic style: "His warm arms, thrilling now with pulses new." Within another year, in the sonnet "On Seeing the Elgin Marbles," the portrayal of mind, brain, and body interaction has become enriched in a manner that is unmistakably Keatsian: "Such dim-conceived glories of the brain / Bring round the heart an undescribable feud." In *Endymion* (1818), that poem of "pulses and throes" (3: 791), Keats's verbal ingenuity – particularly his penchant, learned from Shakespeare, for making one part of speech do the work of another – renders this style for mingling thought and passion, soma and psyche, even more indisputably his own:

> Poor Cynthia greeted him, and sooth'd her light
> Against his pallid face: he felt the charm
> To breathlessness, and suddenly a warm
> Of his heart's blood.   (3: 104–7)

This is a poetry that refuses to distinguish psychology and physiology, that repeatedly confronts the conscious subject with the surprising swiftness of bodily cognition. Meditating on such bodily knowledge in his notorious lecture to the College of Surgeons "On Life" (which must have caused a considerable buzz in the London medical world Keats belonged to at the time), Lawrence could think of only one term to describe it: "sensibility."[50]

Of all the visceral organs, the most important for Keats was, of course, the skin, with its capacity to blush (especially) or grow pallid, flush or tingle, go hot or cold.[51] The skin was also highly significant for contemporary medical science, as the largest of the viscera and at the same time the locus of the external sense of touch. Lawrence recognized the exemplary status of the skin for an emergent biology of mind at once holistic and ecological in character, both in its dual role as internal and external sensory organ and in serving, moreover, as the human organism's most extensive site of contact with the environment. He defines the skin as the "one great connection between animal existence and that of surrounding substances," permeated by a "vascular network over the whole body, eluding our inquiries and defying calculation by the number and fineness of its tubes." In the "glow of exercise or the flush of shame, in the excitement of fever" the web of "tubes" rapidly fills with blood; their "ramifications are particularly numerous and subtle in those parts of the cutaneous organ which possess the most exquisite sensibility" (*LPZ* 236). Bell (in the lectures attended by Haydon) finds in the interplay of nervous system, heart, blood, and skin a telling example of the embodied mind in action, one that illustrates as well the limits of the conscious "intellectual powers," too "precarious" to be trusted with "vital functions." The "filaments" of the nervous system are "extended to the heart, and wind about the vessels in their course through the body. And thus on one hand the passions of the mind agitate the heart, and often the feelings seem to centre there with palpitations and a sense of sinking; while on the other, the nerves, where affected by emotion, influence in no less a degree the minute ramifications of the vessels, which go to the surface, and produce a visible effect as in blushing, or in the paleness and coldness and shrinking of the skin in fear" (*Essays* 162). Blushing remains rather mysterious for Bell, however; it is "too sudden and too partial" to be traced to the "heart's action" (*AP* 89), and relies on a "peculiar provision" of facial nerves that allow for a unique "susceptibility corresponding to the passions of the mind" (*Essays* 166). As a mode of expression, it is eminently social, "one of the many sources of sympathy which bind us together," universally understood and innately guided. "It is not acquired: it is from the beginning." It is wrong, Bell adds (in a passage of great interest for readers of Keats), to associate blushing too narrowly with embarrassment. "We think of blushes as accompanying shame; but it [*sic*] is indicative of excitement. There is no shame when lively feeling makes a timid youth break through the restraint which modesty and reserve have imposed" (*Essays* 88–89).

Blushing in *Endymion* certainly conveys excitement more than shame, though excitement of a reassuring, humane, even healing kind:

> I'm giddy at that cheek so fair and smooth;
> O let it blush so ever! let it soothe
> My madness! let it mantle rosy-warm
> With the tinge of love, panting in safe alarm.   (IV: 311–14)

This is blushing at its most intense, and Keats at his least guarded. In later poems like *Isabella* and *The Eve of St. Agnes*, blushing, panting, flushing, and like events are portrayed less enthusiastically but more subtly, with a more pointed and sustained attention to their curious psychophysiological status. Though blushing in *Endymion* is the sign of a "very maid" (I: 635), in *Isabella* it is Lorenzo whose face is "flush with love" (215). Throughout, Lorenzo's corporeality is emphasized, most grotesquely in the dismemberment of his corpse. (The severed head dutifully washed and tended by Isabella harks back uncannily to Keats's period as an anatomy student.) The most intricate description of the psychophysiological drama unfolding within Lorenzo's sensorium, early on in the poem, does not reflect so much as extend and enrich the contemporary medical understanding of mind–body commerce represented by Bell and Lawrence. When Lorenzo first determines to reveal his love,

> all day
> His heart beat awfully against his side;
> And to his heart he inwardly did pray
> For power to speak; but still the ruddy tide
> Stifled his voice, and puls'd resolve away –   (41–45)

The heart that conventionally harbors love also, quite inconveniently, registers the fear of rejection by speeding up as anxiety quickens the pulse. Because of the extensive interconnections among the heart, blood, and lungs (demonstrated in detail by Bell and taken for granted by Cooper), the "ruddy tide" of blood chokes up the throat and, in another Shakespearean verbal flourish, "pulses" away his willed behavior. Lorenzo finds himself in the ironic position of beseeching his own heart to slow down and let him speak the passion that the same heart universally symbolizes – on account, as Bell had pointed out, of the neurophysiological connections that enable it to stifle his voice in the first place. Volition (here the "power to speak") is anything but the prerogative of a conscious, disembodied, sovereign subject; rather, it arises from a complex system of mental intentions and physiological operations, physical sensations and unconscious as well as conscious anxieties and desires. Building on their conventional associations with passion, Keats represents motions of the heart and blood in a way that underscores the complications as well as the transports of an embodied sensibility. At the same time, poor Lorenzo's love for wealthy Isabella is rendered more genuine for the reader by its physiological signs; it is, quite overtly, proved upon Lorenzo's pulses.

In *The Eve of St. Agnes* the felt expression of love grows more painful, hotter. Keats points up the physiological parallel between the flush of erotic excitement and that of fever; the heart, now not simply warm but "on fire" (75), becomes "Love's fev'rous citadel" (84). All this is conventional enough – for the reasons adduced by Bell. More interesting are the passages where Keats complicates the interplay among passion, its physiological expression, and cognition both conscious and unconscious.

As does Austen in *Persuasion*, Keats gives a finer-grained and still more dynamic account of such matters even than Bell or Cabanis. Madeline, breathless with excitement ("She clos'd the door, she panted") at the erotic ritual she is about to enact, must not speak: "But to her heart, her heart was voluble, / Paining with eloquence her balmy side" (201, 204–5). The first "heart" here seems to figure a sensibility only partly available to consciousness; *it* fully understands the native language of the second, more purely physical heart, but the painful quality of its eloquence seems more psychological than physical, the effect of her struggle to keep the surprising intensity of her erotic excitement out of full awareness. Porphyro undergoes a related process when the physiological expression of a lascivious plan seems to accompany rather than follow the conscious awareness of the "thought":

> Sudden a thought came like a full-blown rose,
> Flushing his brow, and in his pained heart
> Made purple riot. (136–38)

Porphyro's scheme to take advantage of Madeline's ritual observance comes "full-blown" to consciousness because it has evidently been unconsciously fabricated, with the speed that forms for medical writers from Darwin to Bell the chief advantage of unconscious over conscious thought. His brow flushes (the "rose" image does extra work here) *before* his heart, beating more quickly and irregularly, makes "purple riot" – a sequence in keeping with Bell's model of a specially innervated vascular system in the face, uniquely susceptible to "passions of the mind" and quicker in its operations than the heart. Keats's psychophysiology, in other words, can be as precise as Bell's, while his understanding of mind–body interaction seems more even-handed, less drawn toward yielding primacy to the former.

The uncertain lines between psychology and physiology, conscious and unconscious volition only grow hazier when both subjects – Porphyro and Madeline together – are portrayed interacting in a half-waking, half-dreaming, altogether charged erotic encounter.

> Beyond a mortal man impassion'd far
> At these voluptuous accents, he arose,
> Ethereal, flush'd, and like a throbbing star
> Seen mid the sapphire heaven's deep repose;
> Into her dream he melted, as the rose
> Blendeth its odour with the violet, –
> Solution sweet. (316–22)

The "physiological" parallel between blushing and erection noted long ago by Ricks – "in both cases blood rushes visibly to a part of the body" – is heightened by the fact that both tend to arise spontaneously and both resist (rather notoriously) the control of the conscious will.[52] But nothing in this passage seems to happen with full benefit of consciousness, though to call the encounter unconscious – a kind of sexual somnambulism – would be wrong as well. Madeline is not asleep, but "wide awake," according to the previous stanza, yet she "still beheld . . . the vision of her sleep." It is as though her unconscious mind, with its strong links to "internal sensations" (such as sexual desire), has succeeded in tricking the conscious subject by running a kind of simulation of perceptual activity continuous with the dream from which Madeline has just emerged. Yet her sense, a moment later, that she has been "deceived" not by her unconscious desires but by Porphyro's purposeful design is hard to put aside (332). Porphyro, flushed, throbbing, and beside himself with passion, is evidently in the grip of bodily desires of his own – the traffic between the mind and the glands clearly runs in both directions. Yet in the next stanza he asserts control of the situation, at least retrospectively, in telling Madeline authoritatively and rather coolly, "This is no dream" (326). Keats makes it difficult if not impossible to say whether either character has acted willingly, in the sense of performing a consciously intended act; the question almost seems naive in context. Yet the sinister aura surrounding Porphyro, especially toward the end of the poem, might be calculated to provoke readers to ask this very question. As Romantic psychologies erode the prerogatives of the conscious self in favor of unconscious cognition, "inward" sensation, spontaneous or "natural" physiological expression, and innate propensities and inclinations, the behavior of the "human animal" (as Keats writes in the journal-letter to George and Georgiana) begins to be seen in terms of "instinctiveness" (*JKL* 2: 79–80). This is a conclusion Coleridge struggled against for much of his career; Keats may be expressing a comparable ambivalence in the troubled close of *The Eve of St. Agnes*.

Yet the dominant note in Keats's writing is one of acceptance, sometimes resigned, sometimes joyful, of the full weight of an embodied existence, for all its pains and uncertainties; his ambition was to become a "miserable and mighty Poet of the human Heart" (*JKL* 2: 115). This is especially evident when, in depicting immortals in *Lamia* and in the "Hyperion" poems, he proves unable to describe their emotions and thoughts without lending them a human somatosensory system. Saturn's hand, at the beginning of *Hyperion*, is not just "listless," but "nerveless"

(18); the need to anthropomorphically project a visceral nervous system becomes explicit when Thea discovers Saturn a few more lines further on in the poem.

> One hand she press'd upon that aching spot
> Where beats the human heart, as if just there,
> Though an immortal, she felt cruel pain.   (42–44)

Far from enabling them to transcend the life of the body, the epic proportions of the Titans instead magnifies it:

> Without a motion, save of their big hearts
> Heaving in pain, and horribly convuls'd
> With sanguine feverous boiling gurge of pulse.

When Hyperion aches, he aches with "horrors, portion'd to a giant nerve" (I: 175). These images are so effective partly because they strike home; the gods feel, perceive, and emote as we do, only in a bigger way.

According to *Lamia*, the gods even blush in their own spectacular manner:

> So Hermes thought, and a celestial heat
> Burnt from his winged heels to either ear,
> That from a whiteness, as the lily clear,
> Blush'd into roses 'mid his golden hair.   (I: 22–25).

Keats models this "humanizing" touch on a famous one in *Paradise Lost*, as Ricks points out, but the emphasis on hot cognition ("So Hermes thought") is Keats's own.[53] An even hotter passage follows, when Lamia reveals the nymph that Hermes has been seeking: "One warm, flush'd moment, hovering, it might seem / Dash'd by the wood-nymph's beauty, so he burn'd" (I: 129–30). In the second of the twelve introductory lectures, Cooper had taught Keats that the heat of the blood remains more or less constant ("from 98 to 100 degrees") however cool the environment: "The Body exceeds in heat the surrounding atmosphere" (*JKNB* 4). To be human and alive is to run hot in relation to the external world. (For Lawrence, the most striking effect of death is that the body's "heat is lost, and it soon reaches the temperature of the surrounding medium").[54] Because of Hunter's speculations on the blood as conduit of a mysterious vital force, the blood was an ideologically charged topic during Keats's period at Guy's, subject to a great deal of speculation thanks to the materialist–vitalist controversy set in motion by Lawrence's 1816 lectures. Even Cooper, generally not given to wondering out loud, surmises (Keats reports) that the blood is somehow permeated by "nervous energy" (*JKNB* 5). For Keats, however, the chief philosophical interest of the blood is its pervasive role in mediating between psychological events and bodily expression or, more accurately, in regularly and sensibly effacing the Cartesian psychosomatic divide. Mental states like love and pleasure (not to mention embarrassment and pain) are scarcely imaginable without such motions of the blood, which is why the price Lamia sets Hermes for his wood-nymph is human embodiment: "a sweet body fit for life, / And love, and pleasure, and the ruddy strife / Of hearts and lips" (39–41).

The heart is no valentine for Keats, but a "ruddy" organ, pulsing with blood, charging the body with signs and sensations of affect, racing or throbbing or faltering in secret sympathy with the brain and mind. This medical-model understanding of passion remains with Keats throughout his brief career. One of his last (and most confessional) poems, "To Fanny," begins, significantly, with an image that harks back to Keats's years as a surgeon's apprentice: "Physician Nature! let my spirit blood!" – a striking, rather "metaphysical" conceit that once more points up Keats's difficulty in imagining even a "spirit" without a body. His own heart "fluttering" with love and jealousy, Keats asks Fanny to "let the amorous burn," but adds:

> do not turn
> The current of your heart from me so soon:
> O save, in charity,
> The quickest pulse for me.

Keats begs Fanny not for her thoughts but her sensations; their truth Fanny herself can gauge by placing her hand upon her "snowy side, / Where the heart beats," like a physician. The current of the heart's blood flows through his poetry to the poignant end.

PASSIONATE BREATH, STRENUOUS TONGUE, A PALATE FINE

The human ability to read emotions based on their physiological displays was a favorite topic of Bell's, from the early lectures attended by Haydon to the crowning series in the *Philosophical Transactions*. It is another, major, consequence of the neural web and the "secret sympathies" connecting the brain with the motions of the heart and blood, the actions of the lungs (directly supported by the blood), and the musculature and skin of the face and throat. All this supports a "natural language," Bell states in 1806, "which is to be read in the changes of the countenance"; there is "no emotion in the mind of man which has not its appropriate signs" (*Essays* 85). Baillie had spoken of a neurologically-based "natural language" in his Gulstonian lectures of 1794, anticipating Bell's basic model though by no means its intricate details. "The different emotions of the mind are also conveyed along nerves to different muscles of the body . . . producing a change in the countenance and attitude" which is "expressive" of each basic emotion in turn. "This becomes a natural language," nonarbitrary, universal, and produced independently of "volition."[55] Baillie seems fated by circumstance to have posed the connection between the nerves and emotional expression: before coming to London to study medicine with his uncles, he had studied philosophy in Glasgow with Thomas Reid, who had theorized the need for a natural language in his *Inquiry into the Human Mind* (1764). Bell, emigrating to London from Scotland a few years later – with a letter of introduction to Baillie – may well have begun his work on the anatomy and philosophy of expression from hints in Baillie's lectures. He may even, given his strong interest in the arts, have drawn on Joanna Baillie's extension of her brother's ideas in the "Introductory Discourse" to *Plays on the Passions* as well. Cooper, a colleague of Baillie's who had met Bell in Edinburgh (along with Dugald Stewart, Reid's protégé), was undoubtedly familiar with these ideas, as was Haydon; analogous statements could be found in the works of Darwin and Spurzheim as well.[56]

Cooper had taught Keats how the blood, "forced by the contraction of the heart," moves into the right ventrical, "whence it passes into the pulmonary arteries to circulate through the lungs" (*JKNB* 9). Hence the "strict sympathy" between the heart and lungs that Bell stresses in his lectures to artists (*Essays* 165). For Keats, too, the lungs work closely with the heart in the expression of sexual feeling: "all breathing human passion," "forever panting." Love, in *Endymion*, begins in the "commingling of passionate breath" (I: 833). Sighing, panting, and of course the play of blood in the skin, are for Keats the natural signs of love, along with certain movements of the eyes and vocal tones. Without such a natural language, Lorenzo and Isabella may never have come to an understanding:

> So once more he had wak'd and anguished
>   A dreary night of love and misery,
> If Isabel's quick eye had not been wed
>   To every symbol on his forehead high;
> She saw it waxing very pale and dead,
>   And straight all flush'd; so, lisped tenderly,

> "Lorenzo!" – here she ceas'd her timid quest,
> But in her tone and look he read the rest.   (49–56)

That Isabella's "tone" tells more than her words suggests that for Keats, as for Wordsworth, the extrasemantic properties of speech can be as meaningful as the arbitrary symbols they convey. Bell found in the "system of nerves" joining respiration to the heart, thorax, head, and brain a physiological analog to the continuities between "natural" and arbitrary language posited by eighteenth-century theorists of language like Reid and Herder. "These are not the organs of breathing merely, but of natural and articulate language also, and adapted to the expression of sentiment, in the workings of the countenance and of the breast, that is by signs, as well as by words" (*112*: 310). An extension of this system into the mouth, the "organ of voice and speech, as of taste and exquisite feeling," brings verbal articulation into relation with taste as well: in Bell's quaintly archaic terms, the mouth is "pneumatic as much as manducatory" (*111*: 403).

Unpoetic as Bell's terminology sounds here, the elaborate but pointed network of connections he poses bears great relevance to poetry, especially to the poetic practice of Keats. M. H. Abrams, in an essay on the "material dimensions" of Keats's poetry, argues for a renewed attention to the "articulative aspect" of Keats's verse, his nearly unrivaled ability to place the "kinetic and tactile as well as auditory physicality" of speech into subtle relation with its semantic import.[57] One of his many convincing examples is especially relevant here, a rich phrase from the "Ode on Melancholy": "Though seen of none save him whose strenuous tongue / Can burst Joy's grape against his palate fine." The passage gains much of its feeling of rightness from its physical enacture in the mouth of the reader: the tongue pushes against the teeth and lower palate in "*str*enuous," "*t*ongue," and "bur*st*," then arches to touch higher up on the palate in "pala*t*e fine." These effects are made that much more salient, however, by the semantic appeal to the sense of taste, capitalizing on the links between the mouth's articulative and "manducatory" roles traced out by Bell.

For Keats, as for Bell, language is not an abstract, arbitrary system but another locus where mind and body meet, where thought reveals its embodied character. Words are shaped by and for the body, most obviously in enunciation, requiring the cooperation of the mind and brain with the lungs, the throat, and the mouth. "I had no words to answer," the poet-narrator confesses in the *Fall of Hyperion*, "for my tongue, /

Useless, could find about its roofed home / No syllable of a fit majesty"
(I: 228–30). The semantic appeal to taste underscores the "phonetic symbolism" (to borrow a term from psycholinguistics) in passages highlight-
ing the role of the lips and throat as well, as in *Endymion*:[58]

> Long time ere soft caressing sobs began
> To mellow into words, and then there ran
> Two *bub*bling *sp*rings of talk from their sweet li*p*s.   (II: 736–38)

The continuity described by Bell between the passions, the heart and
thorax ("sobs"), and articulate language could hardly be conveyed more
vividly, while the articulatory role of the "sweet" lips is enacted in the "b's"
and "p's" of the final line. The throat throbs in literal as well as metaphoric sympathy with the heart again in "Lamia" – "Deaf to his *thr*obbing
*thr*oat's long, long melodious moan" (75) – and in *Hyperion*: "his white melodious *thr*oat / *Thr*obb'd with the syllable" (III: 81–2), the "*thr*o" clusters
forcing the tongue back and narrowing the throat for the "r" and then
opening it up again to intone the vowel. Both of these passages, appropri-
ately, describe the voice of Apollo, the god of poetry – and of medicine.

    Keats varies this literally throaty "r" effect ingeniously in the self-
reflexive line (from the "Ode to a Nightingale") "S*i*ngest of summer in
full *thr*oated *ea*se." The throat nearly closes to pronounce "throated," in
contrast to the open-throated long "e" vowels at the beginning and end
of the line, underscoring the disparity between natural spontaneity and
human limitation. Elsewhere Keats creates a phonetic symbol through
repetition rather than contrast, as when the conquistadors, sighting the
Pacific in the sonnet "On First Looking into Chapman's Homer,"
"Look'd at each other with a w*i*ld surm*i*se – / S*i*lent," the reader performing open-mouthed wonder in pronouncing the three long "i"
vowels. Semantic and articulatory oppositions reinforce one another particularly nicely in the image (from "Sleep and Poetry") of an erotic "bite
/ As hard as lips can make it." The witty semantic shift (intensified by the
line-break) is physically enacted as the teeth, touched by the tongue to
pronounce "bi*te*," are abandoned for the lips, pressing against one
another to pronounce "li*ps*." The lingering note of aggression is meant
to disperse as the harmless "biting" of soft lips is directly experienced by
the reader, though the effect is a risky one and the sense of erotic combat
and conquest may verge too nearly on the sadistic for some.

    In contrast to Keats, Bell shows little interest in this third function of
the mouth – erotic contact, most notably in kissing. Keats, however, not
only features the meeting of "sweet lips" throughout his poetry, but does

so in a manner that connects kissing in turn to the mouth's other roles as organ of taste and instrument of poetic speech. Lorenzo, having at last come to terms with Isabella, asks to "taste" her mouth: "So said, his erewhile timid lips grew bold, / And poesied with hers in dewy rhyme" (66–70). Abrams notes the "iconic" effect of the lips touching together (making kisses) to form the "p's" and "b's" of a famously risky phrase in *Endymion*: "Those li*p*s, O sli*pp*ery *b*lisses." This line is followed immediately by praise of Cynthia's "tenderest, milky sovereignties" (II: 758–9). Is Keats here connecting, in the manner of Darwin, the pleasure of kissing to the infant's delight in suckling at the mother's breast, the "milky fountain" of all later pleasurable sensation (Z 145)? Far-fetched, perhaps, though later in *Endymion* the witch Circe seduces Glaucus in explicitly maternal fashion – "She took me like a child of suckling time" – after promising erotic pleasures including "tongues for ardour mute" (III: 441, 456). Circe's lulling speech too resembles the mother's speech as heard by an enamoured infant, its semantic function drowned out by its (temporarily) more meaningful rhythms and tonalities, its "semiotic" aspect: "Thus she link'd / Her charming syllables, till indistinct / Their music came to my o'er-sweeten'd soul" (III: 443–45).[59]

Speech sounds and linguistic sense, at times linked so tightly together in Keats's poetry, can also drift apart – especially when women are speaking, otherworldly, dangerous women like Circe above all. "La Belle Dame Sans Merci" speaks a strange language but makes "sweet moan" (the knight is later "lulled" to sleep by her); when Lamia beguiles Hermes, the "words she spake, / Came, as through bubbling honey" (I: 64–65). Again, the appeal to sweetness underscores the complex role of the mouth, the organ of speech and taste, as well as of suckling and sexual play. These passages add a further wrinkle to Keats's well-known ambivalence toward women and toward heterosexual relations, in the connections they suggest among sexual seduction, maternal nurturing, and the emotive effects of semiotic speech (or, if one prefers, "motherese").[60] At the same time, they serve as reminders that extrasemantic linguistic expression, though it may be "natural," is not for that reason simply or invariably transparent. Language is rendered more intimately but not necessarily more innocently human by its embodiment.

DROWS'D WITH THE FUME OF POPPIES

A corporeal view of the mind generally comes with an enhanced sense of its precariousness. Unlike the transcendent mind or spirit, which tenants the body but remains immaterial, a thoroughly embodied mind can be stunned, wounded, or grow decrepit. Inseparable from the brain and body – at least, as Romantic neuroscience tends cautiously to add, "in this life" – the mind can be subtly or violently affected by material substances ingested or inhaled and then carried by the blood into the brain. An interest in mind-altering substances runs throughout the embodied psychologies of the Romantic era, from Darwin's remarks on the effects of opium and other forms of "drunkenness" (Z 1: 240–48), to Davy's (and Coleridge's) experiments with nitrous oxide, to George Combe's ironic account of the "promiscuous" attacks on Gall and Spurzheim made more heated by collegial drinking. "The deeper the brain was ingulphed in alcohol, and the more the system was proved to be true, by the manifestations becoming in consequence disturbed, the more obstinate became the denial of the functions of the brain, and the louder the laugh against the supposition of its being the organ of the mind."[61]

Keats, with his training in pharmacology and his penchant for claret, had a theoretical as well as a practical interest in psychoactive substances. Expatiating on claret ("the only palate-passion I have") in the long journal-letter to George and Georgiana, he produces one of his best passages of comic banter in describing its effects on the brain.

> You do not feel it quarelling with your liver – no it is rather a Peace maker and lies as quiet as it did in the grape – then it is as fragrant as the Queen Bee; and the more ethereal Part of it mounts into the brain, not assaulting the cerebral apartments like a bully in a bad house looking for his trul and hurrying from door to door bouncing against the waistcoat; but rather walks in like Aladin about his own enchanted palace so gently that you do not feel his step. (*JkL* 2: 64)

This is a medical student's humor, playing off the fantastic aspects of a dated neurology. Here is Willis comparing the action of the "animal spirits" in the nerves to the "spirit of wine": "The rather narrow connection of the nerves and brain serves not only for the separation of the subtle from the gross, the pure from the impure, but also in order that the most spirituous and subtle liquor, as it were distilled from the blood, may acquire a further perfection in the brain: for there it is aerated by a kind of fermentation, whereby it is further volatilized."[62] But the more serious implications of a medical view of intoxication – that thought and emotion are functions of the body and its brain – remain with Keats throughout his career.[63] At the wedding feast of Lycius and Lamia, the guests appear subdued until the "happy vintage touch'd their brains, /

Louder they talk, and louder come the strains / Of powerful instruments" (2: 203–5). It is unclear whether the music grows louder as the players compete with the louder talk, or (at least initially) only appears louder to an artificially heightened sensory system – "powerful instruments" either way. Keats calls the wine's action a "rosy deed" (2: 209) because it works both through and in the blood, quickening the pulse and surging into the face: "Soon was God Bacchus at meridian height; / Flush'd were their cheeks, and bright eyes double bright" (2: 213–14). According to Keats's *Note Book*, Cooper had addressed the "stimulant" effect of wine in a lecture on the arteries (*JKNB* 9).

Keats's pharmocological studies brought him detailed knowledge of more exotic psychoactive substances and effects as well. The considerable medical botany behind Keats's garland, in the "Ode on Melancholy," of wolfsbane, nightshade (belladonna), yew berries (a source of prussic acid), and – more surprisingly – peonies, "nerve poisons" all, has been well-established.[64] Opium and its narcotic effects come up throughout the poetry, from *Endymion* – "through the dancing poppies stole / A breeze, most softly lulling to my soul" (1: 566–9) – to the personified Autumn "drows'd with the fume of poppies" in the last of the great odes. The best known is the passage that sets the strangely pained yet detached tone of the "Ode to a Nightingale":

> My heart aches, and a drowsy numbness pains
> My sense, as though of hemlock I had drunk,
> Or emptied some dull opiate to the drains
> One minute past, and Lethe-wards had sunk.

This passage has been related to an anecdote in one of Cooper's lectures, concerning an "extraordinary case" of head injury in which the "functions of the mind were suspended from an interruption of the circulation in the brain," the patient "having, as it were, drunk from the cup of Lethe" for more than thirteen months and suffered a complete mental "death" throughout the ordeal.[65] The parallel, though tempting, is probably incidental; Keats had already compared a "drug"-spiked drink to "Lethe's wave" in his early lyric "Fill for me a brimming bowl," written before his studies at Guy's. More relevant, perhaps, is Cooper's statement, in a lecture recorded by Tyrell, that "opium produces some of the same effects upon the brain as some of the injuries to which it is liable" (*C/T* 277). (Opiates should be avoided in cases of concussion, Cooper warned, because the symptoms of the drug might interfere with reading those from the injury.) Although opium frequently signifies a dreamless, healing sleep in Keats, it can also evoke the brain's, and therefore the embodied mind's, fragility and its eventual extinction. Sleep, whether induced by or merely compared to opiates, can become death-like, as in *The Eve of St. Agnes*:

> In sort of wakeful swoon perplex'd she lay,
> Until the poppied warmth of sleep oppress'd
> Her soothed limbs, and soul fatigued away;
> Flown, like a thought, until the morrow-day.   (236–39)

Here the soul itself appears, unexpectedly yet revealingly, to be a transient brain function, equivalent to conscious awareness. This usage of "soul" saps the term of its orthodox meaning, all but demanding the charge of materialism that bedeviled corporeal accounts of mind from Hartley and Priestley to Lawrence and Elliotson.

In addition to its associations with death and sleep, opium also evokes dreamlike and visionary states in Keats's poetry, signifying (as its does for Coleridge and De Quincey) an opening to the unconscious mind. The poppy-scented breeze in *Endymion* brings on "visions" of "colours, wings, and bursts of spangly light," then a "tumultuous swim" of sensory overload, then sleep and the visionary dream of Cynthia (I: 568–74). The "domineering potion" that precipitates the dream-vision of *The Fall of Hyperion* makes the effects of "Asian poppy" mild by comparison (I: 47, 54). These narcotic (or super-narcotic) effects suggest that the poetic imagination, like cognition generally, can be aroused and enhanced by fumes and potions, revealing – in the tradition of Coleridge's introduction to "Kubla Khan" – a material side to the Romantic imagination that contrasts markedly with the more familiar transcendentalist account. That alcohol and opiates can alter behavior is taken for granted – "Was't opium, / Or the mad-fumed wine?", Sigifred asks in *Otho*, wondering at Ludolph's departure from "clear reason" (I.iii.34–5). But if the poet's visionary flights can themselves be catalyzed or even shaped by material substances, then the status of such visions remains ambiguous. "Was it a vision, or a waking dream?" How timeless and how authoritative are the productions of a "working brain"?

The "Imagination may be compared to Adam's dream," Keats famously suggests: "he awoke and found it truth" (*JKL* I: 185). Many things could be (and have been) said about this enigmatic phrase, but surely one is that the imagination relies largely on unconscious procedures. As Keats clarifies in the same letter, a few lines below: "The simple imaginative Mind may have its rewards in the repeti[ti]on of its own silent Working coming continually on the spirit with a fine suddenness" – a formula that involves both the psychic fragmentation and the deft rapidity of unconscious cognition emphasized throughout Romantic brain science.[66] (Representative is Bell's assertion of the "guidance of a sensibility more certain in its operation than the will," enabled by the pervasive "re-union and crossing" of the nervous system, in the first of the Royal Society lectures on the "new" neurology [III: 423]). Keats characteristically describes this "silent Working" in a materialist language, although the chemical vocabulary he employs – another legacy of his medical training – long confused commentators with its specialized uses of transcendental-sounding terms like "essence," "sublime," "intensity," "ethereal," and even "spiritual."[67] As Stuart Sperry first demonstrated, all of these terms featured prominently in the chemistry of Keats's time, and Keats often uses them in ways that demand reference to their concrete scientific meanings. When Keats defines the "excellence of every Art" as its "intensity, capable of making all disagreeables evaporate," for example, he is thinking of the chemical process of evaporation, playing on the technical sense of "intensity" as degree of heat or "caloric," refining out impurities or "disagreeables" to produce a purified "essence" (*JKL* I: 192). "Men of Genius" are similarly compared to "certain ethereal Chemicals operating on the Mass of neutral intellect," recalling Davy's definition of *"radiant* or *ethereal matters"* that depend for their effects on "communicating motion to the particles of common matter, or modifying their attractions," rather than "actually entering into combination with them" (*JKL* I: 184).[68]

The link between Keats's pronouncements on the imagination and his chemical studies at Guy's can appear disarmingly tight. In a well-known letter to Haydon of 1818, Keats writes of the "innumerable compositions and decompositions which take place between the intellect and its thousand materials before it arrives at that trembling delicate and snail-horn perception of Beauty" (*JKL* I: 265); the first page of the course syllabus used at Guy's defines chemistry as the *"Science of the Composition and Decomposition of the heterogeneous particles of Matter."*[69] The dynamic conception of matter that helped renew the study of chemistry in the Romantic era owed much to the example and exhortations of Priestley, who argued that matter was not the *"inert* substance" supposed by an earlier mechanistic philosophy, but that *"powers of attraction* or *repulsion* are necessary to its very being, and that no part of it appears to be *impenetrable* to other parts." This axiom is taken not from one of Priestley's books on chemistry, however, but from the *Disquisitions Relating to Matter and Spirit*, making part of Priestley's argument to displace the "vulgar hypothesis" of dualism with a materialist understanding of mind.[70] The new dynamic notion of matter ("innumerable compositions and decompositions") is no less axiomatic for Keats, who probably encountered it as early as his period at Enfield, with its close ties to Priestley and its strong emphasis on scientific progress. It helps explain why for Keats a materialist understanding of mind and imagination would not necessarily prove reductive or mechanistic – though Keats's relation to materialism is often an unhappy or resistant one.

THE NAKED BRAIN

Only toward the end of the Romantic era did the brain become widely accepted as the "organ of the mind," thanks in large part to the work of Gall and his popularizers.[71] Prior to the nineteenth century, poets tend not to use the brain as an image for the mind – unless they want to portray a mind diseased or deranged. Well into the eighteenth century and even beyond, "brain" belongs to the language of satire and tragedy more than to lyric or meditative verse. With the emergence of the literary movement now called Romanticism, however, the brain begins to feature not simply as a cognate for mind but as a term that captures the mind's complexity within a finite compass, its productivity and its near if not perfect identity with the body. The poetry of Keats provides some of the most striking and suggestive examples of the newly lyricized image of the brain.

Renaissance poets tend to prefer heart over brain in figuring the mind, not because they think of the heart as the physical locus of thought, but because the heart is less likely to be taken in a physical sense. The brain, by contrast, threatens to collapse the distinction between immaterial thought and corruptible body. Unlike the heart, as one critic of Early Modern culture has acutely noted, the brain seems "tied to its own physicality and function, oddly separate from the more evocative term 'mind.'"[72] This makes the term "brain" all the more potent to convey dysfunction. In Shakespeare's plays, for example, "brain" tends to occur in compounds like "brain-sicke," "mad-brained," "haire-brain'd," "dull-brain'd," and even "fat-brain'd" (said of Falstaff, of course); it is characteristically "troubled," "empty," "hot," "idle," or "drunken." The brain can also be productive – "How her brain coins!" – characteristically, though of lies, plots, and fantasies (occasionally sonnets).[73] The dysfunctional, even comic, connotations of "brain" continue to predominate throughout the neoclassical era as well, even in those poets who wrench neoclassical conventions into novel poetic modes. George Crabbe, though trained (before the onset of English medical reform) as a surgeon, nevertheless characteristically portrays the brain in a negative sense, variously "burning," "frantic," "muddy," "roving," "fever'd," "disturb'd," "touch'd," and "distempered." For Mary Robinson, another poet pushing the late neoclassical mode to its limits, the brain belongs to the satirical register codified by Butler and Pope, "heated," "darken'd," "shatter'd," "giddy," "restless," and "infected." The brain is tragically or, more often, comically earthly and vulnerable. Rarely, for poets working within early modern or neoclassical modes, does it convey the capacity, intricacy, or sublimity of vaguer and loftier terms like soul, heart, and mind.

By the 1790s, however, poets like Coleridge and Thelwall, with their close links to radical scientific and medical culture, had begun to bring a dynamic and complex sense of the corporeal mind into the poetic lexicon. Coleridge, in "Religious Musings" (1794), praises Hartley for inventing physiological psychology: "he first who marked the ideal tribes / Up the fine fibres through the sentient brain" (369–70). Thelwall's *Peripatetic*, dating from the same year (1793) as his notorious lecture on sensation to the Guy's Physical Society, outlines a model of the brain and its relations to the nervous, vascular, and respiratory systems that deliberately evokes the new medical model of mind.[74]

> Nor less the brain – fair Reason's awful stand!
> Whose subtile dictates all the frame command;
> Doom'd each important function to sustain;
> Mysterious "Lord of Pleasure and of Pain,"
> Of Reason, Knowledge, Sense's varied sway,
> And Fancy's train – fantastic, grave, or gay.
> Where vibrates sound, where splendid Vision lives,
> Where Taste – where Smell her essence all receives,
> And Touch, fine-thrilling, each impression gives!
> From this, when injur'd, all tumultuous fly
> The wond'rous train of sudden Sympathy:
> The Lungs, the Heart, their functions each disclaim:
> Dies thro' each Nerve the paralytic frame!

Wordsworth in the late 1790s, the period when he is evidently responding in his poetic theory as well as his verse to the new science of the mind, employs "brain" in ways that he will later reserve for "soul" or "mind"; the "Pedlar," for example, attains through meditation "An *active* power to fasten images / Upon his brain" (41–42). Blake, with his own links (through the publisher Joseph Johnson) to the radical scientific currents of the 1790s, writes of the brain in a strikingly avant-garde manner.[75] For Blake the brain is at once material, organically and developmentally interconnected with the rest of the bodily system ("His nervous brain shot branches / Round the branches of his heart") and yet limited by its Fallen form of corporal existence from realizing its potentially "infinite" scope. "And they inclos'd my infinite brain into a narrow circle."[76] For Keats too the mind's embodiment humanizes while also circumscribing it; the brain "grounds" the mind in both the enabling and constraining senses of that metaphor.

Already in some of his earliest surviving poems, dating from his period at Guy's (1815–17), Keats had begun to use the term "brain" to evoke a productive and restlessly embodied mind. His verse letter to George ("Full many a dreary hour") begins by seemingly differentiating brain and mind only to posit their equivalence – "My brain bewilder'd, and my mind o'ercast" – and goes on to evoke the speedy and involuntary character of corporeal models of mind: "When some bright thought has darted through my brain" (114). The speed of unconscious mental processing is even more remarkable in "Sleep and Poetry": "The hearty grasp that sends a pleasant sonnet / Into the brain ere one can think upon it" (319–20). (Later, in the sonnet "When I have fears," Keats will depict literary creativity as a "teeming brain" gradually gleaned by the poet's pen.) But the involuntary character of embodied cognition also threatens a loss of control and of mental bearings, as in the apprentice sonnet "On Receiving a Laurel Crown from Leigh Hunt": "Nothing unearthly has enticed my brain / Into a delphic labyrinth." Though mortal and of the earth, the brain-mind yearns to be penetrated by the immortal, the "unearthly," like Apollo's oracle at Delphi: "Till I feel in my brain / A Delphian pain," as Keats writes a year later ("Hence burgundy, claret, and port"). Yet the brain has labyrinthine turnings and oracular glimmerings of its own, "dim-conceived glories of the brain," as "On Seeing the Elgin Marbles" so memorably puts it. Such phrases broach something new in British poetry, a sense of the embodied mind's unconscious and ineffable magnitude that might be termed the "neural sublime."

The brain, within the neural sublime mode, reveals its capacity in moments when consciousness fails just at the point of revelation. Precisely because of its network of interconnections with the rest of the body, "brain" for Keats can convey a fuller sense of mental life than "mind," one that includes emotive, unconscious, intuitive, and involuntary cognition.[77] Lamia's "sciental brain" – deft and powerful enough to "unperplex bliss from her neighbor pain" – bears witness to how the term "brain" can come to exceed "mind" rather than illustrate its debility, as in neoclassical satire. When the brain does fail, then, it fails magnificently, underscoring the extent of the embodied mind in touching its limits. The priest in *Endymion* speaks of "thinkings" that "dodge / Conception to the very bourne of heaven, / Then leave the naked brain" (1: 294–95) – these are cognate both with "immensity" and with the "leaven" that gives earth a "touch ethereal." The brain's nakedness – its vulnerability – paradoxically comes to signify the mind's power as well as its ultimate limits. Similarly, the hollowness that Keats sometimes attributes to the brain (inspired, no doubt, by the ventricles he had observed in studying neuroanatomy) conveys not its emptiness but its vastness. "Pour into the wide hollows of my brain" "enormous" knowledge, Apollo asks Mnemosyne in *Hyperion*, "and deify me" (3: 116–17). The brain, in *The Fall of Hyperion*, is at once theater and womb, a site of "electral" activity and constant development:

> I ached to see what things the hollow brain
> Behind enwombed: what high tragedy
> In the dark secret chambers of her skull
> Was acting.   (1: 276–8)

The knowledge in Moneta's brain does not lie dormant, as if snugly filed away, but "ferments" (1: 290). Like the rest of the body ("completely fresh-materiald" every seven years), the brain exists in a state of constant reorganization and self-renewal (*JKL* 2: 208).[78] Thoughts or memories are dynamic in character and what appear to be "things" are revealed to be activities comparable to dramatic performances.

It is the instability implied by this very dynamism, however, that troubled Coleridge in the *Biographia*, and on occasion it troubles Keats as well. At times the "dull brain perplexes and retards," held down by its corporeality in contrast to the transcendence over mortality and flux represented (in this case) by the Nightingale as "immortal Bird." The poet of *Endymion* yearns for stories "potent to send / A young mind from its bodily tenement" (1: 324–25); the poet of "Fancy" urges the reader to "Open wide the mind's cage-door." Yet even in moments when the mind's door springs shut, it can be unclear whether material brain or immaterial spirit is at fault. Brain and mind oddly switch roles in an unmistakably Keatsian passage from a late letter to Mrs. Brawne: "O what an account I could give you of the Bay of Naples if I could once more feel myself a Citizen of this world – I feel a Spirit in my Brain would lay it forth pleasantly – O what a misery it is to have an intellect in splints" (*JKL* 2: 350). Though the body is clearly out of sorts here (Keats is complaining of indigestion, while dying of tuberculosis), he worries that the world is too little, rather than too much with him. "Spirit" grows out of "Brain" rather than being opposed to it, and it is the mind or "intellect" that (in yet another medical metaphor) hobbles in "splints." Keats flirts with transcendence only to find himself unfit for it – "things won't leave me *alone*" – if not to reject it altogether (*JKL* 2: 174). "Wonders are no wonders to me," he writes his publisher regarding his difficulties with "the marvellous": "I am more at home amongst Men and women" (*JKL* 2: 234). As the "Ode to Psyche" and the *Fall of Hyperion* suggest in their different ways, the greatest marvels exist within the skull, and spirit is not clothed but produced by the "naked brain."

CHAPTER SIX

Embodied universalism, Romantic discourse, and the anthropological imagination

"We have all one human heart," Keats declares (*IL* 2: 80). Keats has been speculating on the "instinctiveness" that the "noble animal Man" shares with his fellow creatures in the same rambling, brilliant journal-letter that records his unforgettable meeting with Coleridge and that culminates in his inscription of the "Ode to Psyche." Characteristically, Keats's figure for a core human nature is a corporeal one, evoking (especially in its context) the nervous, passionate, "ellectric" model of human subjectivity that his poetry shares with the radical brain science he absorbed at Guy's Hospital. Yet this deeply Keatsian phrase is in fact a quotation from Wordsworth, the "more than materialist" Wordsworth of *Lyrical Ballads* who speaks, in its controversial "Preface," of the "primary laws of our nature" and of the "great and universal passions of men" (*WP* 1: 122, 144). Wordsworth returns to this position later in describing an organic and embodied poetic sensibility – "grounded" in "universal intellectual" capacities and the "sensations which all men have felt" – that accounts for the poet's expression of universal "truths," "instinctively ejaculated" in moments of "intuition" (*WP* 2: 78). This embodied, emotive universalism is put most simply in the line Keats quotes (slightly misremembering it) from "The Old Cumberland Beggar," a lyrical ballad striving to represent human nature in its barest essentials: "We have all of us one human heart."[1] For Christopher Ricks, Keats's interest in blushing, that most teasingly psychosomatic function, grows out of a profound concern with the "irreducibly human" that helps account for what seems typically "Romantic" about poets like Keats and Wordsworth. "It was in the name of a common humanity," Ricks adds, "that Romanticism so often spoke – a humanity shared by all the races of man."[2]

The universalist, democratic view of Romanticism invoked without apology by Ricks will strike many as off-kilter or just plain wrong. A line of estimable historians of ideas and culture, from A. O. Lovejoy to

Robert Young, have instead viewed Romanticism in terms of a flight from Enlightenment universalism toward an obsession with difference and diversity – individual, national, cultural, and racial.[3] In an influential article on Romanticism and science published in 1982, Hans Eichner argues that in rejecting the "mechanistic assumptions" of the preceding generation, Romantic writers simultaneously "abandoned" the Enlightenment ethos of human uniformity, displacing the "timeless, the universal, and the general" in human nature with the "temporal, the local, and the individual:"[4] in a word, with "history." Hans Aarsleff, writing on Romantic language theory in a book published the same year, concurs that the "19th century had lost the 18th century's fundamental conviction, its first theory we might say, that of the uniformity of human nature."[5] These are sweeping yet compelling generalizations, with profound implications not only for charting the rise of historicist thinking but for tracing the genealogy of modern racism.

The widespread view that Romanticism entails a rejection of human uniformity represents at best, however, a half truth. It would be more accurate to say that a number of Romantic writers – poets and scientists alike – rejected the "timeless" universalism of the Enlightenment, which located human uniformity in reason, language, and logic, with a time-bound and biological universalism that instead grounded "primary" human features in the body, in the material organization of the mind, and in the emotions. As Wordsworth's thinking on poetry and language suggests, the shift from a mechanistic and dualistic to a biological, embodied view of human nature entails not so much an abandonment as a radical reformulation of human universals. In some cases, their corporeal and emotive approach to human nature enables Romantic writers to reassert shared human features rejected by an earlier generation of thinkers. Wordsworth, for example, argues for a "universal" moral sense in the face of Locke's wholesale dismissal of transcultural "moral Principles."[6] Enlightenment discourse fostered its own version of cultural relativism, stemming from a distaste for innate or universally embodied propensities and a consequent overvaluation of the effects of culture, education, and climate. For some Romantic thinkers, embodied universalism set important limits to the new time-bound (evolutionary, historicist) relativism. But these universalist and relativistic tendencies could be found together, sometimes in tension, sometimes in outright contradiction, as the recent debate over Herder's views on race and culture has made overt.[7]

Not all Romantic-era writers who posit human universals do so from the premise of an embodied mind. Coleridge, for example, advances an "almost Chomskyan" notion of universal syntactic principles rooted, ultimately, in the divine Logos rather than in the human body.[8] Thomas Reid, though a mind–body dualist, also posits a "universal sense of mankind" evident in the "structure of all languages."[9] But the emergent "biomedical" approach to understanding human capacities brought with it a fundamentally new vision of the common human features and behaviors recurring over time and across cultures.[10] This new approach departs decisively from the "decorporealized" model of subjectivity that recent critiques of eighteenth-century culture locate at the fragile center of the rationalist project, a "disembodied" subjectivity exemplified by Harris's postulate (in *Hermes*) of "PERMANENT IDEAS" denoting the "GENUINE PERCEPTIONS OF PURE MIND."[11] For Cabanis, human universals proceed instead from a common bodily organization, the "gestures, voices, looks, physiognomy" that help constitute a system of core feelings with non-verbal signs "common to the entire human race" (*R* 1: 68–9). Darwin's theory of universals places more emphasis on experience, retaining the associationist bias of much eighteenth-century thought. Darwin, however, stresses embodied over linguistic experience, tracing the origin of the universally recognizable human smile, for example, to the muscular relaxation around the infant's mouth following a satisfying bout of nursing (*Z* 1: 148–53). Bell, despite his orthodox belief in an immortal and immaterial human soul, traces the "bond of the human family" to the innate and embodied psychophysiology of emotion, human "uniformity" of mind arising out of a common somatosensory organization (*AP* 82, 134).

Some of the era's strongest claims for human uniformity occur in the works of Gall and Spurzheim. This may surprise those who view the phrenology movement primarily through the lens of its later – blatantly racist – permutations, associated with the invidious practice of "craniometry" so trenchantly described in Stephen Jay Gould's *The Mismeasure of Man*.[12] Gall, however, could not be more clear on this point, grounding the uniformity of human nature in a common (and innately programmed) neural "organization," found in "all people in all ages, however different may be the external influences of climate, of nourishment, laws, customs, religion, and education" (*FB* 1: 148). Dismissing the entire list of Enlightenment explanations for unequal "progress" despite a *potential* equality of mind, Gall instead finds cultural variation to be superficial, the divergent manners and customs of "different nations" all ultimately resting on the "same basis" (*FB* 1: 163). Spurzheim includes a section on the "Uniformity of Mankind" in his popular *Physiognomical System*, deducing from common brain organization an innate and universal set of psychological "faculties" (*PS* 476, 485). This common organization, and with it the "uniformity of the nature of man at all times and in all places," provides for Spurzheim the only valid "basis of anthropology" (*PS* 485).

Embodied universalism and the new conception of human uniformity it implies leave scattered but significant traces throughout Romantic-era writing. They mark not only the anthropological speculations of various Romantic brain scientists but inhere within a number of contemporary literary works as well, which pose a critical relation of their own to the received Enlightenment models of subjectivity and human nature.[13] With language demoted from its central position in the mental science of Locke and Condillac, the possibility of sophisticated non-linguistic thought can be reconsidered. With subjectivity no longer considered "single and indivisible" and "detached from the body," the cognitive others of Enlightenment anthropology – Locke's telling category of "*Children, Ideots, Savages, and illiterate* People" – can be newly and more empathetically reimagined.[14] Enlightenment theories of racial difference are challenged, though not across the board, even as "biological" versions of racism begin to proliferate. The rapidity with which corporeal psychologies become allied with racialist ideologies, at least in Britain, underscores the evanescent quality of embodied universalism, an important but neglected relic of Romantic-era culture, and an instructively fragile one.

THOUGHT WITHOUT LANGUAGE

Gall's discussion of language in the *Functions of the Brain* features a long digression, amounting to a biographical sketch, concerning James Mitchell, a "young Scotchman, born *deaf* and *blind*" (*FB* 5: 38–44). The description of Mitchell, borrowed from Spurzheim's 1825 treatise on *Phrenology*, is both touching and fascinating; if better known, it might be considered a minor classic of Romantic writing (*P* 230–39). Both Spurzheim and Gall frame Mitchell's story as a rebuke to empiricist psychologies, with their neglect of the "internal senses" and "internal mental powers" that, largely innate, owe comparatively little to education (*P* 228, 230). Gall also uses the case of Mitchell to help refute Condillac's "false" doctrine that abstract thought depends on a linguistic system of arbitrary signs (*FB* 5: 35). I will give the outlines of

FRONTISPIECE

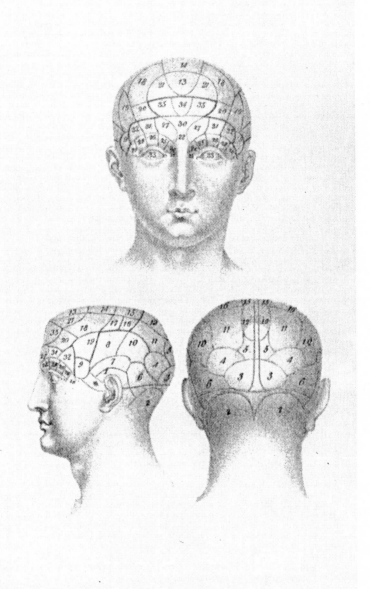

Published by Marsh, Capen & Lyon, Boston.

9 Spurzheim, "Frontispiece" to *Phrenology, or, The Doctrine of the Mind; and of the Relations Between Its Manifestations and the Body* (1825; Boston, 1832).

Mitchell's story as Spurzheim records it in 1825, and then turn to its particular significance for Gall.

"He was born on the 11th of November, 1795," Spurzheim begins, "deaf and blind, of intelligent parents" (*P* 230). This last detail is not incidental. Spurzheim seeks throughout to showcase the significant degree of intelligence demonstrated by Mitchell, though he is limited to the external senses of touch, taste, and smell and lacks access to spoken or signed language. Mitchell can sense sonic vibrations with his "fore teeth" (Henry Brougham tried the clever experiment of placing a "musical snuff-box" between Mitchell's teeth, to his "exquisite delight") but has no sense of hearing. No less a surgeon than Astley Cooper pierced one of his ear drums in 1808 without effect. Two years later Mitchell, now 14 years old, gained limited sight when a cataract was removed from one eye, but (as would now be expected) his visual system remained largely underdeveloped. "He nevertheless continued to examine every thing with his other senses, as if he had been totally blind and deaf" (*P* 231). Yet without the mediation of spoken or other arbitrary signs, with his information about the external world confined to three senses until mid-adolescence and with barely rudimentary sight thereafter, Mitchell exhibits an intense intellectual curiosity dating from early childhood, and manifests a surprisingly rich cognitive, emotional, and ethical life. Far from the apathetic cretin that the Lockean psychologist would expect to find, Mitchell instead "furnishes an evident proof that there are innate dispositions, and that the external senses are not the cause of the affective and intellectual faculties" (*P* 239).

Mitchell was clearly a remarkable subject, and it is no wonder that he attracted the notice of contemporary philosophers and physicians.[15] He learned about other people by touching and smelling them; he spurned those whose smell troubled him and refused to wear clothing that carried any smell but his own. He enjoyed the company of young children and liked to take them up in his arms but (no doubt wisely) sought to avoid "boys of his own age" (*P* 232). He was attached to those closest to him, especially his sister and the boy employed to help him. At his father's funeral, he found his way to the coffin by smell and mournfully embraced it. He developed a liking for pipes and for new clothes; when he got tired of his old clothes, he would throw them in the fire. When his mother gave him a pair of shoes that were too small, however, and locked them away, he asked for the key by pantomime, took them from the closet, and gave them to the boy who looked after him – they were a perfect fit. During his one serious illness he insisted on keeping a favorite aunt near his sick-bed. When his sister grew ill before his own recovery, however, Mitchell motioned his aunt upstairs to nurse her instead. He once injured his foot badly and had to keep it on a "low stool" while it was healing; over a year later, when a "servant boy with whom he used to play" seemed oddly immobile, Mitchell felt him over, found that his foot was bandaged, fetched his old stool out of the garret, and carefully placed the boy's foot on it (*P* 237).

Along with such warm feelings and altruistic tendencies, Mitchell had a distinctive sense of humor. He liked to stand the carcasses of chickens up on their legs and then laugh when they inevitably fell down. He would lock other people up in a room or in the stable, "laughing and jumping about all the while" (*P* 235). On one occasion his sister put a halfpenny in his hand and made signs for him to buy two pipes. When he came back with only one, she signaled her dissatisfaction and Mitchell, "laughing heartily," then produced the other from its hiding place in his clothes. The next Sunday, when his sister gave him a halfpenny for the poor-box in church, "he placed it between his teeth like a pipe and laughed, but she having given him a shake, he dropped it into the box" (*P* 235). He seemed to have formed "ideas of property," leading home and stabling a horse that his mother had sold, without his knowledge, a few weeks before (*P* 236). He would avidly explore the neighborhood and visit the local shops, examining craftsmen's worktables with his hands, and mimicking their activities – carpentry, sewing, weaving – to let his family know where he had been and what he had observed.

According to Spurzheim's first-hand observation, although he acts up and behaves oddly at times, Mitchell evidently experiences the full range of basic emotions, manifesting them by the usual facial and bodily expressions despite never having seen these "in other persons" (*P* 232). He communicates through gesture and pantomime, his self-made language of "natural signs." He shows an appreciation for abstractions like number and time. When his mother once left on a trip, his sister managed to convey the number of nights she would be gone by gently bending Mitchell's head onto an imaginary pillow and closing his eyes so many times in succession. (The anecdote also implies that Mitchell can think metaphorically, though Spurzheim does not point this out.) Spurzheim notes that Mitchell could easily have been taught artificial signs by means of touch and thus educated, had those around him been more enterprising. This represents a loss, not so much to Mitchell as to the "study of mankind," since the "internal activity of his mind" – his evidently rich conceptual life – cannot be conveyed in detail. That

Mitchell's mental powers do develop without benefit of artificial signs gains the notice even of anti-phrenological critics like John Gordon, who remarks on the "extensive" field of Mitchell's knowledge and the connectedness and "rational" character of his thought (*P* 237). And "*why not*," Spurzheim pointedly adds, "*since his brain is very well organized!*"

For Gall, Mitchell similarly serves to illustrate the importance of brain organization and "innate dispositions" (*FB* 5: 44), but in addition he provides a telling counter-example with which to attack Condillac and his school. "They maintain that, without signs we should hardly think; that it is only articulate words which can lead us to abstract ideas; that signs and language develope [*sic*] our faculties, give birth to our inclinations, our sentiments, affections, passions . . . that without language we should have only very few ideas, and those very confused and incomplete" (*FB* 5: 33–34). Against this overvaluation of linguistic signs, Gall adduces a series of examples leading up to Mitchell. Emotions find distinct expression in a bodily language of "natural" signs "anterior to spoken language." Young children evince an "infinity of notions" – including abstractions – before the onset of speech. The deaf, even in the absence of instruction, will find out a way to communicate together, the "precision of their ideas" enabling rather than following from their invention of a signed language (*FB* 5: 36–38).[16] Mitchell, blind, deaf, and unacquainted with "artificial signs," nevertheless "manifests the affective and intellectual faculties in a high degree"; his case provides solid proof of thought in the absence of language (*FB* 5: 44).[17] As Gall states elsewhere, "it is no longer the *signs* so much talked of by modern philosophers which develop our understanding . . . Signs, the language of speech, writing, the language of gestures or action are creations of the brain, and are only understood in proportion as they are addressed to pre-existing faculties" (*FB* 2: 43–44).

Gall could find several precedents in materialist and "corporeal" accounts of mind for the crucial role he gives to pre-linguistic cognition. In *Leviathan* Hobbes had postulated a "*mental discourse*" – an early version of what is now called "mentalese" – that would precede and be transferred into verbal discourse.[18] Herder, though sharing Condillac's emphasis on reason and reflection, nevertheless criticizes him for dismissing innate knowledge of "natural signs" ("what the dumbest animal knows") and describes a "language of the soul" antecedent to verbal language.[19] Cabanis, in the course of his own critique of Condillac, emphasizes the role of "instinct" and indeed of the "entire sensitive system," including the "internal organs," in the "formation of thought" (*R* 2: 570).

Gall seems to echo Cabanis in declaring that "internal sensations" constitute a "mode of thinking" in themselves – a logic of the body that,
unlike Hobbes' mentalese, owes little to external sensations (*FB* 1: 130).
Spurzheim stresses the antecedence of a mental grammar of ideas to
"arbitrary signs" in the *Physiognomical System* of 1815 (*PS* 377). These theories taken together suggest a broader cultural context for analagous
developments in Romantic-era literature than has been noticed to date.
In arguing, for example, that Wordsworth's "anthropological" poetry
sought to redress the "basic weakness of eighteenth-century empiricist
language philosophy" – its "insistence on language as a necessary pre-
condition of thought and feeling" and concommitant neglect of "nature
and preverbal feeling" – Alan Bewell has aptly shown how Wordsworth
significantly revises the Enlightenment models on which he builds.[20] Yet
Wordsworth's interest in nonverbal thought and sensibility should be
viewed as well in relation to analogous contemporary developments,
placing him in a larger and more diverse company than can be found in
Bewell's author-centered study.

Indeed, an interest in thought without language characterizes the literature as well as brain science of the period, from the sublime of
Wordsworth's silent poets – "Theirs is the language of the heavens, the
power, / The thought, the image, and the silent joy" (*1805* 12: 270–1)[21] –
to the pathetic of Mary Robinson's "Savage of Aveyron." Written (in
1800) during the period of her final illness, Robinson's last lyric was
inspired by newspaper accounts of the feral child found in the woods of
the Department of Aveyron, known to posterity as "Victor."[22] In
Robinson's imaginary reconstruction of his discovery, the wild child's
lack of language affects the poem's speaker with something like horror:
"And then to mutter he began, – / But, O! *he could not speak!*"[23] Despite
his inarticulateness, however, the boy reveals a rudimentary notion of
number in attempting to express the story of his mother's murder by
three bandits:

> And though of words he nothing knew,
> And, though his dulcet tones were few,
> Across the yielding bark he drew,
>   Deep sighing, notches THREE.

The child then points "one, two, three" and shrieks "with wild dismay."
This is not the wild child one would expect from reading Condillac, who
assumes that feral children lack reason, memory, and emotions unre-
lated to their immediate needs.[24] The same assumptions condition the

more sober accounts of Victor later published by Itard, Victor's celebrated keeper, teacher, and observer. As an intellectual disciple of Condillac, Itard considers Victor, prior to his (minimally successful) education, a "man-animal," a "stranger to that reflective process which is the first source of ideas."[25] It is only through an elaborate and occasionally harsh program of "civilization" that Itard can slowly arouse Victor from the "torpor" of his "animal existence."[26] In the fictionalized Aveyron of Robinson's ballad, the child has managed to retain a compelling, affecting humanity throughout his years of solitude in the wild, remembering and lamenting his mother, recording and communicating her death in a self-taught iconic language. In Itard's clinical prose, Victor is without ideas, virtually insensible, and limited to the crudest feelings of self-preservation thanks to his ignorance of arbitrary language.[27]

Mary Shelley's *Frankenstein* also bears a revisionary relation, as Marilyn Butler notes, to Enlightenment representations of feral children, describing as it does the mental life of a gigantic "child" abandoned at birth to wander alone in the woods.[28] Subtitled "The Modern Prometheus," *Frankenstein* simultaneously addresses the philosophical convention of the artificial man. From the "automota" and "artificial man" evoked by Hobbes in *Leviathan*, to the "machine man" of La Mettrie (who refers explicitly to a "new Prometheus" [34]), to the animated statue of Condillac's *Traité des Sensations*, artificial human creatures play a significant role in philosophical controversies on the nature of mind, often with materialist overtones.[29] Shelley, however, with her connections to the thought of Darwin (cited in the first sentence of *Frankenstein*'s "Preface"), Cabanis, and Lawrence (the Shelleys' friend and doctor), revisits the mechanical man of Enlightenment thought with the counter-perspective of the new biology in view.[30] Less an automaton than an oversized child or solitary savage, Victor Frankenstein's "creature" enters the world with passions, propensities, and instincts that suggest not Condillac's statue but its contrary, the organic "living machine" ("la machine vivante") of Cabanis (*R* 1: 197).

Critics of *Frankenstein* have made much of the creature's acquisition of language, which strikes the creature himself as a "godlike science" (88).[31] More attention could be paid, however, to the creature's extensive cognitive accomplishments prior to his knowledge of arbitrary signs. Even in his first day of life, the creature functions surprisingly well, suggesting that Victor, having anatomized the "wonders . . . of the brain" (34), has managed to equip his creation with innate mental functions. When Rousseau imagines the emergence of a full-grown infant in *Emile*, he

stresses the sensory confusion, motoric inertia, and blank cognition associated with infancy by empiricist thinkers. He evokes Condillac in
describing the unnatural newborn as an "imbecile, an automaton, an
immobile and almost insensible statue," one that would learn to stand (if
at all) with the greatest difficulty and could not associate hunger-pangs
with the need for food.[32] Shelley portrays her gigantic infant experienc-
ing a "strange multiplicity of sensations" *à la* Rousseau, yet inspired by
"hunger and thirst" the creature spontaneously seeks out berries and
water and feels "half-frightened as it were instinctively" by the dark
(79–80). According to Victor's narration, the creature is able not only to
stand but to walk on its own within hours of birth, and even manifests a
version of an infant's innate capacity to seek out and fix on human faces.
"His eyes, if eyes they may be called, were fixed on me" (40). All of these
abilities must be built in, somehow provided by Victor along with "intricacies of fibres" that constitute the creature's nervous system (35).

During his period as a nomadic wild child, the creature develops a
repertoire of ideas and memories that would astound Condillac or Itard.
His sensations grow "distinct" after a few weeks of wandering and each
successive day brings "additional ideas" (81). The creature is especially
adept at identifying natural kinds, discriminating among various species
of birds, animals, and "herbs." He discovers the use of fire and cookery
on his own and shows a native preference for music (82, 86). His silent
observation of the De Laceys, who unknowingly harbor the creature for
some time, brings out his still more striking innate capacities for social
cognition. The creature can accurately read emotions from facial
expressions, though he has only had momentary contact with human
beings up to this point: "a young man met her, whose countenance
expressed a deeper despondence" (85). In fact, the creature's acquisition
of the "godlike science" of words is facilitated by his inborn ability to
read the "natural" language of facial expressions and gestures, as
Herder, Reid, and Darwin had all theorized. "I perceived that the words
they spoke sometimes produced pleasure or pain, smiles or sadness, in
the *minds* and countenances of the hearers" (88; my italics). Language
acquisition is a matter of arduous work and chance opportunities, but
the mind-reading instinct that supports it comes as part of the neurocognitive package supplied by Victor.[33]

However much Shelley owes to the precedent of Enlightenment
thought experiments like Condillac's living statue or Rousseau's
newborn adult, the cognitive abilities and affective life manifested by
Frankenstein's creature – *before* it discovers speech – suggest an approach

to human nature and development closer to that of Darwin or Cabanis. Like Gall's, Shelley's infant is no automaton but manifests sensations and desires shortly after birth; no more than Gall, that is, does Shelley accept the reduction of man to the "state of a statue" (*FB* 1: 78–9, 114). Are Gall and Spurzheim among the "physiological writers of Germany" linked with Darwin in *Frankenstein's* 1818 "Preface" (3)? (Byron, who took part in the famous 1816 conversations out of which the novel grew, had been examined by Spurzheim two years before, and the Shelleys could have learned about Gall and Spurzheim through Lawrence as well.)[34] What might be termed Shelley's Romantic humanism is complicated, though, by the creature's ambiguous status, what Victor himself terms the "strange nature of the animal" (57). In gathering components for his gigantic science project, Victor has had recourse to the "slaughter-house" as well as the dissecting room (37). His experiment transgresses the "wide chasm between man and the noblest animals of the brute creation" insisted upon by Coleridge but inexorably narrowed by materialist and "corporealist" thinkers from La Mettrie and Herder to Darwin and Lawrence (*SW* 1: 501). As the *Quarterly Review* had complained in attacking Lawrence's *Lectures on Physiology, Zoology, and the Natural History of Man,* for Lawrence (as for "all other persons of the same school") "man is only a superior kind of brute."[35] Shelley's portrayal, in *Frankenstein,* of a human-like creature with animal parts gives vent to such monstrous anxieties while further provoking them.

Did Frankenstein's creature take on a brute's instinctive knowledge with its power? He claims to have been "fashioned" by Victor with humane propensities for "love and sympathy" (188). "I was benevolent and good," he complains; "misery made me a fiend" (78). Yet the creature turns all too readily from sociability to savagery, from human kindness to ferocious rage. "I gave vent to my anguish in fearful howlings. I was like a wild beast that had broken the toils" (111). The reader is left to wonder whether Victor has "endowed" his creation not only with human "perceptions and passions" but with bestial ones as well (114). The return to notions of "instinctiveness" in Romantic thought promised to heal the rift between human beings and mute animals. "I go among the Fields and catch a glimpse of a stoat or a fieldmouse peeping out of the withered grass," Keats writes; "the creature hath a purpose and its eyes are bright with it – I go amongst the buildings of a city and I see a Man hurrying along – to what? The Creature has a purpose and his eyes are bright with it" (*JKL* 2: 80). Yet Shelley's nightmare Creature suggests how the innate and instinctive aspects of mind, with their "brute" heritage, may render human nature more "natural" than most of her contemporaries would care to imagine. Such anxieties were closely linked with the unsettling new biology of mind; the attack on Lawrence in *The Quarterly Review*, for example, places his speculations on "human zoology" in the dubious company of Gall, Spurzheim, and Darwin. As figures like R. L. Stevenson's Dr. Jekyll and H. G. Wells's Dr. Moreau attest, the revival of these anxieties by a second Darwin will make *Frankenstein* paradigmatic for Victorian fictional responses to a renewed biological approach to mind and human nature.

TALES TOLD OF IDIOTS

Among the many doctors, philosophers, and intellectual thrill-seekers who traveled to Itard's clinic to examine the "wild child" were Gall and Spurzheim, who published an initial report in the second volume of their "large work."[36] The "pretended Savage of Aveyron" was, in their opinion, an idiot, as Spurzheim later recalled the meeting (*PS* 464–65). Like most feral children, he was probably abandoned because imbecilic, not imbecilic because abandoned. Had all of his mental organs been intact, they reasoned, he would have shown much more progress under Itard's instruction. Wild children did not point the way back to primitive humanity, Gall stressed, but instead presented an especially blatant example of one or more "defective" intellectual organs (*FB* 164–65).

For a corporeal, and especially for a modular theory of mind, what was then termed "idiocy" held a special interest of its own. Intelligence for Gall and Spurzheim was not a quality spread evenly throughout a unified cognitive system, but rather a misleadingly general term for the superior development of one or more discrete mental organs. Remarkable musical abilities might be accompanied by indifferent verbal or logical skills; an artistic genius could have a terrible memory for names and dates. No longer tied to language, reason, and reflection, intelligence could be discretely localized in one mental organ and psychological faculty or another, giving rise to remarkably different patterns of cognitive strengths and weaknesses among various individuals, even those socialized together. (It was the pronounced variability of talents among his schoolmates, after all, that gave Gall the initial hunch for his organological theory.) Idiots, like "prodigies," showed how great the variation within a given collection of organs – that is, within a given brain – could become (*FB* 2: 275). Spurzheim compared the selective deficiencies found among idiots to the selective impairments following brain injury. "Certain children who are half idiots do not speak, though they do many things like reasonable persons, and sometimes manifest a good deal of cunning; and therefore their parents, relations and even physicians, cannot believe in their partial imbecility" (*PS* 384). Combe devotes several pages of his combative *Letter to Francis Jeffrey* to illustrations of "partial idiocy," impossible to reconcile with the orthodox insistence on an indivisible and immaterial mind and providing especially strong evidence for the "plurality of organs."[37] Locke had considered "*Idiots*" or "*Naturals*" to be barren of reason and distinct ideas, closer to beasts than to "*mad men*," who at least form ideas but combine them improperly.[38] For a brain-based, modular psychology, in contrast, idiots do not lose their title to humanity but rather manifest in extreme form the unequal distribution of cognitive strengths and weaknesses found across any given population.

Coleridge, with his own, post-Enlightenment, bias toward the centrality of language and the integrity of the subject, found idiots and wild children equally repulsive. The latter could not even be considered human, "for who would call Peter the wild Boy a Man?" (*SW* 1: 411). As to idiots, Coleridge worried that Wordsworth's "Idiot Boy," though a "fine poem," did not guard sufficiently against the "disgusting images of *ordinary, morbid idiocy*," might even be said to court them in the repeated mentions of Johnny's "burr, burr, burr" (*BL* 2: 48). Wordsworth's highly empathetic portrayal of Johnny in the "Idiot Boy" takes implicit issue both with the eviscerated, rational subject of Enlightenment anthropology and the transcendental model of subjectivity that Coleridge sought to erect in its place.[39] In its evocation of Johnny's intensely emotive life, his unexpected cognitive strengths, and his moments of verbal and nonverbal eloquence, Wordsworth's ballad bears pronounced affinites with the perspective on idiocy being advanced in the biological psychology of his time. "The Idiot Boy" reflects the corporealist tendencies that mark Wordsworth's thinking on poetry, language, and subjectivity as expressed in the "Preface" to *Lyrical Ballads*, the 1799 *Prelude*, and related works of the same period.[40] It also heralds a series of portrayals of "partial" idiots by Walter Scott, John Galt, and Harriet Martineau that together illustrate another dimension of the convergence of literature and brain science in the Romantic era.

Johnny's "burr" – which has vexed more readers than Coleridge – connects rather than isolates Johnny from the other speakers of *Lyrical Ballads* (including Wordsworth's various poetic personae) with their penchant for extrasemantic yet meaningful sounds. The "burr, burr, burr"

(115), a pointed condensation of the figures of repetition and the emotive interjections found throughout the ballads, is not automatic or mindless behavior but emotionally expressive and other-directed: "His lips *with joy* they burr *at you*" (19, my italics). In his robust defense of "The Idiot Boy" addressed to John Wilson, Wordsworth stresses Johnny's peculiar eloquence: "my Idiot is not one of those who cannot articulate."[41] Yet Johnny articulates as much through gesture and tone as through his limited store of words. He finds a way around his obvious deficits not simply to express his immediate needs but to build and maintain a warm and genuinely dialogical relation with his mother.[42]

> To this did Johnny answer make,
> Both with his head, and with his hand,
> And proudly shook the bridle too,
> And then! his words were not a few,
> Which Betty well could understand.   (72–76)

Her love in turn is unadulterated by pity, her unexpected pride in her son making a striking part of Wordsworth's implicit argument for the idiot boy's title to humanity. "And Betty's face with joy o'erflows, / Proud of herself, and proud of him" (98–99). Betty's flush of joy underscores the links between her embodied human nature and Johnny's, his mute expressiveness and her own.

Perhaps for this very reason Coleridge takes as much exception to Betty Foy as to her idiot son. He calls her behavior a "burlesque on the blindness of anile dotage" and her characterization the "impersonation of an instinct abandoned by judgement" (*BL* 2: 48). This last phrase is a rejoinder to Wordsworth's claim to psychological realism in the "Preface." Tracing Betty's "maternal passion" though its "more subtle windings," Wordsworth offers "The Idiot Boy" not as a study in abnormal psychology but as a representation of the "fluxes and refluxes of the mind when agitated by the great and simple affections of our nature" (*WP* 1: 126). But Coleridge's objection to "instinct abandoned by judgement" might apply equally to Wordsworth's characterization of Johnny. The portrayals both of mother and son, that is, imply a psychology that grants unconscious, emotive, and instinctive mental acts more validity and efficacy than Coleridge is even remotely willing to accept.

The two stanzas that resolve the ballad's narrative crisis – as Betty discovers her son idling on his pony near a "roaring waterfall" – convey the power of Betty's "blind" cognition as well as the complexity masked by the simple term "idiot."

She looks again – her arms are up –
She screams – she cannot move for joy;
She darts, as with a torrent's force,
She almost has o'erturned the horse,
And fast she holds her idiot boy.

And Johnny burrs and laughs aloud,
Whether in cunning or in joy,
I cannot tell; but while he laughs,
Betty a drunken pleasure quaffs,
To hear again her idiot boy.   (382–91)

The mother's rapid transitions between emotions of fear and joy, momentary paralysis and swift action, rival the waterfall itself in channeled spontaneity and "force." If this is "dotage," it is dotage of an unusually lively and energetic sort. As to Johnny, his laughter places the narrator in the uncertain position described by Spurzheim, unsure of how to weigh an idiot's "cunning" against his seemingly mindless behavior. (Johnny has been sent to get a doctor, not to dawdle under the stars while the horse feeds.) The repetitive style – the pronounced anaphora, the partial refrain – pulls the poetry closer to the irrational yet emotionally charged and wordlessly affective behaviors it describes.

Johnny's brief speech in the ballad's final stanza, however – "'The cocks did crow to-whoo, to-whoo, / And the sun did shine so cold'" – is poetic in a different and more challenging manner. Wordsworth called these lines the "foundation of the whole"; he worked backwards from Johnny's terse yet uncannily evocative description of his night's adventure.[13] As Bewell remarks, the "language is highly metaphorical": Johnny creatively distorts his limited daytime vocabulary to describe the unfamiliar world of the night outdoors. Yet in relating Johnny's speech to the "fundamentally metaphoric" consciousness of "primitive perception," as described in the very Enlightenment anthropologies Wordsworth is implicitly criticizing, Bewell underplays the episode's significance for a post-Enlightenment theory of human nature.[14] A rationalist philosopher would not expect an "idiot" to come up with novel metaphors, any more than expecting a wild child to invent an iconic language, or a person deaf and blind from youth to develop an extensive knowledge base. Johnny's spontaneous metaphor-making suggests that limited linguistic abilities can co-exist with powers of poetic invention, unexpectedly aligning Johnny with the silent poets of *The Prelude* ("Words are but under-agents in their souls" [*1805* 12: 272]). A surprisingly rich affective and perceptual life is undiminished by the idiot's

selective cognitive deficits, and he is even given imaginative power sufficient to convey at least a glimmer of that largely wordless inner life.
Wordsworth dares the reader to view Johnny as less than human, all the
while hinting at the intensity of Johnny's perceptions and emotions and
granting a "valid imaginative logic" to his vision of the world.[45]

In the letter to Wilson, Wordsworth insists on the rightness of "the
word Idiot," noting that no other term, such as "lack-wit, half-wit, witless
&c" conveys the *"passion"* attached to "idiot" in the English tongue.[46] Yet
"half-wit" has the advantage of connoting a mind limited only in certain
aspects, and Wordsworth goes this term one better in Betty's characterization of Johnny as "half-wise" (198). Half-wise – severely limited in
some ways, normal or even superior in others – describes the portrayal
of "partial" idiots in later Romantic works by Scott, Galt, and
Martineau, all of whom highlight their subjects' intuitive wisdom and
their active integration into a vital if contracted social sphere. Only
Davie Gellatley, in Scott's *Waverley*, is explicitly compared to the "Idiot
Boy," but Wordsworth's precedent hovers behind all three figures.[47]
Davie displays more than his share of the cunning that both Wordsworth
and Spurzheim associate with certain cases of idiocy, and some indeed
consider him "more knave than fool" (84). But Davie's mental deficits
are genuine, though offset by abilities that both recall and far exceed
those of Johnny Foy.

Davie Gellatley was in good earnest the half-crazed simpleton which he
appeared, and was incapable of any constant and steady exertion. He had just
so much solidity as kept on the windy side of insanity; just so much wild wit as
saved him from the imputation of idiocy; some dexterity in field sports (in which
we have known as great fools excel), great kindness and humanity in his treatment of animals, warm affections, a prodigious memory, and an ear for music.
(105)

What stands out here is the combination of mental "simplicity" (82) in
some respects with "prodigious" cognitive abilities in others, along with
the "warm affections" already seen in Wordsworth's idiot boy. Davie's
late brother had been something of a musical prodigy – "Heaven, as if
to compensate to the family Davie's deficiencies, had given him what the
hamlet thought uncommon talents" (106) – suggesting that Davie's
powers as well as his deficits may be congenital, a matter of familial
inheritance. Within the Romantic psychological discourse of the time,
the prodigy stands only at one remove from the idiot savant. Scott was
no fan of the phrenology movement, fashionable as it was in the
Edinburgh of his day. He called it "turnipology" and pretended, after

learning that a group of ladies had gone to see the "German quack Spurzheim dissect a human head," that he could no longer "look at an Edinburgh belle with[out] thinking of raw head and bloody bones."[48] Yet his characterization of Davie Gellatley could have made a case-study for one of Spurzheim's popular treatises.

Galt, another Scotch novelist working in the local idiom inaugurated by *Waverley*, published a short piece entitled "The Idiot" in the October 1829 number of *Blackwood's*. He argues that the term "idiot" encompasses a whole range of conditions, noting that "under the zero of reason there are many degrees before the human intelligence sinks to that of the animal instincts." Citing Garrick's famous impersonation (incorporated into his performance of *Lear*) of a "father struck with fatuity on beholding his only infant child dashed to pieces," Galt suggests that "histrionic tragedy" has yet to fully exploit the "unexplored regions of the mind, below the ordinary understanding, amidst the gradations of idiocy."[49] This might seem no less a challenge for the serious novel as well. In fact, Galt had made just such a study a few years before in *The Entail* (1822), with its arresting characterization of the "natural," Watty.

Variously called "daft," "defective," a "haverel," a "gouk," a "sumph," "the Natural," and an "idiot," Watty (Walter) nevertheless manages to inherit his father's estate over the claims of his elder brother, thanks to the unconventional "entail" of the novel's title.[50] Watty's claim is duly challenged on the grounds of his legal competence, but he manages to squeak through thanks to his "glaiks and gleams o' sense" – and a clever lawyer (193). In some ways Watty falls only a few degrees shy of the "zero of reason." He can read verses from the Bible (though with little apparent comprehension) and can recite part of the catechism and at least one school-maxim from memory (25, 63, 88). Yet from early childhood everyone sees him, at best, as barely "superior to an idiot." He has "something like" the "instinct" of a colley-dog (though not, his father adds, its "sense") and manifests the "artless affections" commonly associated with idiots in the period (72, 116). Like Wordsworth's "idiot boy," he has a knack for figurative language, inventing the occasional metaphor ("when the winter comes, sowing the land wi' hailstones to grow frost and snaw" [88]) and simile: "I'll sit quiet as ony ane o' the images afore Baillie Glassford's house at the head o' the Stockwell. King William himsel, on his bell-metal horse at the Cross, is a popular preacher, Mr Keeleven, compared to what I'll be" (182).

Surprisingly, but the less so given his fortune and "handsome" looks, Watty marries a local heiress, the strapping and frolicsome Betty Bodle

(197). Brought up by her father – that is, hardly brought up at all – Betty does little to hide her "knowledge of her husband's defective intellects" yet likes having the upper hand, appreciates his "simple affections and harmless character," and enjoys him sexually as well (111, 218). Watty, for his part, grows positively "uxorious," and Betty's death in childbirth sends him into a deep, nearly crushing "melancholy" (111, 116). At this low point, however, Watty's turn for metaphor comes to his aid in a bizarre but affecting fashion. As the body of his wife is coffined, Watty shudders "from head to foot" and turns to his infant daughter, born healthy. "He immediately quitted the death-room, and, going to the nursery where the infant lay asleep in the nurse's lap, he contemplated it for sometime, and then, with a cheerful and happy look and tone, said, – 'It's a wee Betty Bodle, and its my Betty Bodle noo'" (116). It becomes clear as the narrative progresses that Watty has not entered into a delusional state regarding the status of his wife or daughter, but rather has "blended" the two identities in a creative and, if anything, psychologically healthy manner. The absolute quality of the identification remains strange (and one wonders how Watty would deal with his daughter's adolescence), but it makes for an unusually affectionate and devoted father, at once Betty's playfellow and protector. It even gives him a greater degree of agency, enabling him finally to resist his father's overbearing influence by opening up a "deeper and more intractable" side to his character (132).

When his young daughter in turn falls ill and dies and Watty moves on to "his third Betty Bodle," it proves his undoing (167). Again, the transference is a matter not of delusional but of metaphoric substitution, which Watty describes using a trope that might have come from Wordsworth. He mourns over his daughter's corpse three days and nights, until a "kirkyard smell" comes from the bed. "And then I saw, wi' the eye o' my heart, that my brother's wee Mary was grown my wee Betty Bodle, and so I gaed and brought her hame in my arms, and she is noo my dochter" (200). The transference of identity, however irrationally it begins, makes good ethical as well as emotional sense. Mary has been left penniless by her father's death, and she and her mother and brother are barely surviving when Watty's *de facto* adoption of Mary brings the entire family under his protection. In stark contrast to their other relatives, Watty is more than happy to share his prosperity and to atone (however naively) for the injustice done to his brother's children, cut off from their potential inheritance by the entail. "Some idiots," Combe notes, "are as remarkable for correct moral feelings as some great

geniuses are for the reverse."[51] Watty's inability to explain his actions logically, however, constitutes "indisputable proof of idiocy according to
the notions of society," leaving him fair game for his younger brother's
legal machinations (167). Defining competence in Enlightenment terms
– the ability to "originate such motions or volitions of mind as are req-
uisite to constitute what may be denominated a legal modicum of understanding" (187) – the court hands in a "verdict of Fatuity" (201). The
estate passes to the self-regarding, morally bankrupt, eminently rational
George.

    Idiocy gets a chapter to itself in the *Letters on the Laws of Man's Nature
and Development* (1851), a popular introduction to phrenology co-written
by Harriet Martineau and the mesmerist H. G. Atkinson.[52] Sweeping
aside legal, philosophical, and medical definitions of idiocy as one
chaotic "mess" of misstatement and confusion, Martineau suggests that
a proper understanding of idiocy can only begin with principles first
enunciated by Gall: rejecting the "idea that the mind is one thing, and
the body another," acknowledging the importance and extent of human
"Instinct," and accepting the "plurality and independence" of various
mental faculties and the brain organs underlying them (90–93). She
notes that the definition of idiocy enshrined in English law equates idiots
with persons born deaf, dumb, and blind, characterized by Blackstone
as "incapable of any understanding" and "wanting all those senses
which furnish human beings with ideas." That is, from the rationalist
"metaphysical assumptions" of a Blackstone or Condillac, a subject like
James Mitchell and an "idiot" would equally forfeit any claim to understanding or legal agency, observed facts of "nature" notwithstanding
(91). Martineau gathers facts from her own observation that suggest the
uneven pattern of mental deficits and strengths seen both in phrenological and Romantic fictional representations of idiots. She recalls a man
who (like Galt's Watty) could mechanically read and copy the Scriptures
though mentally "deficient from birth" (90), and sketches the portrait of
an idiot boy who lacks speech but boasts "marvellous" acuteness and delicacy of sense, innate notions of time and number, and pronounced
artistic abilities (69–71). Only phrenological "science" can begin to bring
the law into some conformity with the observed range of mental deficits
grouped under idiocy, while studying the varieties of "deficient senses
and defective or impaired organs" can in turn help advance knowledge
of the structure and functions of the organic mind (91, 96).

    Martineau's conversion to phrenology (or more precisely "phreno-
mesmerism") did not take place till well into the 1840s, in the wake of

her own mesmeric cure. Born into a Unitarian family, however, she grew up in the culture of Dissent and had long been familiar with brain-based accounts of mind, serving an intellectual apprenticeship to Hartley and Priestley as Coleridge and Wordsworth had done a generation before.[53] Her memorable portrayal of Archie, the heroine's "idiot brother" in *Ella of Garveloch* (1832), remarkably anticipates her later phrenological thinking on "defective" minds and organs.[54] In Archie one finds yet another representation (set yet again in Scotland) of an idiot who exhibits admirable human traits despite his lack of reason, who shows considerable instinctive judgment, and who forms strong affective bonds with those around him.

Archie has some linguistic ability, but will speak with virtually no one but his sister, Ella, and their two brothers. He can be left to himself on familiar ground but nowhere else; even the very small island on which they live is mostly alien territory to him. Yet however foolish and "lost" he appears to strangers, his brothers insist that he is "wiser" than they are "about many things, and sees farther" (17). His insight comes not from preternatural abilities (though local superstitions hold otherwise) but from a combination of instinct and pronounced powers of observation and imitation. "He is always housed before a tempest, or safe in a hole in the rock, like the birds he seems to learn from, while we breast the wind as we may, far from home" (17–18). As much naturalist as natural, Archie picks up subtle signs from the local wildlife that others miss, and his siblings use him as a kind of human barometer before risking the weather in their light boats. "He has a keener sight into the place of storms than we" (56). He finds "pleasures of his own" in nature that go beyond what Wordsworth (in "Tintern Abbey") calls "glad animal movements" to include an unusual but recognizably human "love of what is beautiful to the eyes God gave him" (136). He takes to music and has a naive capacity for metaphor, comparing the northern lights to the fires used locally to process kelp: "It was but lately that he pointed to the northern lights one clear evening, and told me that kelping time was come again over the sea" (135).

For all its Romantic setting (the "Isles of Rough Rock" off the west coast of Argyleshire), *Ella* does not market itself as a picturesque tale but as Number Five of the "Illustrations of Political Economy." Openly didactic and anti-sentimental, the "Illustrations" were intended to expose a wide audience to the fundamentals of laissez-faire economic doctrine. Martineau includes *Ella* to show that even a tiny, isolated community can play its part in the burgeoning global economy. And within

that tiny community, even the "idiot brother" makes his economic contribution, an important one given the lean and unforgiving island environment. Archie frequents a "high rock" (surrounded by water at full
tide) where he gathers puffin eggs and catches gannets, twisting their
necks as he has seen his brothers do (48). Ella takes pride in his birding
and, in speaking to others, "represented Archie as adding to the
resources of her house-hold, in no small degree" (59). At the same time,
she wants to keep Archie unconscious of the economic aspects of their
life, refusing to give him a turn at rent-paying and worrying that their
mutual affection would be compromised if he knew the extent of her
financial support. "The birds are his playmates while they wheel round
his head, and when he takes them on the nest he has no thought of gain
. . . He does not look beyond the pleasure to his eyes and to his heart,
and he never shall; and gold and silver are not the things to give pleasure to such an eye and such a heart, and he shall never know them" (64).
Archie is to be kept from the very economic knowledge that his portrayal
is meant didactically to convey. Such Romantic inconsistencies help
make the "Illustrations" far more interesting than the utilitarian tract
fiction they superficially resemble, and *Ella* may be the most interesting
of all.

    Archie's death is also Romantic in a carefully understated way.
Representations of idiots – literary and scientific alike – frequently
feature death because a sense of mortality is seen as one crucial sign of
a genuinely human mind. According to Enlightenment discourse, idiots
and those characteristically grouped with them – the deaf and blind,
wild children, "savages" – lack the very "idea" of death. A young man
of Chartres who learns to speak only at 23, for example, is said by
Condillac to lack real knowledge of life up to then because he "did not
distinctly know what death was."[55] Both Gall and Spurzheim are at
pains to show (contrary to the reports of Gordon and other critics) that
James Mitchell not only understands the meaning of his father's death,
but (in the wake of his own illness) becomes "apprehensive of dying"
himself (*P* 235). Robinson's "Savage of Aveyron" and Galt's "Idiot"
anecdote in *Blackwood's* center on their subject's awareness of a mother's
death, providing at once a sentimental crisis and a quietly polemical
assertion of a common human nature independent of language. Davie
"breaks into tears" when reminded of his dead brother in *Waverley* (106),
and Watty's legal competency is challenged when his compensatory
response to the death of his daughter seems to imply his lack of any conventional idea of mortality.

At the emotional climax of *Ella*, Martineau significantly varies this convention, having Archie save his brother from imminent death at certain risk of his own life. Much is left ambiguous in this charged episode. Archie senses his brother's danger (he is about to drown) by correctly reading the expressions of those looking on from shore, but whether he fully comprehends the underlying emotions remains uncertain. "He was strongly wrought upon; for no one understood better the signs of emotion, whether or not he understood the cause" (199). He acts in a manner that objectively appears daring and decisive, but the subjective status of the act remains unclear. "He acted with rapidity and strength, as if suddenly inspired by reason; but, alas! his energy could only manifest itself in the way of imitation." Seeing a rescue boat launched from shore, Archie (watching from his offshore rock) leaps into a cask he likes to play with. The cask is sucked under by an eddy, drowning Archie, but resurfaces within reach of Archie's brother, keeping him afloat till the rescue boat can arrive. Archie has "no doubt foreseen" something of this, since one of his favorite games is to float feathers and the like into the same eddy, launching them from precisely the spot where he launches his cask (200). He is also canny about the tides and exceptionally "cautious" under ordinary circumstances (48). Whether he consciously sacrifices himself for his brother becomes an unresolvable question. But no one suggests that his action is inspired by folly rather than love and concern. However opaque his state of mind, however irrational his behavior, he still acts empathically, and dies heroically.

All of these texts follow Wordsworth in recalibrating the "undue value set upon that faculty which we call reason" in favor of the affections, of blind or instinctive actions, and of judgments made with the body. (We do not rely on logic to test the goodness of our actions, Wordsworth continues: "we feel internally their beneficent effect; we are satisfied with this delicious sensation" [*WP* I: 103–4]). Wild children, idiots, those born deaf and blind – the mental outcasts of rationalist theory – are granted profound feelings and keen sensations within these revisionary Romantic accounts, whether they take the form of psychological case-studies or fictional tales. As M. H. Abrams has argued in relation to Wordsworth, an interest in such figures reflects not a rejection but a rethinking of human uniformity, eliciting "those feelings and thoughts whose very presence in peasants, children, and idiots is what proves them to be the property, not of the cultivated classes alone, but of all mankind."[56] In contrast to Abrams, however, I see this new, embodied conception of human nature not as a "simple extension" of neoclassical thought but as a significant departure from it, one that places far more emphasis on sensations, emotions, nonverbal thought and communication, and unconscious or instinctive mental acts. In this, Wordsworth exemplifies an important but rarely noted strain within Romantic discourse, both literary and scientific, that far from repudiating human uniformity, broadens and extends it in unprecedented ways.

ROMANTIC DISCOURSE AND RACIAL SCIENCE

In equating idiots, feral children, and the deaf and blind with "savages," Enlightenment writers inevitably raise issues of race and racial classification, issues that become no less important for their critical Romantic heirs. This is not the place for an extended discussion of race in Romantic discourse, a large and difficult topic that scholars have only begun to explore in depth.[57] However, the relation between corporeal theories of mind and issues of race and racism qualifies what I have termed embodied universalism in serious ways. Those who see a marked shift from Enlightenment universalism to a Romantic cult of difference have not failed to implicate Romanticism in the rise of modern, pseudo-scientific racism. Studies by Martin Bernal and Robert Young, by relating the Romantic emphasis on diversity, bloodlines, and "national" character to the emergence of racist science in the early nineteenth century, have revived an argument first made in the early 1930s, a time that saw the rise of Nazism and other extreme racialist ideologies.[58] Writing on the "diversitarian" character of Romanticism in *The Great Chain of Being*, Lovejoy warned: "It has lent itself all too easily to the service of man's egotism, and especially – in the political and social sphere – of the kind of collective vanity which is nationalism or racialism."[59] More troubling in this context, embodied conceptions of human nature play a notable role within the racialist strains of various Romantic discourses, helping to displace "older ways of regarding difference in terms of civilization versus savagery" with an "allegedly scientific set of hierarchies inscribed upon the body."[60]

It would be misleading, however, to pose too simple an equation between the emergence of biological accounts of mind and of "scientific" racism in the Romantic era. For some writers, embodied theories of mind could in fact militate against the racialist aspects of Enlightenment thought, which tends to make human equality merely *potential*, while relegating "uncivilized" groups to a childlike or even proto-human status.[61] Monboddo, for whom "man, in his natural state, is a wild animal, without language or arts of any kind," represents the extreme form of this view.[62] Notoriously, Monboddo considers orang-utans an example of humanity "in one of the first stages of society," not far removed from other peoples of Africa, "a country which we are sure at all times has abounded with wild men" and where "arts and civility appear to have made less progress than any where else."[63] Though Monboddo's equation of orangutans and other "barbarous nations" of Africa found few adherents, his view of Africans as primitive, bereft of arts and culture, and effectively "wild" is all too common among Enlightenment writers.[64] Rousseau is representative in relying on "moral" (that is, cultural) rather than biological differences in account-ing for the superiority of European over "uncivilized" sensibilities: "Why is our most touching music only a pointless noise to the ear of a West Indian? Are his nerves of a different nature from ours?"[65]

For those Romantic brain scientists who answered "no" to Rousseau's question, the basic neuroanatomical similarities found among all known peoples could render the dichotomy of savage and civilized a crude and misleading one. For Gall, there is "no essential difference" between "brutal ignorance and refined learning – between the savage and the civ-ilized man" (*FB* 6: 282). Each is comparably equipped to negotiate a challenging physical and social environment, and their similarities far outweigh their alleged differences. Bell holds that man "in his state of nature" uses his brain no less than the "man at his desk," since the basic process of taking in the world – creating it through active perception – already involves a good deal of cognitive work. If civilization implied greater mental activity and power, Bell archly observes, "we should find the gamekeeper inferior to his master in a greater degree than my expe-rience warrants" (*AP* 67). The new biology of mind could thus serve to demolish the "moral" and intellectual hierarchy that for Enlightenment writers grants European man justified dominion over the "savage" groups found, conveniently enough, in the areas of the world being col-onized or otherwise exploited in an era of slavery and imperial expan-sion.[66] Spurzheim attacked the apologists for slavery ("this most selfish of all barbarities") for presuming the mental inferiority of black Africans, countering that the brains of Africans and Europeans showed no more variation across than within racial and ethnic groups and that no human group could be considered "superior to the others."[67] Gall concurred: "Hence, as I find in the brain of the negro, the same parts as in that of the European, it is certain, that they both occupy the same degree in the same scale of the animal kingdom" (*FB* 2: 113). Both scorn the Dutch physiognomist Camper's theory of a "facial angle" revealing racial differences in intellectual capacity and marking the gradations from ape to white European (with black Africans somewhere near the former). "We know of negroes whose jaw-bones are extremely prominent, but who manifest great intellectual faculties because their foreheads are much developed. According to their facial angle, they ought to come after many stupid Europeans who have a small forehead but whose jaw-bones are inclined backward" (*PS* 199). Measuring skulls did not always mean endorsing racial hierarchies.

What accounts like Lovejoy's ignore, then, is that Romantic-era writers could draw on the new biology of mind to oppose the racist and "elitist" tendencies of the Enlightenment paradigm they came to challenge.[68] Herder provides an especially fraught example, given the transitional character of his thought. Both Bernal and Young have argued that Herder's unprecedented emphasis on local, indigenous cultures helped prepare the ground for a "right-wing anthropology focused on ideas of race and nation," whereas Bernal's critics have pointed instead to the "liberal, pluralistic" elements of Herder's thinking.[69] In fact, both tendencies co-exist, however uneasily, in Herder's *Outlines of a Philosophy of the History of Man*, which in places affirms the uniformity of human nature while elsewhere indulging in chauvinistic asides on the "primitive savage races" of sub-Saharan African (*Outlines* 18, 96). Significantly, it is Herder's cultural relativism – part of his Enlightenment inheritance – that fuels his hierarchical vision of a "progressive scale" from the lowly "New-Zealand cannibal" to a Newton or Fenelon, representing the flower of European civilization and the "purest genius in human form" (*Outlines* 93).[70] On the other hand, his denial of racial differences ("there are neither four or five races, nor exclusive varieties, on this Earth") and his affirmation of human uniformity stem from his biological understanding of man's "organic structure" ("organischen Bau"), so "fixed" and "delicate" that it allows for only limited human variation (*Outlines* 96, 166).[71] Herder's embodied universalism acts as a brake on his cultural relativism, which otherwise tends to exaggerate human differences in terms of the "various Degrees of Civilization" separating the primitive African from the polished European (*Outlines* 450).

Yet along the way Herder endorses Camper's facial angle and the "acute observations" it entails regarding "that which distinguishes nations from each other" (*Outlines* 84); he also views the African body as inferior and degrading: "their forefathers purchased it [Africa] at a dear rate, at the price of the negro form and complexion" (*Outlines* 170).[72] If Herder anticipates the embodied universalism of the Romantic era, he also demonstrates its tentative character, how readily it could give way to a science of human differences marked upon racialized bodies. Despite the examples of Gall and Spurzheim, the phrenology movement in Britain rushed to place craniology at the service of racial supremacy. Combe includes a chapter on "National Character" and brain development in his widely read *System of Phrenology*, ascribing a whole list of mental "deficiencies" to the "Negro," and a raft of later popularizers followed suit.[73] Lawrence finds occasion to praise Camper and suggests that as the "nobler attributes of man reside in the cerebral hemispheres . . . we shall find, in the comparison of the crania of the white and dark races, a sufficient explanation of the superiority constantly evinced by the former" (*LPZ* 19–20, 432). Bell dismisses Camper only to put forth his own racialist theory to prove that the "cranium of the Negro" manifests inferior mental "capacity" in comparison with the "perfect cranium of an European" (*AP* 40). Without abandoning the notion of a single human species, any more than did Herder, each of these writers attempts to assert European racial superiority on the basis of skull capacity and brain organization.

My purpose in this chapter has been to complicate an influential model for understanding Romanticism that finds its way into numerous cultural histories, old and new. Romantic writers simply did not, as a group, "abandon" an earlier era's postulate of a universal human nature. Not at all. Instead, at least some Romantic-era writers fundamentally revised that postulate, looking to the body with its nervous system, brain, and "organic" mind rather than to a disembodied Reason as the ground for human uniformity and equality. The earlier standard of reason guaranteed potential equality but allowed for "gradations" within the hierarchical classificatory schemes dear to Enlightenment thought. Even in acknowledging the claims of black Africans to equal treatment, a neoclassical writer like Hannah More cannot resist asserting her civilized superiority: "Tho' dark and savage, ignorant and blind, / They claim the common privilege of kind" (137–38). "Few can reason," she helpfully adds, but "all mankind can feel" (150).[74] This crippling note of condescension disappears in a younger anti-slavery poet like Mary Birkett, who locates the African's humanity in the body, a body that manifests its equivalence, actual not potential, with the body and hence the mind of the British reader.[75]

Look at the Negro's sun-burnt, grief-worn frame!
Examine well each limb, each nerve, each bone,
Each artery – and then observe *thy own*;
The beating pulse, the heart that throbs within,
All, (save the sable tincture of his skin,)
Say, Christians, do they not resemble you?
If so, their feelings and sensations too.   (70–76)

In stark contrast to the "untutor'd" nerve that signifies cultural inferiority in More's poem (159), the "Negro's . . . nerve" evinced by Birkett
makes part of an intricate, living somatosensory system that does not
require civilizing or education to manifest full kinship with that of the
pulsing, feeling British subject. For an early Romantic sensibility like
Birkett's, the body and mind constitute a single system, with anatomical
and physiological sameness (under the literally superficial difference of
skin color) underwriting a conviction of human equality.

The new, embodied universalism of the Romantic era extended to
embrace those considered only marginally human within Enlightenment
philosophical and anthropological discourses. Departing from the trinity
of reason, reflection, and artificial language central to the accounts of
human nature put forward by Locke, Condillac, and their followers,
Romantic writers, both literary and scientific, radically rethought the
claims of the "savage," the mute, the mentally impaired. Hunter-gath-
erers, considered wild or bestial by an earlier generation, could now
appear fully human, pursuing a rich perceptual, emotional, physically
active existence by means of the same neuroanatomical organs as their
more urbane contemporaries. The "savage" is reclaimed for humanity
not from sentimentalist or primitivist impulses – eighteenth-century
vogues that do in fact persist throughout the Romantic era – but on the
basis of a new, embodied conception of human nature. Feral children,
though entirely unsocialized, gain new title to human status and abstract
mental capacity. Even the idiot is drawn back from the margins of
humanity to be granted an unprecedented measure of emotional and
cognitive complexity. The modular approach to brain and mind made
prominent by Gall and Spurzheim, along with the decentering of reason
associated with literary Romanticism, allows for a greater appreciation
of affective, intuitive, and perceptual strengths to counterbalance deficits in rationality and reflection. Sophisticated linguistic ability no longer
serves as the undisputed touchstone for gauging human development,
with new attention brought to nonverbal communication, tonal, rhythmic and other extrasemantic aspects of language, and metaphorical

thought arising in despite of linguistic deficits. The organic, biological, embodied tenor of Romantic approaches to mind and human nature makes for a more, not less, democratic science of man.

Woman fares less well under the new dispensation, assigned a quantitatively (though not qualitatively) different brain in keeping with the different "amatory" and procreative functions of her body. A given woman writer such as Austen or Martineau, however, might adapt and even extend notions articulated in the new, biological theories of mind. Even while these theories perpetuate a psychology of sexual difference, they fundamentally challenge the age-old misogynist ranking of mind over body and reason over emotion, validating registers of bodily knowledge and affective experience conventionally coded as feminine.[76] Notions of racial difference trouble the democratic promise of an embodied psychology and anthropology in a different, more uneven fashion. The anti-racist pronouncements of Gall and Spurzheim demonstrate that even in a period that saw the rise of modern racism, a brain-based conception of human nature does not necessarily entail, and may even militate against, invidious notions of racial difference. But other embodied psychologies, and the debased phrenology of Combe and later popularizers, show how readily brain science may become enlisted in the service of racist ideology. Democratic impulses exist side by side with chauvinistic ones in the new biological psychologies. Cabanis and Lawrence go so far as to recommend eugenics programs, although the political allegiances of both are revolutionary rather than reactionary.[77]

The turn to the body that marks the larger field of Romantic discourse (including literary discourse) manifests the same ambivalence. A conception of human nature that refuses to transcend or deny the body – that *begins* from the body and its brain – can help to affirm a common humanity or to engineer a systemic hierarchy of human differences. If the embodied universalism of the Romantic era has eluded notice, its seeming invisibility is, in part, a reflection of its evanescence. Embodied universalism quickly gave way to (or, in most literary cases, uneasily cohabited with) the cult of difference noted by Lovejoy and others, with its anti-democratic uses and implications. Notions of human nature that seek, instead, to bracket off the body have been historically bound up with misogyny and with the rise of a bourgeois sensibility with elitist impulses of its own. The temptation to scorn universalist conceptions of human nature altogether is understandable. But such a retreat notoriously leaves the guarantee and extension of human rights without a theoretical basis, while rendering the pursuit of cross-cultural under-standing dubious at best.[78] The anthropological imagination of the Romantic era at least broached an embodied universalism that prom-ised to extend human belonging and mutual comprehension beyond the limits set by an earlier era's governing paradigms. That the vision was barely sustained and its promise largely unrealized does not make the attempt less intriguing.

CHAPTER SEVEN

Epilogue

As I write, a century has just turned and with it the "Decade of the Brain" has come to a close. Baptized by Congressional fiat and endorsed by Presidential Proclamation in 1990, the brain's decade has more than lived up to its advance billing. Neuroscientific research, propelled by a host of new developments in neuroimaging, molecular biology, genetics, psychopharmacology, and cognitive science has transformed not only neurology but psychology and psychiatry as well. Hybrid disciplines like cognitive neuroscience, psychobiology, behavioral neurology, and neuropsychology have emerged or become newly prominent as the study of the mind has steadily converged with the study of the brain. Brain science has been "fundamentally changed" and, with it, the science of the mind has entered a "new era."[1]

I am quoting from an ambitious essay, "Neurology and Psychiatry: Closing the Great Divide," published as the lead-off piece in the first issue of *Neurology* for the year 2000. Though forward-looking – one might even say millennial – in character, the essay begins with a backward glance to none other than Gall, said to have begun the "scientific study of the brain and its relationship to complex behaviors" in the early nineteenth century.[2] For the authors, two neurologists and a psychiatrist based at the Harvard Medical School, Gall's fundamental intuition that "all mental processes are ultimately biological" has been borne out, and the "historic debates about mind versus brain, nurture versus nature, and functional versus organic" have now run their course. This has come about, moreover, despite the virtual abandonment of biological psychology throughout much of the twentieth century and the ascendance, during the same period, of a dualistic and "doctrinaire" psychoanalytical approach to psychiatry.[3]

Given this emphatically discontinuous history, it is all the more remarkable, not only that Gall's central claim has been so widely reasserted, but that a whole set of postulates and propositions once advocated by Gall and other Romantic brain scientists has returned to prominence over the past several decades. When giving a seminar to a group of professors and graduate students a few years ago, having pre-circulated a draft of the introduction to this book, I began (disconcertingly enough) with the following "pop quiz." What brain scientist claimed (a) that the "mind is a system of organs designed by natural" processes over many thousands of years; (b) that this system of "mental organ[s]" gives rise to a "universal psychology" supported by "complex innate structures"; (c) that the "supposedly immaterial human soul . . . can be bisected with a knife" or "extinguished by a sharp blow"; (d) that human behaviors are often motivated by "versions of animal instincts"; (e) that "facial expressions" are "universal" and reliable indicators of basic emotions; and (f) describes, at the beginning of his book, self-experiments for the reader to perform with afterimages and other visual illusions? It was, I confess, a trick question. Though readers of my introduction might well hear in these brief passages an amalgam of Gall, Lawrence, Cabanis, Bell, and Darwin – no wonder no one at the seminar wanted to take the first guess – all of them in fact come from a book first published in 1997, Steven Pinker's *How the Mind Works.*[4]

Ironically, however, Pinker portrays himself as working *against* the Romantic tradition, unaware of the many points of contact between Romantic brain science and his own popular synthesis of cognitive science and evolutionary biology. Instead, Pinker scorns the "Romantic movement" for its "dreamy" notion of creative genius and, worse, for placing the "emotions and the intellect" into separate "realms," locating the former in the body and the latter in a "cool" and disembodied mind.[5] Although understandable in light of anti-Romantic pronouncements going back to Irving Babbitt, this characterization of Romanticism could hardly be more wrong.[6] It prevents Pinker from even beginning to consider the significance of the Romantic provenance of many of his own views, or to think through the implications of the historical recurrence of an anti-dualistic, naturalistic, holistic, adaptationist, "organic" approach to human psychology.

Pinker is by no means alone in allowing an inadequate notion of Romanticism to block recognition of the Romantic tenor of some of his central notions. Mark Johnson opens *The Body in the Mind* with a set of propositions instantly familiar to readers versed in the Romantic tradition: "Without imagination, nothing in the world could be meaningful. Without imagination, we could never make sense of our experience. Without imagination, we could never reason toward knowledge of reality." Yet for Johnson the "Romantic" notion of the imagination is badly misleading in its presumed bias toward fantasy and novelty.[7] Johnson's account of the constant, quotidian acts of imagination that bring the lived world into being – the "exceedingly complex interaction with your environment in which you experience significant patterns and employ structured processes that give rise to a coherent world of which you are able to make sense" – aptly evokes the central notion of an "active mind" that links the poetic psychologies of Wordsworth and Coleridge to the scientific theories of Darwin, Cabanis, and Bell. Yet Johnson presents this "mundane" account of meaning-making as the *contrary* to meaning in the "Romantic sense of being profoundly moving or significant."[8]

Like Johnson, Antonio Damasio returns to ground staked out by the Romantics not only in the anti-dualist ethos of his work on the "body-minded brain" but in some of its more detailed concerns as well. His key distinction between the (divided) self and the (integral) organism, his emphases on nonconscious mental processes, "internal" sensations, and "background" emotions, his acceptance of a universal set of basic human emotions with a "shared biological core," his assumption of a "nonverbal" conceptual system that gets translated into linguistic expression, his appreciation of the extrasemantic, prosodic element of speech and its affective qualities, and his view of perception as a creative process all have robust analogs in Romantic brain science and Romantic esthetic theory alike.[9] Even his set of governing assumptions reads less like an updating than a faithful paraphrase of Gall: "that the processes of mind, including those of consciousness, are based on brain activity; that the brain is part of a whole organism with which it interacts continuously; and that we, as human beings, in spite of remarkable individual traits that make each of us unique, share similar biological characteristics in terms of the structure, organization, and function of our organisms." And yet Damasio restates Pinker's caricature view that the "Romantics placed emotion in the body and reason in the brain," rather than looking to the Romantic era for historical allies in his quest to overcome mind-brain dualism and rectify Descartes' error.[10]

However unmerited, does the bad reputation the "Romantics" have gained among cognitive and neuroscientific circles really make a difference? Perhaps not much of one. Yet by misconstruing the histories, or prehistories, of their fields, neuroscientists and cognitive theorists fail to take advantage of the perspective that a richer and more accurate history might bring to their work. Contemporary discussions of facial-expression theory, to take one example, usually look back to the work of Charles Darwin and no further, though Darwin himself cites Bell as having "laid the foundations" for future work in the field.[11] A fuller history of facial expression theory, however, in uncovering some of the hypotheses and connections made in the past, might provoke new questions for scientific investigation in the present. The links between facial expression, nonverbal communication, and what is now called "theory of mind" – the human ability to model the intentions, emotions, and mental dispositions of other human agents – theorized by Bell, Reid, and the Baillies have recently been proposed anew.[12] But current researchers tend to feature the visual aspect of "mindreading" while paying little attention to the role of extrasemantic properties of speech, including the conveyance of emotions through "prosody" recently emphasized by Damasio.[13] The example of Romantic-era work on the expression and communication of emotions and intentions might well prompt new lines of research in the present, possibly leading to a more complex and compelling scientific picture.

Other, more critical, lessons could be gained from reexamining the connections posed within the embodied psychologies of the Romantic era. A widespread tendency in recent accounts of cognition and behavior, for example, involves a reliance on adaptationist arguments to answer or anticipate theoretical problems. The mind-brain works the way it does simply because it has been "designed" to, optimizing its fit to the natural and social environment under the constant pressure of natural selection. So prevalent and uncritical has the recourse to adaptationism become that Francisco Varela, Evan Thompson, and Eleanor Rosch have characterized it as a new "orthodoxy" badly in need of conscientious reappraisal.[14] The strategic reliance on adaptationist logic in biological accounts of mind, however, is an old story. Expanding on hints in Erasmus Darwin and Herder, Gall, and Cabanis both rely extensively on adaptationist arguments in expounding their views on mind and behavior; Lawrence makes key use of adaptationism in his materialist polemics as well. Even Bell, though writing as a creationist, makes use of adaptationist logic; the difference is that for Bell, the optimal fit between organism and environment is the result of divine, rather than natural, design. That adaptationist arguments have been used in the past to develop, promote, and defend biological theories of mind does not, of course, speak to their truth value in the present. But if adaptationist logic proved seductive even *before* Charles Darwin had given it a sophisticated theoretical justification, it seems to add point to the contention of Varela, Thompson, and Rosch that "optimization" is being overworked and underexamined in recent cognitive science.[15] As long as the issue remains under debate, the suspicion arises that adaptationist logic may prove so convenient for grounding embodied accounts of mind that its legitimacy in relation to specific accounts of cognition and behavior may be too readily taken for granted rather than rigorously demonstrated.

The intellectually charged atmosphere of recent work on cognition and the brain has made a new history of neuroscience possible, one that restores prominence to issues and debates – on modularity, innateness, human universals, the "pre-Freudian" unconscious, and much more – that had long seemed of merely antiquarian interest. With this new history have come important new perspectives for literary and cultural history, as I hope to have demonstrated above in relation to British Romanticism. These new histories – scientific, cultural, literary – may in turn inspire critical reflection on the state of brain science in the new century. Sherry Turkle was among the first to note the "Romantic" character of second-generation cognitive science, as biological, emergent, and "fuzzy" approaches came to challenge the mechanistic models of early theorists inspired by the computer revolution.[16] Rediscovering the Romantic pre-history of many of the concepts and connections at play in the brain sciences today may help to extend and complicate the informed critical analysis exemplified by Turkle's work at the border between the humanities and the cognitive sciences. At a time when biological accounts of mind are again becoming ascendant, better knowledge of the embodied psychologies of the past may provide not just a richer and more accurate history, but a more useful one.

Notes

PREFACE

1 Christopher Wordsworth, *Memoirs of William Wordsworth, Poet-Laureate, D. C. L.*, 2 vols. (London: Edward Moxon, 1851), 2: 322. Robert Southey claimed that "Wordsworth has no sense of smell" in the ninth of his autobiographical letters (written in July, 1822) included in *The Life and Correspondence of the Late Robert Southey*, ed. Charles Cuthbert Southey, 6 vols. (London: Longman, Brown, Green, and Longmans, 1849–50), 1: 63.
2 Jerome J. McGann, *The Poetics of Sensibility: A Revolution in Literary Style* (Oxford: Clarendon, 1996), 125.
3 Henry George Atkinson and Harriet Martineau, *Letters on the Laws of Man's Nature and Development* (London: John Chapman, 1851), 121.
4 John Sutton, *Philosophy and Memory Traces: Descartes to Connectionism* (Cambridge University Press, 1998), 1, 23, 30.
5 Nicholas Roe, *John Keats and the Culture of Dissent* (Oxford: Clarendon, 1997), ix.

1 INTRODUCTION: NEURAL ROMANTICISM

1 James Ralston Caldwell, *John Keats' Fancy: The Effect on Keats of the Psychology of His Day* (Ithaca: Cornell University Press, 1945), 8.
2 See, for example, Maria Tatar, *Spellbound: Studies in Mesmerism and Literature* (Princeton University Press, 1978).
3 M. H. Abrams, *The Mirror and the Lamp: Romantic Theory and the Critical Tradition* (Oxford University Press, 1953), Tilottama Rajan, *Dark Interpreter: The Discourse of Romanticism* (Ithaca: Cornell University Press, 1980), and Charles J. Rzepka, *The Self as Mind: Vision and Identity in Wordsworth, Coleridge, and Keats* (Cambridge: Harvard University Press, 1986) all remain indispensable. Douglas B. Wilson reduces "psychological approaches" to British Romanticism entirely to psychoanalitical approaches in his survey, "Psychological Approaches," in *A Companion to Romanticism*, ed. Duncan Wu (Oxford: Blackwell, 1998), 420–30.
4 Especially valuable studies in the history of science, medicine, and psychology include: F. N. L. Poynter, ed., *The History and Philosophy of Knowledge of the*

Brain and Its Functions (Oxford: Blackwell, 1958); Robert Young, *Mind, Brain, and Adaptation in the Nineteenth-Century: Cerebral Localization and Its Biological Function from Gall to Ferrier* (Oxford: Clarendon, 1970); Edwin Clarke and L. S. Jacyna, *Nineteenth-Century Origins of Neuroscientific Concepts* (Berkeley: University of California Press, 1987); Graham Richards, *Mental Machinery: The Origins and Consequences of Psychological Ideas*, Part I: *1600–1850* (Baltimore: Johns Hopkins University Press, 1992); and Edward S. Reed, *From Soul to Mind: The Emergence of Psychology from Erasmus Darwin to William James* (New Haven: Yale University Press, 1997).

5 See Roger Cooter, *The Cultural Meaning of Popular Science: Phrenology and the Organization of Consent in Nineteenth-Century Britain* (Cambridge University Press, 1984); Maureen McNeil, *Under the Banner of Science: Erasmus Darwin and His Age* (Manchester University Press, 1987); Simon Schaffer, "States of Mind: Enlightenment and Natural Philosophy," in *The Languages of Psyche: Mind and Body in Enlightenment Thought: Clark Library Lectures 1985–1986*, ed. G. S. Rousseau (Berkeley: University of California Press 1990), 233–90; and Jan Golinski, *Science as Public Culture: Chemistry and Enlightenment in Britain, 1760–1820* (Cambridge University Press, 1992).

6 Jerry A. Fodor, *The Modularity of Mind: An Essay on Faculty Psychology* (Cambridge: MIT Press 1983), 22. As Fodor notes, the revival of interest in Gall among cognitive scientists was sparked by John C. Marshall's essay "The New Organology," *Behavioral and Brain Sciences* 3 (1980): 23–25, although Young had already established Gall's importance for the history of science in *Mind, Brain, and Adaptation*. Prominent contemporary neuroscientists who have helped rehabilitate Gall's reputation include Francis Crick in *The Astonishing Hypothesis: The Scientific Search for the Soul* (New York: Scribner, 1993), 85–86; Stephen Kosslyn and Olivier Koenig in *Wet Mind: The New Cognitive Neuroscience* (New York: Free Press, 1992), 4–5; and Antonio Damasio in *Descartes' Error: Emotion, Reason, and the Human Brain* (New York: Avon, 1994), 14.

7 Anne Harrington, *Medicine, Mind, and the Double Brain: A Study in Nineteenth-Century Thought and Culture* (Princeton University Press, 1987), 4–5.

8 William Keach, "'Words Are Things': Romantic Ideology and the Matter of Poetic Language," in *Aesthetics and Ideology*, ed. George Levine (New Brunswick: Rutgers University Press, 1994), 221.

9 For "organic" used in this sense, compare Coleridge's 1817 fragment "On Animal Magnetism": "no man has yet discovered any organic apparatus for Thought, Passion, Volition – we have discovered the Instrument set in action by them but not the specific organs – but simply this, that in some way or other the whole nervous system is the organ" (*SW* 1: 591).

10 Roy Porter, "Medical Science and Human Science in the Enlightenment," in *Inventing Human Science: Eighteenth-Century Domains*, ed. Christopher Fox, Roy Porter, and Robert Wolker (Berkeley: University of California Press 1995), 53–87.

11 For the term "psychology" and the challenges of discriminating the

"psychological" from among various eighteenth-century discourses of mind, see G. S. Rousseau, "Psychology," in *The Ferment of Knowledge: Studies in the Historiography of Eighteenth-Century Science*, ed. Rousseau and Roy Porter (Cambridge University Press, 1980), 143–210 and Christopher Fox, "Defining Eighteenth-Century Psychology: Some Problems and Perspectives," *Psychology and Literature in the Eighteenth Century*, ed. Fox (New York: AMS Press 1987), 1–22. I have summarized the problems with and defended the continuing usefulness of the term "Romanticism" in *Literature, Education, and Romanticism: Reading as Social Practice, 1780–1832* (Cambridge University Press, 1994), 3–4.

12 M. H. Abrams states in his classic study *The Mirror and the Lamp* (Oxford University Press, 1953) that the "Copernican revolution in epistemology" associated with Kant and the "concept that the perceiving mind discovers what it has itself partly made" was independently "effected in England by poets and critics before it manifested itself in academic philosophy" (58). This basic point has been often restated since: for example, Joel Black's remark that the "Kantian revolution" had its "literary counterpart" among English and German Romantic writers in "Newtonian Mechanics and the Romantic Rebellion: Introduction," in *Beyond the Two Cultures: Science, Technology, and Literature*, ed. Joseph W. Slade and Judith Yaroll Lee (Ames: Iowa State University Press, 1990), 134. What seems to have been consistently overlooked is that this "revolution" was simultaneously taking place in contemporary brain science, in Germany, Britain, and France, and that the international scientific culture of the era may have facilitated the transmission of "active mind" conceptions across several European traditions.

13 Mary A. B. Brazier, "The Evolution of Concepts Relating to the Electrical Activity of the Nervous System 1600–1800," in *The History and Philosophy of Knowledge of the Brain*, ed. F. N. L. Poynter (Oxford: Blackwell, 1958), 191–222. For the significance of Galvani's experiments in their bearing on the central nervous system, see John D. Spillane, *The Doctrine of the Nerves: Chapters in the History of Medicine* (Oxford University Press, 1981), 111; Eric T. Carlson and Meribeth M. Simpson, "Models of the Nervous System in Eighteenth Century Psychiatry," *Bulletin of the History of Medicine* 43 (1969), 111; and Reed, *From Soul to Mind*, 13–14.

14 John Frederick William Herschel, *Preliminary Discourse on the Study of Natural Philosophy* (1830; rpt. University of Chicago Press, 1987), 342–43.

15 Brazier, *Evolution of Concepts*, 215.

16 G. S. Rousseau, "Nerves, Spirits, and Fibres: Towards Defining the Origins of Sensibility," in *Studies in the Eighteenth Century 3: Papers Presented at the Third David Nichol Smith Memorial Seminar, Canberra 1973*, ed. R. F. Brissenden and J. C. Eade (University of Toronto Press, 1976), 144.

17 Rousseau, "Nerves," 145, 154–55, 157.

18 Isobel Armstrong, "The Gush of the Feminine: How Can We Read Women's Poetry of the Romantic Period?" in *Romantic Women Writers: Voices*

and Countervoices, ed. Paula R. Feldman and Theresa M. Kelley (Hanover: University Press of New England, 1995), 27–28.

19 Jerome J. McGann, *The Poetics of Sensibility: A Revolution in Literary Style* (Oxford: Clarendon, 1996), 18.

20 On Hartley as the first physiological psychologist, see Benjamin Rand, "The Early Development of Hartley's Doctrine of Association," *Psychological Review* 30 (1923): 306–20.

21 David Hartley, *Observations on Man*, 2 vols. (1749; rpt. Hildesheim: Olms, 1967), 1: 5–8, 60–1. Hereafter cited in the text. For useful accounts of Hartley's model of mental functioning, see Carlson and Simpson, "Models of the Nervous System in Eighteenth-Century Psychiatry," 109–10 and Stanley Jackson, "Force and Kindred Notions in Eighteenth-Century Neurophysiology and Medical Psychology," *Bulletin of the History of Medicine* 44 (1970): 404–8.

22 John Thelwall, *Poems Written Chiefly in Retirement* (1801; rpt. Oxford: Woodstock, 1989), xxii–xxiii. See also Cooter, *Cultural Meaning*, 209.

23 Quoted in John W. Yolton, *Thinking Matter: Materialism in Eighteenth-Century Britain* (Minneapolis: University of Minnesota Press 1983), 113.

24 Clarke and Jacyna, *Nineteenth-Century Origins*, 157–60; Reed, *From Soul to Mind*, 39.

25 For the parallel between Hartley and Hebbs, see Richards, *Mental Machinery*, 151. John Sutton discusses "Hartley's neurophilosophy" more broadly in relation to connectionism and neural network theories, *Philosophy and Memory Traces, Descartes to Connectionism* (Cambridge University Press, 1998), 248–59.

26 Thomas Reid, *Essays on the Intellectual Powers of Man*, ed. Baruch A. Brody (Cambridge: MIT Press, 1969), 88.

27 Sutton provides a pointed discussion of Coleridge's objections to Hartley in *Philosophy and Memory Traces*, 233–34.

28 This is a criticism sometimes leveled today at connectionist theories of cognition by those who characterize them in terms of a "new associationism." See, for example, Hilary Putnam, "Against the New Associationism," in *Speaking Minds: Interviews with Twenty Eminent Cognitive Scientists*, ed. Peter Baumgartner and Sabine Payr (Princeton University Press, 1995), 177–88.

29 According to Desmond King-Hele, Darwin's own experiments with electrotherapy led him to believe that "nerve impulses were electrical," but he never pursued or elaborated this notion, *Erasmus Darwin and the Romantic Poets* (New York: St. Martin's Press 1986), 16.

30 [George Canning *et al.*], "The Loves of the Triangles: A Mathematical and Philosophical Poem, Inscribed to Dr Darwin," *Anti-Jacobin, or Weekly Examiner*, 4th rev. edn., 2 volumes (London: J. Wright, 1799), 2: 162–64, 200–5, 274–80. The satire was initially published in three installments dated April 16, April 23, and May 7, 1798. The third installment begins by mocking Darwin's enthusiasm for Galvani's theory of neural transmission: "Thrills with *Galvanic* fire each tortuous nerve, / Throb her blue veins, and dies her cold reserve" (2: 275).

31 Thomas Brown, *Observations on the Zoonomia of Erasmus Darwin, M. D.* (Edinburgh: J. Mundell, J. Johnson, and J. Wright, 1798), xvi-xx. At best, Brown argued, Darwin's murky "spirit of animation" represented a waffling desire to have it both ways: "We shall be at once materialists and immaterialists, libertarians and necessarians, phlogistians and anti-phlogistians" (11).

32 Christopher Lawrence, "The Power and the Glory: Humphry Davy and Romanticism," in *Romanticism and the Sciences*, ed. Andrew Cunningham and Nicholas Jardine (Cambridge University Press, 1990), 223.

33 McNeil, *Under the Banner*, 80–85.

34 This notion returns to philosophy of mind and neuroscience in what Mark Johnson calls the "body in the mind" and Antonio Damasio the "body-minded brain." Mark Johnson, *The Body in the Mind: The Bodily Basis of Meaning, Imagination, and Reason* (University of Chicago Press, 1987); Damasio, *Descartes' Error*, 223–44.

35 Julien Offray de La Mettrie, *Machine Man and Other Writings*, ed. and trans. Ann Thomson (Cambridge University Press, 1996), 15, 26. For Cabanis and French intellectual traditions, see Martin S. Staum, *Cabanis: Enlightenment and Medical Philosophy in the French Revolution* (Princeton University Press, 1980); Elizabeth A. Williams, *The Physical and the Moral: Anthropology, Physiology, and Philosophical Medicine in France, 1750–1850* (Cambridge University Press, 1994); and Sergio Moravio, "From *Homme Machine* to *Homme Sensible*: Changing Eighteenth-Century Models of Man's Image," *Journal of the History of Ideas* 39 (1979): 45–60.

36 An overview of Cabanis' ideas was published as part of a review of the *Mémoires de l'Institut National* in the *Monthly Review*, new series, 34 (1801): 302.

37 Porter, "Medical Science," 69–70.

38 One can read in Cabanis' critique of the mechanical man an almost uncanny anticipation of the quarrel between a "strong AI" approach to cognition (the "hardware" doesn't matter) and those that insist on the embodied and organic nature of the "wet mind." For an introduction to this debate, see Terence J. Sejnowski, "The Hardware Really Does Matter," in *Speaking Minds*, ed. Baumgartner and Payr, 215–30.

39 The continuities between Gall and Cabanis are usefully discussed by Williams, *Physical and Moral*, 105–10.

40 Harrington notes that Gall's division of the mind-brain into functionally and anatomically distinct organs was in part a response to the "sensorium commune" problem run up against in assocationist psychology, *Medicine, Mind, and the Double Brain*, 7–9.

41 On the importance of adaptation for Gall's thought, see Young, *Mind, Brain, and Adaptation*.

42 Francis Jeffrey, review of George Combe, *A System of Phrenology*, *Edinburgh Review* 88 (1826): 256. Hereafter cited in the text.

43 Thomas Brown, review of *A Letter from Charles Villier to Georges Cuvier*, *Edinburgh Review* 2 (1803): 147; [John Gordon,] review of F. J. Gall and G.

Spurzheim, *Anatomie et Physiologie du Système Nerveux en général, et du Cerveau en particulier, Edinburgh Review* 25 (1815): 227–68.

44 Review of [Henry Crabb Robinson], *Some Account of Dr. Gall's New Theory of Physiognomy, Monthly Review* 55 (1808): 36–39; review of J. G. Spurzheim, *The Physiognomical System of Doctors Gall and Spurzheim, Monthly Review* 78 (1815): 147–65; review of J. G. Spurzheim, *Observations sur la Phrenologie, Monthly Review* 94 (1821): 517–26; for the *Quarterly Review* see note 48 below.

45 M. A., "The Craniological Controversy: Some Observations on the Late Pamphlets of Dr Gordon and Dr Spurzheim," *Blackwood's Edinburgh Magazine* 1 (1817): 35; Peter Morris, "On the Nature of the Imitative Principle, and Some Other Faculties, Pointed out by Gall and Spurzheim," *Blackwood's Edinburgh Magazine* 6 (1819): 309–14; "Essays on Cranioscopy, Craniology, Phrenology, etc., by Sir Toby Tickletoby, Bart.," *Blackwood's Edinburgh Magazine* 10 (1821): 73–82; "Essays on Phrenology, etc.," *Blackwood's Edinburgh Magazine* 10 (1821): 682–91; "Anti-Phrenologia; a Plain Statement of Objections against the System of Drs Gall and Spurzheim," *Blackwood's Edinburgh Magazine* 13 (1823): 100–8, 199–206.

46 For a full bibliographical account of articles on Gall, Spurzheim, and the phrenology movement pro and con, see Roger Cooter, *Phrenology in the British Isles: An Annotated, Historical Biobibliography and Index* (Metuchen: Scarecrow Press, 1989).

47 Hazlitt's anti-phrenological essays include "On Dr. Spurzheim's Theory," published in *The Plain Speaker* in 1826 (*HW* 12: 137–56); and two essays published in *The Atlas* in 1829, "Burke and the Edinburgh Phrenologists" (*HW* 20: 200–4) and "Phrenological Fallacies" (*HW* 20: 248–53).

48 Review of J.G. Spurzheim, *The Physiognomical System of Doctors Gall and Spurzheim, founded on an Anatomical and Physiological Examination of the Nervous System in general, and of the Brain in particular, and indicating the Dispositions and Manifestations of the Mind, Quarterly Review* 13 (1815): 173; John Gordon, review of F. J. Gall and G. Spurzheim, *Anatomie et Physiologie du Système Nerveux en général, et du Cerveau en particulier, Edinburgh Review* 25 (1815): 232, 245.

49 An anonymous pamphlet entitled *Sir William Hamilton and Phrenology* (Edinburgh, 1826), cited in Cooter, *Cultural Meaning*, 40.

50 Marilyn Butler, "Introduction" and "Appendix C" to Mary Shelley, *Frankenstein or The Modern Prometheus: The 1818 Text* (Oxford University Press, 1993), ix–li, 229–51.

51 *The Radical Triumvarite* is a pamphlet of 1820 mentioned by Butler, "Introduction" (230); *Thought, Not a Function of the Brain: A Reply to the Arguments for Materialism Advanced by W. Lawrence, in his Lectures on Physiology* (London, Rivington, 1827).

52 William Lawrence, *An Introduction to Comparative Anatomy and Physiology; Being the Two Introductory Lectures Delivered at the Royal College of Surgeons, On the 21st and 25th of March, 1816* (London: J. Callow, 1816), 115 (see also *LPZ* 7). Lawrence seems to be drawing on Priestley, who argues that the "powers of sensation and perception, and thought, as belonging to man, have never

been found but in conjunction with a certain *organized system of matter*; and therefore, that those powers necessarily exist in, and depend upon, such a system." Joseph Priestley, *Disquisitions Relating to Matter and Spirit* (London: J. Johnson, 1777), 26.

53 [D'Oyley, George], Review of John Abernethy, *An Enquiry into the Probability and Rationality of Mr. Hunter's Theory of Life*, etc., *Quarterly Review* 22 (1819): 1. Hereafter cited in the text.

54 Later in the essay Coleridge uses "Darwinian flight" as a synonym for irresponsible evolutionary theorizing (*SW* 1: 542).

55 Reed, *From Soul to Mind*, 14; Cooter, *Cultural Meaning*, 63–200.

56 Carlile in *The Republican* 11 (22 April 1825), cited in Cooter, *Cultural Meaning*, 208. For Carlile's printing of Lawrence's lectures (initially in "twice-weekly numbers at threepence each,") see Hugh J. Luke, Jr., "Sir William Lawrence: Physician to Shelley and Mary," *Papers on Language and Literature* 1 (1965): 150–52. According to Luke, "as late as 1840 James Watson, shopman of Richard Carlile and a leader of the Chartist Movement, was issuing an excerpt from the *Lectures* entitled *Facts versus Fiction! An Essay on the Functions of the Brain*" (152).

57 Review of Charles Bell, *An Exposition of the Natural System of the Nerves of the Human Body*, *Edinburgh Review* 47 (1828): 444, 446, 480.

58 Darwin is called a "materialist (even if vitalist) thinker" by Gary Hatfield in "Remaking the Science of Mind: Psychology as Natural Science," in Fox, et al., *Inventing Human Science*, 209. Staum describes Cabanis as "closer to panpsychism" than "mechanical materialism," though remarking that Cabanis was usually labelled a materialist. Staum also notes, however, that in the thought of Cabanis, "mechanism" and "vitalism" can be seen converging (*Cabanis*, 7, 49, 179). Some recent work on Romanticism and science has been hampered by confusion regarding the terms "vitalism," "materialism," and "mechanism," no two of which can be opposed (and no one of which can be defined) in any simple manner. See, for example, the confusing account of Lawrence's views which aligns vitalism and biology on the one hand against materialism and mechanism on the other (rendering even a rudimentary understanding of Lawrence's biological materialism impossible), in D. L. Macdonald and Kathleen Scherf, "Introduction" to Mary Shelley, *Frankenstein: Or, The Modern Prometheus*, 2nd edn. (Peterborough: Broadview Press, 1999), 18–20.

59 Brown, *Observations*, 9–10.

60 Charles Bell, *Idea of a New Anatomy of the Brain: A Facsimile of the Privately Printed Edition of 1811 With a Bio-Bibliographical Introduction* (London: Dawsons, 1966), 3. Hereafter cited in the text.

61 Everard Home had already described the nerves as bundles or "fasicules" of fibres in his Croonian lecture on "Experiments and Observations on the Structure of the Nerves" published in the *Philosophical Transactions* for 1799 (89: 1–12). "These experiments show," he summarized, "that the nerves do not consist of tubes conveying a fluid, but of fibres of a peculiar kind, differ-

ent from everything else in the body, with which we are acquainted. The course of these fibres is very curious; they appear to be constantly passing from one fasiculus to another, so as to connect all the fasculi together by a mixture of fibres" (12).

62 Cf. Karl M. Figlio, "Theories of Perception and the Physiology of Mind in the Late Eighteenth Century," *History of Science* 12 (1975): 177–79.

63 William Wordsworth, "Prospectus" to *The Recluse*, lines 63–71.

64 Frederick Burwick, "Sir Charles Bell and the Vitalist Controversy in the Early Nineteenth Century," in *The Crisis in Modernism: Bergson and the Vitalist Controversy*, ed. Burwick and Paul Douglass (Cambridge University Press, 1992), 121.

65 Clarke and Jacyna, *Nineteenth-Century Origins*, 1–2, 229–31.

66 Clarke and Jacyna, *Nineteenth-Century Origins*, 20–1, 39.

67 Erwin H. Ackerknecht, "Contributions of Gall and the Phrenologists to Knowledge of Brain Function," *The History and Philosophy of Knowledge of the Brain*, ed. Poynter, 149–53.

68 Clarke and Jacyna, *Nineteenth-Century Origins*, 33–34.

69 "Ham-slicing" is Acherknechts memorable phrase ("Contributions," 151). According to Clarke and Jacyna, neuroanatomy retains a "romantic" character to this day (*Nineteenth-Century Origins*, 56).

70 Jason Y. Hall, "Gall's Phrenology: A Romantic Psychology," *Studies in Romanticism* 16 (1977): 306, 312–15. Hall's pioneering essay on Gall and Burwick's equally unprecedented essay on Bell (see note 64) represent the two most important attempts to date to explore links between literary Romanticism and the neuroscience of the period.

71 Burwick, "Bell," 121; Staum, *Cabanis*, 176.

72 Robert Darnton, *Mesmerism and the End of the Enlightenment in France* (Cambridge: Harvard University Press, 1968), 127, 156.

73 Stefano Poggi, "Neurology and Biology in the Romantic Age in Germany: Carus, Burdach, Gall, von Baer," in *Romanticism in Science: Science in Europe, 1790–1840*, ed. Poggi and Maurizio Bossi (Dordrecht: Kluwer Academic Publishers, 1994), 143–60. See also the essays collected in *Romanticism and the Sciences*, ed. Cunningham and Jardine.

74 Simon Schaffer, "Self Evidence," *Critical Inquiry* 18 (1992): 360.

75 Trevor Levere, "S. T. Coleridge and the Human Sciences: Anthropology, Phrenology, and Mesmerism," in *Science, Pseudo-Science and Society*, ed. Marsha P. Hanen, Margaret J. Osler, and Robert G. Weyant (Waterloo: Wilfrid Laurier University Press, 1980), 171–92.

76 [Henry Crabb Robinson], *Some Account of Dr. Gall's New Theory of Physiognomy, Founded upon the Anatomy and Physiology of the Brain, and the Form of the Skull* (London: Longman, Hurst, Rees, and Orme, 1807). For Robinson's claim of authorship, see the *Diary, Reminiscences, and Correspondence of Henry Crabb Robinson*, ed. Thomas Sadler, 2 vols. (Boston: Fields, Osgood, 1869), 1: 141; in fact much of the work was translated by Robinson from a German work by Christian Heinrich Ernst Bischoff.

77 King-Hele, *Erasmus Darwin and the Romantic Poets*, 39; Reed, *From Soul to Mind*, 41.

78 G. S. Rousseau and Roy Porter, "Introduction: Toward a Natural History of Mind and Body," in *The Languages of Psyche: Mind and Body in Enlightenment Thought*, ed. G. S. Rousseau (Berkeley: University of California Press, 1990), 32–33; King-Hele, *Erasmus Darwin*.

79 See Anne K. Mellor, *Mary Shelley: Her Life, Her Fiction, Her Monsters* (New York: Methuen, 1988), 89–114 and Butler, "Introduction."

80 For Percy Shelley's interest in contemporary science and medicine, see Carl Grabo, *A Newton Among Poets: Shelley's Use of Science in Prometheus Unbound* (Chapel Hill: University of North Carolina Press 1930) and Nora Crook and Derek Guiton, *Shelley's Venomed Melody* (Cambridge University Press, 1986).

81 Reed, *From Soul to Mind*, 38–59.

82 Donald C. Goellnicht, *The Poet-Physician: Keats and Medical Science* (University of Pittsburgh Press, 1984); Hermione De Almeida, *Romantic Medicine and John Keats* (New York: Oxford University Press, 1991).

83 On Baillie's family, see Dorothy McMillan, "'Dr' Baillie," in *1798: The Year of the Lyrical Ballads*, ed. Richard Cronin (Houndmills: Macmillan, 1998), 68–92. On Baillie and Matthew Baillie's neuropathology, see Frederick Burwick, "The Romantic Drama," in *A Companion to Romanticism*, ed. Wu, 329, and Janice Patten, "Joanna Baillie, *A Series of Plays*," *A Companion to Romanticism*, 169–78.

84 Richards, *Mental Machinery*, 124, 243.

2 COLERIDGE AND THE NEW UNCONSCIOUS

1 Allan Paivio, "The Mind's Eye in Arts and Science," *Poetics* 12 (1983), 16.

2 Steven Pinker, *The Language Instinct: How the Mind Creates Language* (New York: Harper, 1994), 70. Quotations from the relevant poems and Coleridge's introductory notice follow the facsimile reprint of the 1816 edition of *Christabel: Kubla Kahn, A Vision; The Pains of Sleep*, ed. Jonathan Wordsworth (Oxford: Woodstock Books, 1991).

3 Margaret A. Boden, *The Creative Mind: Myths and Mechanisms* (New York: Basic Books, 1990), 18–19.

4 Sir David Brewster, "The Connexion of Intellectual Operations with Organic Action," *Quarterly Review* 45 (1831): 357.

5 For discussions of Coleridge's interest in contemporary medicine and science, see John Harris, "Coleridge's Readings in Medicine," *The Wordsworth Circle*, 3 (1972): 85–95; Trevor Levere, *Poetry Realized in Nature: Samuel Taylor Coleridge and Early Nineteenth-Century Science* (Cambridge University Press, 1981); Ian Wylie, *Young Coleridge and the Philosophers of Nature* (Oxford: Clarendon Press, 1989); Marilyn Gaull, "Coleridge and the Kingdoms of the World," *The Wordsworth Circle*, 22 (1991): 47–52; and Jennifer Ford, *Coleridge on Dreaming: Romanticism, Dreams, and the Medical Imagination* (Cambridge University Press, 1998).

6 Among the few known to have read the poem or heard Coleridge recite it are Mary Robinson (who had herself written a poem, "The Maniac," in an opium-induced reverie), Charles Lamb, Lord Byron (a recitation just missed by Leigh Hunt) and, almost certainly, William and Dorothy Wordsworth. See Elisabeth Schneider, *Coleridge, Opium, and Kubla Khan* (University of Chicago Press, 1953), 22, 83, 216; Molly Lefebure, *Samuel Taylor Coleridge: A Bondage of Opium* (London: Victor Gollancz, 1974), 254; and Edmund Blunden, *Leigh Hunt: A Biography* (London: Cobden-Sanderson, 1930), 93–94.

7 For a pioneering account of Coleridge's early interest in the theories of Darwin, Priestley, and other radical scientists, see H. W. Piper, *The Active Universe: Pantheism and the Concept of Imagination in the English Romantic Poets* (London: Athlone Press, 1962), 29–51.

8 This distancing strategy is noted by both K. M. Wheeler, *The Creative Mind in Coleridge's Poetry* (Cambridge: Harvard University Press, 1981), 12–13 and Jerome Christensen, *Coleridge's Blessed Machine of Language* (Ithaca: Cornell University Press, 1981), 63–4.

9 See the discussion in chapter one, above. In his useful discussion of the letter to Godwin, J. A. Appleyard argues that "organic" would have had "no special meaning" for Coleridge in 1801 but would connote instead the "physiological functioning of an organ, as in the Hartleyan system," *Coleridge's Philosophy of Literature: The Development of a Concept of Poetry* (Cambridge: Harvard University Press, 1965), 81. James McKusick, in his important book on Coleridge and language, reads "organic" in terms of the "materialistic" linguistic theories being advanced at the time, *Coleridge's Philosophy of Language* (New Haven: Yale University Press, 1986), 41. Neither mentions the crucial significance of terms like "organ" and "organic" in the brain science of the time.

10 Trevor H. Levere, "S. T. Coleridge and the Human Sciences: Anthropology, Phrenology, and Mesmerism," in *Science, Pseudo-Science and Society*, ed. Marsha P. Hanen, Margaret J. Osler, and Robert G. Weyant (Waterloo: Wilfrid Laurier University Press, 1980), 182–84.

11 By Spurzheim's "Anatomical Demonstrations of the Brain" Coleridge is almost certainly referring not to a book (there is no such title by Spurzheim) but to one of the public dissections or "demonstrations" frequently exhibited by Spurzheim and other phrenologists in London and elsewhere in Britain.

12 *Table Talk*, ed. Carl Woodring, 2 vols. (London and New York: Routledge & Kegan Paul, Princeton University Press, 1990), 1: 183, hereafter *TT*.

13 In a letter to Thelwall a year later, Coleridge calls Darwin the "first *literary* character in Europe, and the most original-minded man" (*STCL* 1: 305–6).

14 John Beer, *Coleridge's Poetic Intelligence* (London: MacMillan, 1977), 70–94. Coleridge can also be found sparring with Matthew Baillie, for his high opinion of Gall and Spurzheim (*TT* 1: 184), and with Charles Bell, who confounds "stimulability with sensibility" (*SW* 2: 1426), in his *obiter dicta* and

unpublished writings. The overall picture is clear: Coleridge was an avid and critical reader of contemporary brain science.

15 Graham Richards, *Mental Machinery: The Origins and Consequences of Psychological Ideas*, Part 1: *1600–1850* (Baltimore: Johns Hopkins University Press, 1992), 128.

16 Thomas MacFarland, *Coleridge and the Pantheist Tradition* (Oxford: Clarendon, 1969), 187. On Coleridge's specific debts to German science, idealism, and *natürphilosophie*, see also Levere, *Poetry Realized in Nature*, and Raimonda Modiano, *Coleridge and the Concept of Nature* (Tallahassee: Florida State University Press, 1985).

17 See especially David Miall, "The Meaning of Dreams: Coleridge's Ambivalence," *Studies in Romanticism*, 21 (1982): 57–87; "Coleridge on Emotion: Experience into Theory," *The Wordsworth Circle*, 22 (1991): 35–39; and "'I see it feelingly': Coleridge's Debt to Hartley," *Coleridge's Visionary Languages: Essays in Honor of J. B. Beer*, ed. Tim Fulford and Morton D. Paley (Cambridge: Brewster, 1993), 151–63. See also Daniel Sanjiv Roberts, "Exorcising the Malay: Dreams and the Unconscious in Coleridge and De Quincey," *The Wordsworth Circle* 24 (1993): 91–96 and Ford, *Coleridge on Dreaming*, 51–3.

18 See my essay "Romanticism, the Unconscious, and the Brain" in *Romantic Prose*, ed. Virgil Nemoainu and Steven Sondrup, a forthcoming volume of the *Comparative History of Literatures in European Languages*.

19 The 1801 account of Cabanis' views in the *Monthly Review* stressed this very point: "The result of his chain of reasoning is that sleep, as well as thought, is produced by a real and peculiar action of the brain," review of *Mémoires de l'Institut National*, 302.

20 *The Botanic Garden*, book III, line 74; from *The Poetical Works of Erasmus Darwin, M.D., F.R.S.*, 3 vols. (London: J. Johnson, 1806).

21 See especially Henri Ellenberger, *The Discovery of the Unconscious: The History and Evolution of Dynamic Psychiatry* (New York: Basic Books, 1970) and Catherine Belsey, "The Romantic Construction of the Unconscious," in *Literature, Politics, and Theory: Papers from the Essex Conference 1976–84*, ed. Francis Barker *et al.* (London: Methuen, 1986), 57–76.

22 Coleridge, *Lectures 1808–19 on Literature*, ed. R. A. Foakes, 2 vols (London and New York: Routledge & Kegan Paul, Princeton University Press, 1987) 2: 266, hereafter *LL*. See also Schneider, *Coleridge, Opium*, 95–97.

23 Hazlitt writes similarly in his intriguing essay "On Dreams" that the "bundles of thought are, as it were, untied, loosened from a common centre, and drift along the stream of fancy as it happens" (*HW* 12: 20). Although Hazlitt begins this essay by dismissing the "disgusting cant" of Gall and Spurzheim, he agrees with contemporary brain science – and Coleridge – that in dreaming the "voluntary power is suspended" and speculates that the vividness of dreams is "rather physical than mental," an "effervesence of the blood or of the brain, physically acting" on the dreaming mind (*HW* 12: 19, 22–23).

24 This striking image occurs in a passage on the difference between waking and dreaming in a letter to Sara Hutchinson dated 6 August 1802: "if this Reality were a Dream, if I were asleep, what agonies had I suffered! what screams! – When the Reason & the Will are away, what remain to us but Darkness & Dimness & a bewildering Shame, and Pain that is utterly Lord over us, or fantastic Pleasure, that draws the Soul along swimming through the air in many shapes, even as a Flight of Starlings in a Wind" (*STCL* 2: 842).

25 Coleridge's interest in physiological accounts of dreaming and in medical approaches to the imagination are helpfully discussed by Ford, *Coleridge on Dreaming*, 159–202.

26 In addition to the essays mentioned in note 17, see Miall, "The Body in Literature: Mark Johnson, Metaphor, and Feeling," *Journal of Literary Semantics* 26 (1997): 191–210.

27 John Mackenzie Robertson, *New Essays Towards a Critical Method* (London: John Lane, 1897), 140, 190.

28 George Combe, *Essays on Phrenology, or, An Inquiry Into the Principles and Utility of the System of Drs. Gall and Spurzheim, and Into the Objections Made Against It*, ed. John Bell (Philadelphia: Carey and Lea, 1822), 93.

29 Kenneth Burke, *Language as Symbolic Action: Essays on Life, Literature, and Method* (Berkeley: University of California Press, 1966), 218.

30 Wheeler, *Creative Mind*, 26.

31 Desmond King-Hele, *Erasmus Darwin and the Romantic Poets*, 92–93.

32 Julien Offray de La Mettrie, *Machine Man*, 6.

33 Jack Stillinger, *Coleridge and Textual Instability: The Multiple Versions of the Major Poems* (New York: Oxford University Press, 1994), 78.

34 Suzanne R. Hoover, "Coleridge, Humphry Davy, and Some Early Experiments with a Consciousness-altering Drug," *Bulletin of Research in the Humanities* 81 (1978): 10.

35 Jan Golinski, *Science as Public Culture*, 168.

36 Hoover, "Coleridge, Humphry Davy," 14.

37 Golinski, *Science as Public Culture*, 172.

38 Lawrence, "Power and the Glory," 223.

39 Hoover, "Coleridge, Humphry Davy," 19, 22.

40 Simon Schaffer, "Self Evidence," 358–59.

41 Combe, *Letter from George Combe to Francis Jeffrey, Esq. in Answer to His Criticism on Phrenology, Contained in No. LXXXVIII of the Edinburgh Review* (Edinburgh: John Anderson, 1826), 29.

42 Robertson, *New Essays*, 187; cf. Eli Marcovitz, "Bemoaning the Lost Dream: Coleridge's 'Kubla Khan' and Addiction," *International Journal of Psychoanalysis* 45 (1964): 411–25.

43 John Livingston Lowes, *The Road to Xanadu: A Study in the Ways of the Imagination* (Boston: Houghton Mifflin, 1927), 423.

44 Schneider, *Coleridge, Opium*, 90; Norman Fruman, *Coleridge, the Damaged Archangel* (New York: George Braziller, 1971), 349.

45 Lefebure, *Samuel Taylor Coleridge*, 254.

46 Wheeler, *Creative Mind*, 23.

47 Fruman, *Coleridge*, 336. David Perkins points out that in describing "Kubla Khan" as a dream poem Coleridge would not, as some critics have assumed, have minimized its "import" but rather the opposite, given the new attention being paid to dreams and dreaming at the time; see "The Imaginative Vision of *Kubla Khan*: On Coleridge's Introductory Note," in *Coleridge, Keats, and the Imagination: Romanticism and Adam's Dream; Essays in Honor of Walter Jackson Bate*, ed. John L. Mahoney and J. Robert Barth, S.J. (Columbia: University of Missouri Press, 1990), 104. Perkins does not, however, consider the philosophical and ideological issues at stake, instead arguing that Coleridge included the introductory notice largely for esthetic reasons.

48 Beer, *Coleridge's Poetic Intelligence*, 118.

49 Ironically, Coleridge himself at times made use of secretion and digestion metaphors in discussing mind and thought. In a note added to his tranlation, in the *Biographia*, of a passage from Herder, he writes, for example, that "what medical physiologists affirm of certain secretions, applies equally to our thoughts; they too must be taken up into the circulation, and be again and again re-secreted to ensure a healthful vigor, both to the mind and to its intellectual offspring" (*BL* 1: 231). M. H. Abrams gathers a number of related metaphors (including digestion, as in "the Mind must in turn assimilate and digest the food which it thus receives from without") in his helpful discussion of Coleridge's recourse to recent developments in biology and physiology in his figures for mind and imagination, not least in his distinction between "organ" and "machine," *The Mirror and the Lamp*, 169–73.

50 Lefebure, *Samuel Taylor Coleridge*, 257.

51 I discuss the changing valence of the word "brain" in English poetry in chapter 5, below. For the reception of the 1816 volume, see Jonathan Wordsworth's introduction to the *Christabel* facsimile reprint.

52 Wheeler, *Creative Mind*, 38; Reuven Tsur, *The Road to Kubla Khan: A Cognitive Approach* (Jerusalem: Israel Science Publishers, 1987), 74.

53 Beer, *Coleridge's Poetic Intelligence*, 118; Burke, *Language*, 208–9.

54 Wheeler, *Creative Mind*, 26.

55 Peretz Lavie and J. Allan Hobson, "Origin of Dreams: Anticipations of Modern Theories in the Philosophy and Physiology of the Eighteenth and Nineteenth Centuries," *Psychological Bulletin* 100 (1986): 230.

56 Jonathan Miller, "Going Unconscious," *New York Review of Books*, April 20, 1995, 64.

57 Lancelot Law Whyte, *The Unconscious Before Freud* (New York: Basic Books, 1960), 117.

58 Denis Diderot, *Rameau's Nephew and Other Works*, trans. Jacques Barzun and Ralph H. Bowen (Indianapolis: Bobbs-Merrill, 1964), 155, 162.

59 *De Quincey's Works*, ed. David Masson, 14 vols. (Edinburgh: A. and C. Black, 1896–97), 10: 390; *HW* 8: 31–2, 35; William Godwin, *Thoughts on Man, His*

Nature, Productions, and Discoveries (London: Effingham Wilson, 1831), 152, 159.

60 Sandra Gilbert and Susan Gubar, "The Mirror and the Vamp: Reflections on Feminist Criticism," in *The Future of Literary Theory*, ed. Ralph Cohen (New York: Routledge, 1989), 162.

61 Gilbert and Gubar, "Mirror," 162; Marcowitz, "Lost Dream," 414; Eugene Sloane, "Coleridge's *Kubla Khan*: The Living Catacombs of the Mind," *American Imago* 29 (1972): 106–7; Fruman, *Coleridge*, 400.

62 Gilbert and Gubar, "Mirror," 160; William Benzon, "Articulate Vision: A Structuralist Reading of 'Kubla Khan,'" *Language and Style* 18 (1985): 11.

63 Wheeler, *Creative Mind*, 34; Burke, *Language*, 206.

64 Sloane, III; Marcowitz, 416.

65 Wheeler, *Creative Mind*, 26; Gilbert and Gubar, "Mirror," 163; M. W. Rowe, "'Kubla Khan' and the Structure of the Psyche," *English* 41 (1992): 150; Fruman, *Coleridge*, 399.

66 Benzon, "Articulate Vision," 10; Gilbert and Gubar, "Mirror," 161; Marcowitz, "Lost Dream," 414.

67 Tsur, *Road to Kubla Khan*, xxxi.

68 Burke, *Language*, 210, 220.

69 Links between Freud and Romantic biology and medicine have been posited by Iago Galdston, "Freud and Romantic Medicine," *Bulletin of the History of Medicine* 30 (1956): 489–507; for a broader study, see Frank J. Sulloway, *Freud, Biologist of the Mind: Beyond the Psychoanalytic Legend* (New York: Basic Books, 1983).

70 Burke, *Language*, 220.

71 Darwin, *The Temple of Nature*, book III, lines 167–76.

72 Cabanis adds that "men of letters" are especially subject to these "disturbing" visitations, thanks to the heightened activity of their nerves and brains (*R* 1: 136).

73 Ashton Nichols, "The Anxiety of Species: Toward a Romantic Natural History," *The Wordsworth Circle* 28 (1997): 135.

74 Fruman, *Coleridge*, 401.

75 Schneider, *Coleridge, Opium*, 318, n. 75.

76 Dan J. Stein, "Introduction: Cognitive Science and the Unconsious," and George Lakoff, "How Unconscious Metaphorical Thought Shapes Dreams," in *Cognitive Science and the Unconscious*, ed. Stein (Washington, D.C.: American Psychiatric Press, 1997), 6–7, 89.

77 See, for example, Stephen Kosslyn and Olivier Koenig, *Wet Mind: The New Cognitive Neuroscience* (New York: Free Press, 1992) and Antonio Damasio, *Descartes' Error: Emotion, Reason, and the Human Brain* (New York: Avon, 1994).

78 Burke, *Language*, 221.

79 Burke, *Language*, 221; Gilbert and Gubar, "Mirror," 163.

80 Tsur, *Road to Kubla Khan*, xiii.

81 Perkins, "Imaginative Vision," 103.

82 Stillinger, *Coleridge and Textual Instability*, 74; Wheeler, *Creative Mind*, 41; Perkins, 102–3.
83 Perkins, "Imaginative Vision," 99.
84 Tsur, *Road to Kubla Khan*, 79–81.

3 A BEATING MIND: WORDSWORTH'S POETICS AND THE "SCIENCE OF
FEELINGS"

1 On Churchill's translation of Herder and its reception, see Henri Tronchon, *Le Jeune Edgar Quinet ou L'Aventure d'un Enthousiaste* (Paris: Publications de la Faculté des Lettres de Strasbourg, 1937) and V. Stockley, *German Literature as Known in England 1750–1830* (London: Routledge, 1929), 7, 108–11.
2 *The Letters of William and Dorothy Wordsworth: The Early Years*, ed. Ernest de Selincourt, rev. Chester Shaver (Oxford: Clarendon Press, 1967), 213.
3 Jonathan Wordsworth has speculated about the importance of Wordsworth's period with Coleridge in Göttingen in April, 1799, wondering whether notions of "organic power" and of the active mind that become salient in Wordsworth's verse just at this time may owe something to conversations with Coleridge and in turn to Coleridge's readings in German. If so, Coleridge's request for Herder's volume in November ("Herder's Ideas of the History of the Human race – I do not accurately remember the German title") points to the *Ideen zur Philosophie* as the German work that may have played a part in the April conversations. As Jonathan Wordsworth points out, it is unlikely that Coleridge is thinking at this time in terms of the conception of "organic form" he will later borrow from Schlegel and *natürphilosphie*, so the different but equally suggestive notion of "organic" ("*organische*") development in Herder's *Ideen*, with its analogues in English materialist and quasi-materialist thought, becomes all the more noteworthy. Jonathan Wordsworth, "As with the Silence of the Thought," in *High Romantic Argument: Essays for M. H. Abrams*, ed. Lawrence Lipking (Ithaca: Cornell University Press, 1981), 62–64.
4 See Richards, *Mental Machinery*, esp. 198–99.
5 H. W. Piper, *The Active Universe*, 60, 115. See also David Miall, "Wordsworth and *The Prelude*: The Problematics of Feeling," *Studies in Romanticism* 31 (1992): 233–53. For Wordsworth's radical and revolutionary contacts, see Nicholas Roe, *Wordsworth and Coleridge: The Radical Years* (Oxford: Clarendon Press, 1988).
6 For Wordsworth and Darwin, see James Averill, "Wordsworth and 'Natural Science': The Poetry of 1798," *Journal of English and Germanic Philology* 77 (1978): 232–46, and Richard Matlak, "Wordsworth's Reading of *Zoonomia* in Early Spring," *The Wordsworth Circle* 21 (1990): 76–81.
7 Priestley, *Disquisitions*, xiii, 27–8. For Wordsworth's reading of Priestley, see Charles Pittman, "An Introduction to Wordsworth's Reading in Science," *Furman Studies* 33 (1950): 55.

8 John Thelwall, *Poems Written Chiefly in Retirement*, xxii–xxiii.
9 Simon Schaffer, "Self Evidence," 359.
10 Basil Willey, *The Eighteenth Century Background* (London: Chatto and Windus, 1940), 149; James Averill, "Wordsworth and 'Natural Science'," 232–46, 239; Duncan Wu, *Wordsworth's Reading 1770–1799*, 45.
11 John Jones, *The Egotistical Sublime: A History of Wordsworth's Imagination* (London: Chatto and Windus, 1954), 9.
12 E. D. Hirsch, Jr., *Wordsworth and Schelling: A Typological Study of Romanticism* (New Haven: Yale University Press, 1960), 1–14; Alan Grob, *The Philosophic Mind: A Study of Wordsworth's Poetry and Thought 1797–1805* (Columbus: Ohio State University Press, 1973), x; Newton P. Stallknecht, *Strange Seas of Thought: Studies in Wordsworth's Philosophy of Man and Nature* (Bloomington: Indiana University Press, 1958), 13; Herbert Read, *Wordsworth: The Clark Lectures* (New York: Jonathan Cape, 1931), 195; John Hodgson, *Wordsworth's Philosophical Poetry, 1797–1814* (Lincoln: University of Nebraska Press, 1980), 35; Arthur Beatty, *Wordsworth: His Doctrine and Art in Their Historical Relations*, 2nd edn (Madison: University of Wisconsin Press, 1962), 121; James Averill, "Wordsworth and 'Natural Science'," 232–46: 235. Alan Bewell, *Wordsworth and the Enlightenment: Nature, Man, and Society in the Experimental Poetry* (New Haven: Yale University Press, 1989), ix; Richard E. Brantley, *Wordsworth's Natural Methodism* (New Haven: Yale University Press, 1975), xi; James K. Chandler, *Wordsworth's Second Nature: A Study of the Poetry and Politics* (University of Chicago Press, 1984), 31–32; Nicholas Roe, *The Politics of Nature: Wordsworth and Some Contemporaries* (New York: St. Martin's Press, 1992), 137.
13 Jones, *Egotistical Sublime*, viii.
14 Jones, *Egotistical Sublime*, 35.
15 Piper, *The Active Universe*, 9–10; Roy Porter, "Medical Science," 57.
16 Paul Hamilton similarly argues (though with a good deal less nuance) that in the "spiritualised" English materialist traditions "shared by Hartley, Priestley, Darwin, and the usual suspects, materialism could be argued not to deny but to give an alternative account of an animated, active universe ostensibly more congenial to, or building a more helpful launching pad for, the idealist adventures of Wordsworth and Coleridge." "A French Connection: From Empiricism to Materialism in Writings by the Shelleys," *Colloquium Helveticum* 25 (1997): 171.
17 Alan Bewell, *Wordsworth and the Enlightenment: Nature, Man and Society in the Experimental Poetry* (New Haven: Yale University Press, 1989), 40–41.
18 McGann, *The Poetics of Sensibility*, 121.
19 [Henry Crabb Robinson], *Some Account*, 24, 33.
20 *Outlines*, 118. This usage is consistent with Priestley, who argues in the *Disquisitions* (1777) that "*perception*, as well as the other powers that are termed *mental*, is the result (whether necessary, or not) of such an organical structure as that of the brain" (*Disquisitions*, xiii–xiv). Blake, in *The Marriage of Heaven and Hell* (1793), contrasts "finite organical perception" with the

visionary apprehension of the "infinite in every thing," *The Complete Poetry and Prose of William Blake*, rev. edn, ed. David V. Erdman (Garden City: Anchor Press, 1982), 38.

21 See the "Preface," note 1, above.

22 For a feminist analysis of this tendency in Wordsworth, see my essay "Romanticism and the Colonization of the Feminine" in *Romanticism and Feminism*, ed. Anne K. Mellor (Bloomington: Indiana University Press, 1988), 13–25.

23 Matlak, "Wordsworth's Reading of Zoonomia," 76–78.

24 Matlak, "Wordsworth's Reading of Zoonomia," 77.

25 Thomas Beddoes, *Hygëia: or Essays Moral and Medical, on the Causes Affecting the Personal State of Our Middling and Affluent Classes*, 3 vols. (Bristol: R. Phillips, 1802–3), 3: 73 (Essay x).

26 Miall, "Wordsworth and *The Prelude*," 237.

27 Wordsworth may have found the phrase "a beating mind" in Shakespeare's *Tempest*, where it is also used to convey the sense of an embodied psyche:

> Sir, I am vex'd;
> Bear with my weakness, my old brain is troubled.
> Be not disturb'd with my infirmity.
> If you be pleas'd, retire into my cell,
> And there repose. A turn or two I'll walk
> To still my beating mind. (4.i.158–63)

28 Thomas Reid, *Essays*, 107–9.

29 See especially Essay vi, "Of the Economy of the Human Body as It Relates to Expression and Character in Painting," in the first edition of Bell, *Essays on the Anatomy of Expression in Painting* (London: Longman, Hurst, Rees, and Orme, 1806), 161–86.

30 Hans Aarsleff, *From Locke to Saussure: Essays on the Study of Language and Intellectual History* (Minneapolis: University of Minnesota Press, 1982), 372–81.

31 A. W. Phinney, "Wordsworth's Winander Boy and Romantic Theories of Language," *The Wordsworth Circle* 18 (1987): 66–82; William Keach, "Romanticism and Language," in *The Cambridge Companion to British Romanticism*, ed. Stuart Curran (Cambridge University Press, 1993), 95–119.

32 Wordsworth, *Prelude*, p. 495.

33 George Lakoff, *Women, Fire, and Dangerous Things: What Categories Reveal about the Mind* (University of Chicago Press, 1987), 154; Eve Sweetser, *From Etymology to Pragmatics: Metaphorical and Cultural Aspects of Semantic Structure* (Cambridge University Press, 1990), 2, 16. Both titles hereafter cited in the text.

34 M. H. Abrams, *The Mirror and the Lamp*, 105.

35 See chapter six, below.

36 John Locke, *An Essay Concerning Human Understanding*, ed. Peter H. Nidditch (Oxford: Clarendon Press, 1975), 43, 405. Hereafter cited in the text.

37 James Harris, *Hermes* (1751; rpt. Menston, England: Scolar Press, 1969), x, 305–6, 330.

38 James Burnet, Lord Monboddo, *Of the Origins and Progress of Language*, 2nd edn, 5 vols. (Edinburgh: J. Balfour, 1774–1809) 1: 81, 159, 207, 489.

39 Monboddo, *Of the Origins*, 1: 481–82.

40 Etienne Bonnot de Condillac, *An Essay on the Origin of Human Knowledge*, trans. Thomas Nugent (1756; rpt. Gainesville: Scholar's Facsimile Reprints, 1971), 51, 58; hereafter cited in the text.

41 Condillac, *Essay*, 172, 174.

42 Jean-Jacques Rousseau, "Essay on the Origin of Languages Which Treats of Melody and Musical Imitation," trans. John H. Moran, *On the Origin of Language*, ed. Moran and Alexander Gode (University of Chicago Press, 1966), 5–6, 12. Hereafter cited in the text.

43 Thomas Reid, *Essays*, 635–36.

44 Thomas Reid, *An Inquiry into the Human Mind, on the Principles of Common Sense* (1785; rpt. Bristol: Thoemmes Antiquarian, 1990), 93.

45 Reid, *Inquiry*, 95.

46 Johann Gottfried Herder, "Essay on the Origin of Language," trans. Alexander Gode, *On the Origin of Language*, ed. John H. Moran and Gode, 99. Hereafter cited in the text.

47 Erasmus Darwin, *Poetical Works* 3: 342 n.

48 Matthew Baillie, *Lectures and Observations on Medicine* (London: Richard Taylor, 1825), 145–46.

49 Joanna Baillie, *The Dramatic and Poetical Works of Joanna Baillie*, 2nd edn (London: Longman, Brown, Green, and Longmans, 1853), 3.

50 For a view of Wordsworth's poetic theory as backward-looking, see Abrams, *Mirror and the Lamp*, 103–4.

51 Stuart Sperry notes that critics are "frequently puzzled" by these connections: see "Wordsworth and the Grounds of Human Consciousness," in *The Cast of Consciousness: Concepts of the Mind in British and American Romanticism*, ed. Beverley Taylor and Robert Bain (New York: Greenwood Press, 1987), 63; McKusick finds Wordsworth's view of poetic meter an "embarrassment" in *Coleridge's Philosophy of Language*, 113.

52 Condillac, *Essay*, 182.

53 Reid, *Essays*, 637.

54 Reid, *Essays*, 787.

55 Darwin, *Poetical Works*, 3: 314.

56 Sperry, "Wordsworth," 66–67, 73–74.

57 Brennan O'Donnell calls attention to the importance of "extrasemantic elements of poetry" for Wordsworth in *The Passion of Meter: A Study of Wordsworth's Metrical Art* (Kent State University Press, 1995), 3.

58 Wordsworth's note to "The Thorn," *Wordsworth's Literary Criticism*, ed. W. J. B. Owen (London: Routledge & Kegan Paul, 1974), 97.

59 W. J. B. Owen argues for a tension or divergence between these two positions in *Wordsworth as Critic* (University of Toronto Press, 1969), 63–64.

60 John Horne Tooke, Επεα Πτεροεντα, *or, the Diversions of Purley*, ed. Richard Taylor, 2 vols. (London: Thomas Tegg, 1829), 1: 61. Hereafter cited in the text.

61 As Stephen K. Land writes, eighteenth-century "theorists of primitivism," by selectively combining previously distinct notions of "organic" language, "vindicated their intuition that the early stages of language were based in emotional responses and constructed largely of picturesque metaphors." "The Silent Poet: An Aspect of Wordsworth's Semantic Theory," *University of Toronto Quarterly* 42 (1973): 158.

62 In addition to Abrams, *Mirror and the Lamp*, see Owen, *Wordsworth as Critic*, 65; Bewell, *Wordsworth and the Enlightenment*, 30, Land, "The Silent Poet", 159, and Frances Ferguson, *Wordsworth: Language as Counter-Spirit* (New Haven: Yale University Press, 1977), 17.

63 Olivia Smith, *The Politics of Language 1791–1819* (Oxford: Clarendon Press, 1984), 213–26.

64 Don Bialostosky, "Coleridge's Interpretation of Wordsworth's Preface to *Lyrical Ballads*," *PMLA* 93 (1978): 912–24.

65 Mark Johnson, *The Body in the Mind*, pp. 68–69. Hereafter cited in the text.

66 McKusick, *Coleridge's Philosophy of Language*, 112.

67 Aarsleff, *Locke to Saussure*, 375.

68 Mark Turner, *Reading Minds: The Study of English in the Age of Cognitive Science* (Princeton University Press, 1991), 1.

69 Turner, *Reading Minds*, 6; cf. Mark Johnson, *Body in the Mind*, 1–2.

70 Reid, *Essays*, 39, 388, 100.

71 Adam Smith, "Considerations Concerning the First Formation of Languages, and the Different Genius of Original and Compounded Languages," appended to *The Theory of Moral Sentiments*, 6th edn (Dublin: Beatty and Johnson, 1777), 393–94; Darwin, *Poetical Works*, 3: 182.

72 On Condillac, see Aarsleff, *Locke to Saussure*, 163–5 and *The Study of Language in England, 1780–1860* (Princeton University Press, 1967), 21–23.

73 John R. Taylor, *Linguistic Categorization: Prototypes in Linguistic Theory*, 2nd edn (Oxford: Clarendon Press, 1995), 135; Sweetser, *Etymology to Pragmatics*, 30.

74 Francisco J. Varela, Evan Thompson, and Eleanor Rosch, *The Embodied Mind: Cognitive Science and Human Experience* (Cambridge: MIT Press, 1991), 177.

75 See also Eleanor Rosch, "Principles of Categorization," in *Cognition and Categorization*, ed. Rosch and Barbara B. Lloyd (Hillsdale: Erlbaum, 1978), 29. For a helpful discussion of the theoretical issues involved, see N. Katherine Hayles, "Constrained Constructivism: Locating Scientific Inquiry in the Theater of Representation," *Realism and Representation: Essays on the Problem of Realism in Relation to Science, Literature, and Culture* (Madison: University of Wisconsin Press, 1993), 27–43.

76 Rosch, "Principles," 35.

77 Eleanor Rosch and Carolyn B. Mervis, "Family Resemblance: Studies in the Internal Structure of Categories," *Cognitive Psychology* 7 (1975), 586–87.

78 Lakoff, *Women, Fire*, 51; Taylor, *Linguistic Categorization*, 50.
79 Owen, *Wordsworth as Critic*, 13–14.
80 For an important discussion of Wordsworth's tendency to see the world in terms of "separate blockish units" (analogous to basic categories) and its relation to his organic approach to language, see Jonathan Wordsworth, *William Wordsworth: The Borders of Vision* (Oxford: Clarendon Press, 1982), 203–30.
81 Raymond W. Gibbs, Jr., *The Poetics of Mind: Figurative Thought, Language, and Understanding* (Cambridge University Press, 1994); Mark Turner, *The Literary Mind* (New York: Oxford University Press, 1996).
82 Miall, "Body in Literature," 194.
83 See Keach, "Romanticism," 108–9 and Ferguson, *Wordsworth*.

4 OF HEARTACHE AND HEAD INJURY: MINDS, BRAINS, AND THE
SUBJECT OF *PERSUASION*

1 Reed, *From Soul to Mind*, 43–59.
2 M. A., "The Craniological Controversy," 35.
3 Cooter, *Cultural Meaning*, 29.
4 See Chapter Five.
5 William Godwin, *Enquiry Concerning Political Justice and Its Influence on Modern Morals and Happiness*, ed. Isaac Kramnick (Harmondsworth: Penguin, 1976), 97–98, 111–12.
6 Godwin, *Thoughts on Man*, 29–30, 41, 32.
7 Godwin, *Thoughts on Man*, 363–65, 370.
8 Jerome Kagan, *Galen's Prophecy: Temperament in Human Nature* (New York: Basic Books, 1994), esp. 1–37; Lawrence Stone, *The Family, Sex, and Marriage in England 1500–1800*, abridged edn (New York: Harper, 1979), 255.
9 Mary Hays, *Memoirs of Emma Courtney*, ed. Gina Luria, 2 vols. (New York: Garland, 1974) 1: 4.
10 Alan Richardson, *Literature, Education, and Romanticism*, 185–202.
11 Susan Ferrier, *Marriage*, ed. Rosemary Ashton (Harmondsworth: Penguin, 1986), 299, 444, 475.
12 Mary Shelley, *The Last Man*, ed. Brian Aldiss (London: Hogarth Press, 1985), 47 (my italics).
13 See Sally Shuttleworth, *Charlotte Brontë and Victorian Psychology* (Cambridge University Press, 1996) and Janet Oppenheim, *"Shattered Nerves": Doctors, Patients, and Depression in Victorian England* (New York: Oxford University Press, 1991).
14 For an extended statement of this claim, see D. D. Devlin, *Jane Austen and Education* (London: Macmillan, 1975).
15 For the role of the "false hero" and "object" see V. Propp, *Morphology of the Folktale*, 2nd edn, trans. Laurence Scott and Louis A. Wagner, ed. Alan Dundes (Austin: University of Texas Press, 1968), 50–62.
16 Jane Austen, *Persuasion*, ed. D. W. Harding (London: Penguin, 1965), 67; hereafter cited in the text.

17 Mary Lascelles, quoted in John Wiltshire, *Jane Austen and the Body* (Cambridge University Press, 1992), 186.

18 Gloria Sybil Gross, "Flights into Illness: Some Characters in Jane Austen," in *Literature and Medicine during the Eighteenth Century*, ed. Marie Mulvey Roberts and Roy Porter (London: Routledge, 1993), 195; Anita Sokolsky, "The Melancholy Persuasion," in *Psychoanalytic Literary Criticism*, ed. Maud Ellman (London: Longman, 1994), 136.

19 Wiltshire, *Jane Austen*, 187.

20 Wiltshire, *Jane Austen*, 196.

21 Hartley, *Observations* 1: 19; cf. Priestley, *Disquisitions*, 27, Lawrence, *Lectures on Physiology*, 6, Robinson, *Some Account*, 27, and Spurzheim, *PS* 137. Thomas Beddoes believed that "blows on the head" could cause insanity by affecting the brain (*Hygëia* 3 [Essay x]: 71–2).

22 Andrew Combe, "On the Effects of Injuries of the Brain upon the Manifestations of the Mind," *Transactions of the Phrenological Society* 1 (1825); rpt. in George Combe, *A System of Phrenology* (New York: Colyer, 1841), 473.

23 Hartley, *Observations*, 1: 399. Nor is Louisa the only young woman to fall out of love from what appear to be physiological causes. Thomas Brown, in the course of a skeptical view of phrenology, mentions a "young lady, of very good understanding," who married a "person whom she passionately loved" despite "much opposition from her relatives." After a "long illness," however, "she completely lost memory of all the time that had elapsed since her marriage," though her memory was otherwise intact. "From the sight of her child, presented to her as her own, she turned with amazement and horror; and though she now, on the faith and assurance of her friends, consents to consider herself, as a wife and mother, she 'still looks upon her husband, and her child, without being able to conceive, by what magic she has acquired the one, and given birth to the other.'" Review of *A Letter from Charles Villier to Georges Cuvier, Member of the National Institute of France, on a New Theory of the Brain, as the immediate organ of intellectual and moral faculties, by Dr Gall of Vienna, Edinburgh Review* 2 (1803): 152.

24 Damasio, *Descartes' Error*, 3–33; see also H. Damasio *et al.*, "The Return of Phineas Gage: The Skull of a Famous Patient Yields Clues about the Brain," *Science* 264 (1994): 1102–5.

25 Sir Everard Home, "Observations on the Functions of the Brain," *Philosphical Transactions of the Royal Society of London* 104 (1814): 469. Home's essay was also discussed in the *Monthly Review*, 2nd series, 76 (1815): 40.

26 Review of Sir Everard Home, "Observations on the Functions of the Brain," *Edinburgh Review* 24 (1815): 443. Hereafter cited in the text.

27 Wiltshire, *Jane Austen*, 195.

28 Tony Tanner notes, in this novel, the "increased presence of sudden unanticipated and unpredictable inward intensities" in his study *Jane Austen* (Cambridge: Harvard University Press, 1986), 219; Marilyn Butler discusses Austen's representation of Anne's "rich and feeling" "inner life" in *Jane*

Austen and the War of Ideas, 2nd edn (New York: Oxford University Press, 1987), 283.

29 For a careful study of the "sentimental" novel in a wider cultural and scientific context, see John Mullan, *Sentiment and Sociability: The Language of Feeling in the Eighteenth Century* (Oxford: Clarendon Press, 1988).

30 A. Walton Litz, "*Persuasion*: Forms of Estrangement," in *Jane Austen: Bicentenary Essays*, ed. John Halperin (Cambridge University Press, 1975), 228.

31 Butler, *Jane Austen*, 277.

32 Wiltshire, *Jane Austen*, 177.

33 Richardson, *Literature, Education, and Romanticism*, 191–92. For a reading of Austen's *Pride and Prejudice* that emphasizes the social significance of blushing and related physiological phenomena, see Mary Ann O'Farrell, *Telling Complexions: The Nineteenth-Century Novel and the Blush* (Durham: Duke University Press, 1997), 13–27.

34 Butler, *Jane Austen*, 290 and Litz, "*Persuasion*," 228.

35 Litz discusses the novel in terms of Austen's "new-found Romanticism" in "*Persuasion*," 227.

36 O'Farrell coins the term "organic mechanics" to describe such wordless, meaningful exchanges between couples in *Persuasion* (*Telling Complexions*, 52).

37 J. F. Blumenbach was an important source for Romantic-era ideas on heredity; his *Essay on Generation* had been translated into English in 1792. James Prichard's *Researches into the Physical History of Man* (1813) was another important source within the British context. For Lawrence's role in disseminating these and other early notions of heredity, both through his lectures and various encyclopedia articles, see Kentwood D. Wells, "Sir William Lawrence (1783–1867): A Study of Pre-Darwinian Ideas on Heredity and Variation," *Journal of the History of Biology* 4 (1971): 319–61.

38 Spurzheim includes "imbecility" among other examples of how the "same organic constitution of brain" can be "transmitted from parents to children" in his popular *Physiognomical System* of 1815 (*PS* 438–9). It is the more noteworthy, then, that Austen had both a maternal uncle (Thomas Leigh) and an elder brother (George) who were considered mentally "handicapped" and in each case were "boarded out from the family," though remaining near enough for family supervision and visits. It has been surmised that Austen learned the "deaf and dumb alphabet" in order to communicate with George. Whether or not hereditary transmission was suspected, having both a brother and uncle who were considered so mentally "abnormal" as to be brought up insulated from the family might well have inspired a sympathetic interest in "organic" approaches to mind. See William Austen-Leigh and Richard Arthur Austen-Leigh, *Jane Austen: A Family Record*, rev. and enlarged by Deirdre Le Faye (New York: G. K. Hall, 1989), 8, 19–20.

39 Sokolsky, "Melancholy Persuasion," 133. See also Elizabeth Dalton, "Mourning and Melancholia in *Persuasion*," *Partisan Review* 62 (1995): 49–59 and Frances L. Restuccia, "Mortification: Beyond the Persuasion

Principle," in *Melancholics in Love: Representing Women's Depression and Domestic Abuse* (Lanham: Rowman & Littlefield, 2000), 17–34.

40 Claudia L. Johnson, *Jane Austen: Women, Politics, and the Novel* (University of Chicago Press, 1988), 151–52.

41 Oppenheim, "*Shattered Nerves*," 185.

42 Quoted in Shuttleworth, *Charlotte Brontë*, 82.

43 In this, the new brain-based psychologies departed not only from vague notions of "universal" sexual difference like Hazlitt's, but from the neurological models of the earlier eighteenth century, which tended to assign "different nervous systems" to men and women. See G. J. Barker-Benfield, *The Culture of Sensibility: Sex and Society in Eighteenth-Century Britain* (University of Chicago Press, 1992), 27.

44 Marina Benjamin, "Elbow Room: Women Writers on Science, 1790–1840," in *Science and Sensibility: Gender and Scientific Inquiry*, ed. Marina Benjamin (Oxford: Blackwell, 1991), 27–28.

45 See Kagan, *Galen's Prophecy*, 34–35 and Sweetser, *From Etymology to Pragmatics*, 28.

46 Carol Shields, "Jane Austen Images of the Body: No Fingers, No Toes," *Persuasions* 13 (1991): 132.

5 KEATS AND THE GLORIES OF THE BRAIN

1 Charles Bell, "On the Nerves: giving an account of some experiments on their structure and functions, which lead to a new arrangement of the system," *Philosophical Transactions* 111 (1821): 398–424 [cited in the text as "*111*"] and "Of the Nerves which associate the muscles of the Chest, in the actions of breathing, speaking, and expression. Being a continuation of the paper on the Structure and Functions of the Nerves," *Philosophical Transactions* 112 (1822): 284–312 [cited in the text as "*112*"]. A third lecture, "On the motions of the Eye, in illustration of the uses of the Muscles and Nerves of the Orbit," appeared in 1823.

2 *The Lectures of Sir Astley Cooper, Bart. F.R.S. Surgeon to the King, &c. &c. on the Principles and Practice of Surgery; with Additional Notes and Cases, by Frederick Tyrell, Esq.* 3 vols. London: Thomas and George Underwood, 1824–27. Cited in the text as "*C/T*."

3 *John Keats's Anatomical and Physiological Note Book*, ed. Maurice Buxton Forman (Oxford University Press, 1934).

4 Richardson, *Literature, Education, and Romanticism*, 247–50.

5 "On the Cockney School of Poetry," no. 4, *Blackwood's Edinburgh Magazine* 3 (1818): 524. "Z" is usually identified as John Gibson Lockhart.

6 Donald C. Goellnicht, *The Poet-Physician: Keats and Medical Science* (University of Pittsburgh Press, 1984), 24; Hermione De Almeida, *Romantic Medicine and John Keats* (New York: Oxford University Press, 1991), 7.

7 Nicholas Roe, *John Keats and the Culture of Dissent* (Oxford: Clarendon, 1997), 160–81.

8 De Almeida, *Romantic Medicine*, 30.

9 On Cooper and Darwin, see Desmond King-Hele, *Doctor of Revolution: The Life and Genius of Erasmus Darwin* (London: Faber & Faber, 1977), 301 and King-Hele, *Erasmus Darwin and the Romantic Poets*, 227.

10 Barnsley Blake Cooper, *The Life of Sir Astley Cooper, Bart.*, 2 vols. (London: John W. Parker, 1843), 1: 249.

11 Cooper, *Life*, 1: 211–12.

12 See Goellnicht, *Poet-Physician*, 123–24.

13 Roe, *John Keats*, 27–50.

14 Roe, *John Keats*, 171–72.

15 Robert Gittings, *John Keats* (London: Heinemann, 1968), 72–73; Andrew Motion, *Keats: A Biography* (1997; University of Chicago Press, 1999), 98.

16 F. J. Gall and J. G. Spurzheim. *Anatomie et Physiologie du Système nervaux en général, et du Cerveau en particulier, avec des observations sur le possibilité de reconnaître plusiers dispositions intellectuelles et morales de l'homme et des animaux, par le configuration des leurs têtes*. 4 vols. and *Atlas*. Paris: F. Schoell, 1810–19.

17 Review of Gall and Spurzheim, *Anatomie*, *Critical Review*, 3rd series, 18 (1810): 497.

18 R. S. White, "'Like Esculapius of Old': Keats's Medical Training," *Keats–Shelley Review* 12 (1998): 30.

19 *The Diary of Benjamin Robert Haydon*, ed. Willard Bissell Pope, 2 vols. (Cambridge: Harvard University Press, 1960), 1: 419; Henry Crabb Robinson, *Diary*, 1: 276.

20 *The Autobiography and Memoirs of Benjamin Robert Haydon*, ed. Tom Taylor, 2nd edn, 2 vols. (New York: Harcourt Brace, [1926]), 1: 32–33.

21 Sir William Hale-White, *Keats as Doctor and Patient* (London: Oxford University Press, 1938), 24–25.

22 *The twelve first lectures of Mr Astley Coopers anatomical course delivered at St. Thomas' theatre, A.D. 1817*. Taken by E[dward] Reynolds. A single manuscript bound in leather. I.K.13. Boston Medical Library in the Francis A. Countway Library of Medicine. Cited in the text as "*C/R.*"

23 See note 26 to chapter 4.

24 Cooper may have been inspired by Bell's discussion of the contrasting papillae for taste and feeling on the tongue, a key example in the *Idea of a New Anatomy*, 9–10.

25 Ackerknecht, "Contributions," 151.

26 Joshua Waddington's notes for the 1816 lecture course on Anatomy and Surgery, cited by Goellnicht, *Poet–Physician*, 143–44. Cooter, on the other hand, cites indirect evidence that Cooper was sympathetic to Gall (*Cultural Meaning*, 29).

27 The passage is misunderstood by Henry Pettit in "Scientific Correlatives of Keats' *Ode to Psyche*," *Studies in Philology* 40 (1943): 563 and by Charles Hagelman, Jr., who notes Pettit's misreading, only to supply a different one, in "Keats's Medical Training and the Last Stanza of the 'Ode to Psyche,'" *Keats-Shelley Journal* 11 (1962): 74–75. These are both on the whole, however, valuable essays to which I am indebted in this chapter.

28 Spurzheim, *PS*, 32–33. Ackerknecht comments that Gall "not only definitely

proved the decussation of the pyramids but differentiated between 'convergent' (or 'reentrantes,' our association) and 'divergent' (or 'sortantes,' our projection) fibres" ("Contributions," 151).

29 De Almeida comments that the "Beauley Abbey" poem "reveals knowledge of the basic phrenology of Gall and Spurzheim even as it borrows Hamlet's sardonic manner to read the life-styles of the brethren through the 'psychological' evidence of their skulls," *Romantic Medicine*, 55.

30 As Stuart Sperry has demonstrated in his important study, *Keats the Poet* (Princeton University Press, 1973), 3–29.

31 Goellnicht, *Poet-Physician*, 64–65.

32 Goellnicht, *Poet-Physician*, 128–29.

33 See especially Pettit, "Scientific Correlatives," Hagelman, "Keats's Medical Training," and Goellnicht, *Poet-Physician*, 135–39.

34 Edwin Clarke and Kenneth Dewhurst, *An Illustrated History of Brain Function* (Berkeley: University of California Press, 1972), 81–88, 101–2.

35 Spurzheim, *PS*, 32.

36 Hagelman, "Keats's Medical Training": 75–77.

37 "The word signifies the *soul*, and this personification of Psyche first mentioned by Apuleius, is posterior to the Augustan age, though still it is connected with ancient mythology," from the entry for "Psyche" in J. Lemprière, *A Classical Dictionary*, 6th edn (London: T. Cadell and W. Davies, 1806), [unpaginated].

38 Walter Jackson Bate, *John Keats* (1963; New York: Oxford University Press, 1966), 488–89.

39 See chapter two, above.

40 Keats's reading of Coleridge's poems is authoritatively examined by Beth Lau in *Keats's Reading of the Romantic Poets* (Ann Arbor: University of Michigan Press, 1991), 69–114. As Lau points out, there is every reason to assume that Keats was familiar with the 1816 volume *Christabel: Kubla Khan, A Vision; The Pains of Sleep*, including direct quotations by Keats of "Christabel" (71). Critics have found echoes of "Kubla Khan" in *Endymion*, "La Belle Dame sans Merci," and other poems, but not (so far as Lau's and my own supplementary research has discovered) in the "Ode to Psyche" (101–2).

41 Cooter notes that Green included an abstract of Gall and Spurzheim's system in his *Dissector's Manual*; *Cultural Meaning*, 31.

42 Keats had been re-reading the "Paulo and Francesca" story in Dante's *Inferno*.

43 Yet, in Apuleius, the nightly visits seem those of a demon lover, until Psyche first sees Eros in the light.

44 Goellnicht, *Poet-Physician*, 259.

45 La Mettrie, *Machine Man*, 29.

46 Priestley, *Disquisitions*, 28.

47 Damasio's *Descartes' Error* is the single most influential statement of this view. For the phrase "hot cognition," see Willie Van Peer, "Towards a Poetics of

Emotion," in *Emotion and the Arts*, ed. Mette Hjort and Sue Laver (New York: Oxford University Press, 1997), 219.

48 Bell, *Idea of a New Anatomy*, 14, 29.

49 Christopher Ricks, *Keats and Embarrassment*, 20.

50 William Lawrence, *Introduction*, 153.

51 For a recent discussion of the skin's importance as visceral as well as sensory organ, see Damasio, *Descartes' Error*, 205–6, 230.

52 Ricks, *Keats and Embarrassment*, 158.

53 Ricks, *Keats and Embarrassment*, 23.

54 Lawrence, *Introduction*, 128.

55 Baillie, *Lectures*, 146–47.

56 On Cooper, Stewart, and Bell, see De Almeida, *Romantic Medicine*, 31–32.

57 M. H. Abrams, "Keats's Poems: The Material Dimensions," in *The Persistence of Poetry: Bicentennial Essays on Keats*, ed. Robert M. Ryan and Ronald A. Sharp (Amherst: University of Massachusetts Press, 1998), 38–39.

58 Pinker discusses "phonetic symbolism" in *The Language Instinct*, 166–67.

59 On the "semiotic" aspect of language, see Julia Kristeva, *Revolution in Poetic Language*, ed. Leon S. Roudiez, trans. Margaret Walker (New York: Columbia University Press, 1984) and *Desire in Language: A Semiotic Approach to Literature and Art*, ed. Leon S. Roudiez, trans. Thomas Gora, Alice Jardine, and Leon Roudiez (New York: Columbia University Press, 1980), where the "semiotic" is explicitly connected with "instinctual and maternal" processes that "prepare the future speaker for entrance" into meaningful language (136).

60 For a review and discussion of work on "motherese," a notion in psycholinguistics that overlaps significantly with Kristeva's conception of the "semiotic," see Anne Fernald, "Human Maternal Vocalizations to Infants as Biologically Relevant Signals: An Evolutionary Perspective," in *The Adapted Mind: Evolutionary Psychology and the Generation of Culture*, ed. Jerome H. Barkow, Leda Cosmides, and John Tooby (New York: Oxford University Press, 1992), 391–428.

61 Combe, *Essays on Phrenology*, 138.

62 W. P. D. Wightman, "Wars of Ideas in Neurological Science – from Willis to Bichat and from Locke to Condillac," in Poynter, ed., *The Brain and Its Functions*, 136.

63 Keats's interest in wine and its intoxicating effects is discussed by Anya Taylor in *Bacchus in Romantic England: Writers and Drink, 1780–1830* (New York: St. Martin's Press, 1999), 172–90.

64 See De Almeida, *Romantic Medicine*, 168–72 and White, "'Like Esculapius of Old': Keats's Medical Training," *Keats–Shelley Review* 12 (1998): 46–48.

65 Goellnicht, *Poet-Physician*, 226–27.

66 Leon Waldoff discusses Keats's interest in "unconscious mental processes" from a psychoanalytical perspective in *Keats and the Silent Work of Imagination* (Urbana: University of Illinois Press, 1985), 1–31.

67 Sperry, *Keats the Poet*, 37.

68 Sperry, *Keats the Poet*, 38.

69 Sperry, *Keats the Poet*, 36.

70 Priestley, *Disquistions*, xxxviii, xiii.

71 Young, *Mind, Brain and Adaptation*, 3; Cooter, *Cultural Meaning*, 2–7.

72 Scott Manning Stevens, "Sacred Heart and Secular Brain," in *The Body in Parts: Fantasies of Corporeality in Early Modern Europe*, ed. David Hillman and Carlo Mazzio (New York: Routledge, 1997), 278.

73 In this section, I have made use both of the "search" feature of *Literature Online* (18 August 1999, Chadwyck-Healey, accessed 5 November, 1999, <http://lion.chadwyck.com/>) and of conventional concordances, here Marvin Spevack, *A Complete and Systematic Concordance to the Works of Shakespeare*, 9 vols. (Hildesheim: Georg Olms, 1968–1980). Full references are given only for longer quotations.

74 [John Thelwall], *The Peripatetic; or, Sketches of the Heart, of Nature and Society; in a Series of Politico-Sentimental Journals, in Verse and Prose, of the Eccentric Excursions of Sylvanus Theophrastus; Supposed to be Written by Himself* (Southwark, 1793), 164–65. The lines on the brain occur in a section entitled "A Digression for the Anatomists."

75 For a concise account of Johnson's circle and publishing activities, see Marilyn Gaull, "Joseph Johnson: Literary Alchemist," *European Romantic Review* 10 (1999): 265–78.

76 William Blake, *The Book of Urizen*, iv [b], plate 12, lines 11–12; *Visions of the Daughters of Albion*, plate 2, line 32.

77 This is equally true, though in a somewhat different manner, for P. B. Shelley, who uses the term "brain" more extensively than any other canonical Romantic poet, and in ways that reflect his interest in materialist or quasi-materialist thinkers like Priestley, Darwin, and Cabanis. For some ninety instances of Shelley's use of "brain," see F. S. Ellis, *A Lexical Concordance to the Poetical Works of Percy Bysshe Shelley* (London: Bernard Quaritch, 1892), 69–70.

78 William Lawrence speaks of the body's "continual change" through such processes as nutrition and excretion, claiming that the "body cannot be called the same in any two successive instants," in the 1816 lecture "On Life" (*Introduction*, 138–39).

6 EMBODIED UNIVERSALISM, ROMANTIC DISCOURSE, AND THE
ANTHROPOLOGICAL IMAGINATION

1 See chapter two, above.

2 Ricks, *Keats and Embarrassment*, 51.

3 Arthur O. Lovejoy, *The Great Chain of Being: A Study in the History of an Idea* (1936; Cambridge: Harvard University Press, 1974), 294–313; Robert J. C. Young, *Colonial Desire: Hybridity in Theory, Culture and Race* (London: Routledge, 1995), 42.

4 Hans Eichner, "The Rise of Modern Science and the Genesis of Romanticism," *PMLA* 97 (1982): 16.

5 Aarsleff, *Locke to Saussure*, 110.

6 Locke, *An Essay*, 66; *WP* 1: 76.

7 See the relevant discussion below and the citations in note 69.

8 Richards, *Mental Machinery*, 129; cf. McKusick, *Coleridge's Philosophy of Language*, 2, 70, 125–27.

9 Reid, *Essays*, 39.

10 Porter, "Medical Science," 69–70. See also Williams, *Physical and the Moral*, 107.

11 Francis Barker, *The Tremulous Private Body: Essays on Subjection* (London: Methuen, 1984), 24, 77; Peter Stallybrass and Allon White, *The Politics and Poetics of Transgression* (Ithaca: Cornell University Press, 1986), 105; Harris, *Hermes*, 372.

12 Stephen Jay Gould, *The Mismeasure of Man* (New York: Norton, 1981).

13 This relation has been discussed at length with regard to Wordsworth by Alan Bewell in his important study, *Wordsworth and the Enlightenment*.

14 Condillac, *Essay*, 16; Locke, *An Essay on the Origin of Human Knowledge*, 63–64. On the importance of these and related "marginal" groups as limit-cases for empiricist philosophy and anthropology, see Bewell, *Wordsworth and the Enlightenment*, 25–28.

15 Among the accounts that Spurzheim and in turn Gall borrowed from, the most prominent are James Wardrop, *History of James Mitchell, A Boy Born Blind and Deaf, With an Account of the Operation Performed for the Recovery of His Sight* (London: John Murray and Archibald Constable, 1813) and Dugald Stewart, "Some Account of James Mitchell, a Boy Born Deaf and Blind," first published (with supplementary material by John Gordon) in the *Transactions of the Royal Society of Edinburgh* (volume 7, 1812) and later appended to Part 3, chapter 2 of his *Elements of the Philosophy of the Human Mind* (*Collected Works of Dugald Stewart*, ed. Sir William Hamilton, 11 vols. [Edinburgh: Thomas Constable, 1854–60], 4: 300–61). Stewart's account in the *Transactions* was reviewed with generous excerpts in the *Edinburgh Review* 20 (1812): 462–71.

16 Condillac, in contrast, supplies a sketch of a young man, born deaf and dumb, who regained his hearing in his twenty-third year; up to that point, he "led a mere animal life," incapable of forming "one single reasoning." *Essay on the Origin of Human Knowledge*, 124, 127.

17 At least one contemporary champion of the brain-based, modular mind would concur: Steven Pinker, in discussing "mentalese" and other kinds of "nonverbal thought" in *The Language Instinct*, draws similar conclusions from the example of "languageless adults" (67–68).

18 Thomas Hobbes, *Leviathan: Or the Matter, Forme and Power of a Commonwealth Ecclesiastical and Civil*, ed. Michael Oakeshott (New York: Collier, 1962), 28, 34.

19 Herder, "Essay on the Origin of Language," 100, 125. Aarsleff notes that

Herder's conception of a "complete language of concepts" prior to speech constitutes an important departure from Condillac, *Locke to Saussure*, 196.

20 Bewell, *Wordsworth and the Enlightenment*, ix, 66–67.

21 Piper notes the importance of "mute poets" for Wordsworth's thinking about language and subjectivity in *The Active Universe*, 125. See also Land, "The Silent Poet," and Jonathan Wordsworth, "As with the Silence of the Thought."

22 *The Poetical Works of the Late Mrs. Mary Robinson*, 3 vols. (1806; rpt. London: Routledge/Thoemmes, 1996), 2: 1–8.

23 This is the "Wild Child," "*L'Enfant Sauvage*," again made famous in the 1969 Francois Truffaut film of that title. For the definitive study of Victor and his importance within the linguistic, medical, and anthropological debates of the time, see Harlan Lane, *The Wild Boy of Aveyron* (Cambridge: Harvard University Press, 1979).

24 Etienne Bonnot de Condillac, *Condillac's Treatise on the Sensations*, trans. Geraldine Carr (Los Angeles: University of Southern California School of Philosophy, 1930), 224–27.

25 Jean-Marc-Gaspard Itard, *The Wild Boy of Aveyron*, trans. George and Muriel Humphrey (Englewood Cliffs: Prentice-Hall, 1962), 53.

26 Itard, *Wild Boy*, 87.

27 Lane includes a telling anecdote on this score in his thoughtful study of Victor and of Itard, an important pioneer in the field of sign language and the education of the deaf. "Itard's favorite pupil Allibert was asked at a dinner if he had had ideas before receiving instruction at the institute; to the general amazement he said that he had, and proceeded to describe a few of the ideas of his childhood. Whereupon Itard commented, 'If you had ideas such as those you have told us about, all of Condillac's theory would be destroyed'" (Lane, *Wild Boy*, 243).

28 Butler, "Introduction" to *Mary Shelley, Frankenstein or The Modern Prometheus: The 1818 Text*, xxxvii. The citations to *Frankenstein* below follow this edition.

29 Burton R. Pollin, "Philosophical and Literary Sources of *Frankenstein*," *Comparative Literature* 17 (1965): 97–108; Bruce Mazlish, "The Man-Machine and Artificial Intelligence," *Stanford Humanities Review* 4 (1995): 21–45. For a discussion more particularly concerned with La Mettrie, see Hamilton, "A French Connection: From Empiricism to Materialism in Writings by the Shelleys."

30 On Shelley and Darwin see King-Hele, *Erasmus Darwin and the Romantic Poets*, 259–60 and Reed, *From Soul to Mind*, 49–53. On Shelley and Lawrence, see Hugh J. Luke, Jr., "Sir William Lawrence," 141–52 and Butler, "Introduction." Cabanis is widely considered an important source for the youthful "materialism" of Percy Bysshe Shelley, who cites the *Rapports* in the notes to *Queen Mab*. David Lee Clark, *Shelley's Prose or The Trumpet of a Prophecy* (Albuquerque: University of New Mexico Press, 1954), 173, 175, 340.

31 See especially Peter Brooks, "'Godlike Science/Unhallowed Arts': Language, Nature, and Monstrosity," in *The Endurance of Frankenstein: Essays*

on Mary Shelley's Novel, ed. George Levine and U. C. Knoepflmacher (Berkeley: University of California Press, 1979), 205–21.

32 Jean-Jacques Rousseau, *Emile or On Education*, trans. Allan Bloom (New York: Basic Books, 1979), 61–62.

33 The phrase "mindreading instinct" is from Simon Baron-Cohen, *Mindblindness: An Essay on Autism and Theory of Mind* (Cambridge: MIT Press, 1995), 10.

34 Byron describes his meeting with Spurzheim (who duly examined Byron's cranium) in a letter to Annabella Milbanke, 26 September 1814. *Byron's Letters and Journals*, ed. Leslie A. Marchand, 12 vols. (Cambridge: Harvard University Press, 1973–82), 4: 182.

35 George, D'Oyley, review of John Abernethy, *An Enquiry*, . . . etc., *Quarterly Review* 22 (1819), 27.

36 Gall and Spurzheim, *Anatomie*, 2: 41–44.

37 Combe, *Letter*, 20–23.

38 Locke, *An Essay*, 159–61.

39 For "The Idiot Boy" and Wordsworth's "debunking" of Enlightenment anthropology (65), see Bewell, *Wordsworth and the Enlightenment*, 64–70. For an examination of the poem in terms of Wordsworth's philosophical differences with Coleridge, see Ross Woodman, "The Idiot Boy as Healer," in *Romanticism and Children's Literature in Nineteenth-Century England*, ed. James Holt McGavran, Jr. (Athens: University of Georgia Press, 1991), 72–95.

40 See chapter 3, above.

41 *Letters of William and Dorothy Wordsworth*, 357.

42 Bewell, *Wordsworth and the Enlightenment*, comments of a later passage, "It is crucial to recognize that the basic function of language in this joyful reunion is not to represent ideas, but to create *contact*" (67). This is a needful correction of the claim, in an essay that I find in other ways remarkably perceptive, that "The Idiot Boy" represents a "one-sided relationship." Mary Jacobus, "*The Idiot Boy*," in *Bicentenary Wordsworth Studies in Memory of John Alban Finch*, ed. Jonathan Wordsworth and Beth Darlington (Ithaca: Cornell University Press, 1970), 254.

43 Wordsworth's comments on "The Idiot Boy," as reported to Isabella Fenwick, in Owen (ed.), *Lyrical Ballads 1798*, 143.

44 Bewell, *Wordsworth and the Enlightenment*, 68–69.

45 Jacobus, "*Idiot Boy*," 261.

46 *Letters of William and Dorothy Wordsworth: The Early Years*, 357.

47 Sir Walter Scott, *Waverley*, ed. Andrew Hook (Harmondsworth: Penguin, 1985), 439. Hereafter cited in the text.

48 Scott, *The Journal of Sir Walter Scott*, ed. W. E. K. Anderson (Oxford: Clarendon Press, 1972), 257; *The Letters of Sir Walter Scott 1826–1828*, ed. H. J. C. Grierson (London: Constable, 1936), 10: 312.

49 John Galt, "The Idiot. An Anecdote," *Blackwood's Edinburgh Magazine* 26 (1829): 631–32. For Galt's authorship, see Ian A. Gordon, *John Galt: The Life of a Writer* (University of Toronto Press, 1972), 91.

50 John Galt, *The Entail or The Lairds of Grippy*, ed. Ian A. Gordon (Oxford University Press, 1984), 24, 25, 61, 73, 92, 111. Hereafter cited in the text. There is an overt connection between Watty, who as a child compulsively sings "lal, lal, lal, lal" to himself (25), and the "idiot" of Galt's *Blackwood's* piece, whose only sound is the repetitive "ditty," "pal-lal" (631).

51 Combe, *Letter*, 21.

52 Henry George Atkinson and Harriet Martineau, *Letters on the Laws of Man's Nature and Development* (London: John Chapman, 1851), 89–96. Hereafter cited in the text.

53 *Harriet Martineau's Autobiography* (1877; rpt. London: Virago Press, 1983), 1: 103–6.

54 Harriet Martineau, *Illustrations of Political Economy*, no. v, *Ella of Garveloch. A Tale* (Boston: Leonard C. Bowles, 1832), 23. Hereafter cited in the text.

55 Condillac, *Essay on the Origin of Human Knowledge*, 128.

56 Abrams, *The Mirror and the Lamp*, 107.

57 For an introduction to the issues involved, including the difficulty of defining "race" in the Romantic era, see Alan Richardson, "Darkness Visible? Race and Representation in Bristol Abolitionist Poetry, 1770–1810," in *Romanticism and Colonialism*, ed. T. J. Fulford and Peter J. Kitson (Cambridge University Press, 1998), 129–47. Kitson provides a helpful survey of Romantic-era racial theories and reproduces some key texts in *Theories of Race*, volume 8 of *Slavery, Abolition, and Emancipation: Writings in the British Romantic Period*, ed. Kitson and Debbie Lee (London: Pickering and Chatto, 1999).

58 Martin Bernal, *Black Athena: The Afroasiatic Roots of Classical Civilization*, vol. 1, *The Fabrication of Ancient Greece 1785–1985* (New Brunswick: Rutgers University Press, 1987), 204–6; Robert J. C. Young, *Colonial Desire*, 36–42.

59 Lovejoy, *Great Chain*, 313.

60 Kitson, *Theories of Race*, xxv.

61 Ronald L. Meek, *Social Science and the Ignoble Savage* (Cambridge University Press, 1976).

62 Monboddo, *Of the Origins*, 367.

63 Monboddo, *Of the Origins*, 358, 361.

64 A number of examples have been collected by Emmanuel Chukwudi Eze in *Race and the Enlightenment: A Reader* (Oxford: Blackwell, 1997).

65 J. J. Rousseau, "Essay on the Origin of Languages," 59; by "West Indian" Rousseau almost certainly means an Afro-Caribbean slave or freedman.

66 This view is neatly summarized by Tzvetan Todorov: "reason belongs to all climates, but we are its most advanced representatives; thus, we have not only the right but also the duty to spread it everywhere – and for this we must first occupy the territories." *On Human Diversity: Nationalism, Racism, and Exoticism in French Thought*, trans. Catherine Porter (Cambridge: Harvard University Press, 1993), 392.

67 J. G. Spurzheim, *A View of the Elementary Principles of Education, Founded on the Study of the Nature of Man*, 2nd edn. (Boston: Marsh, Capen, and Lyon, 1833), 19.

68 Todorov, *On Human Diversity*, 49.
69 Young, *Colonial Desire*, 43; cf. Bernal, *Black Athena*, 206. This view of Herder
    has been criticized by Robert E. Norton, "The Tyranny of Germany over
    Greece?: Bernal, Herder, and the German Appropriation of Greece," *Black
    Athena Revisited*, ed. Mary R. Lefkowitz and Guy MacLean Rogers (Chapel
    Hill: University of North Carolina Press, 1996), 403.
70 Given the controversy over Herder's views and the date of Churchill's trans-
    lation, I include the following references to *Ideen zur Philosophie der Geschischte
    der Menschheit* in volume 4 of *Herders Werke in Fünf Bänden*, ed. Wilhem
    Dobbek (Berlin and Weimar: Aufbau-Verlag, 1964): "die ürsprungliche
    Rauheit dieses Erdgeschlechts" ("wilden Völkern") (36); "ein Stufengang
    sichtbar vom Menschen," "Der Menschenfresser in Neuseeland" (99).
71 Herder, *Ideen*, 103.
72 "Unterscheid . . . der verschiedenen Nationen" (*Ideen*, 86); "Ihr Väter hatten
    ihn um den höchsten und schwersten Preis erkauft, um ihre Negergestalt
    und Negerfarbe" (*Ideen*, 161).
73 George Combe, *System of Phrenology*, 433–34.
74 Hannah More, *Slavery, A Poem* (London: T. Cadell, 1788); cited by line
    number.
75 Mary Birkett, *A Poem on the African Slave Trade* (Dublin: J. Jones, 1792); cited
    by line number.
76 See the discussion of Austen in chapter 4, above, and Roger Cooter,
    "Dichotomy and Denial: Mesmerism, Medicine, and Harriet Martineau,"
    in *Science and Sensibility*, ed. Benjamin, esp. 160–65.
77 Cabanis proposes the "audacious enterprise" of selective breeding of
    humans as a form of "social hygiene" (*R* 1: 308–10); Lawrence similarly
    declares that the "hereditary transmission of physical and moral qualities,
    so well understood and familiarly acted on in domestic animals, is equally
    true of man. A superior breed of human beings could only be produced by
    selections and exclusions similar to those so successfully employed in rearing
    our more valuable animals" (*LPZ* 397).
78 See Todorov, *On Human Diversity*, 387–90.

EPILOGUE

1 Bruce H. Price, Raymond D. Adams, and Joseph T. Coyle, "Neurology and
   Psychiatry: Closing the Great Divide," *Neurology* 54 (2000): 8, 12.
2 Price, Adams, and Coyle, "Neurology": 8.
3 Price, Adams, and Coyle, "Neurology": 8, 10.
4 Steven Pinker, *How the Mind Works* (New York: Norton, 1997), 20, 32, 64, 185,
   365–66, 8–9.
5 Pinker, *How the Mind Works*, 361, 369.
6 The prevalence of this anti-Romantic understanding of Romanticism may
   be traceable to certain disparaging remarks in the popular defense of scientific method by Paul Gross and Norman Levitt, *The Higher Superstition: The*

Academic Left and Its Quarrels with Science (Baltimore: Johns Hopkins University Press, 1994). See George Bornstein, "Constructing Literature: Empiricism, Romanticism, and Textual Theory," in *The Flight from Science and Reason*, ed. Gross, Levitt, and Martin W. Lewis (New York: New York Academy of Sciences, 1996), 459–60.

7 Johnson, *Body in the Mind*, ix, 139.

8 Johnson, *Body in the Mind*, 31.

9 Antonio Damasio, *The Feeling of What Happens: Body and Emotion in the Making of Consciousness* (New York: Harcourt, Brace, 1999), 40, 46, 51–52, 92–93, 107, 150, 185, 228, 285–86, 320.

10 Damasio, *Feeling of What Happens*, 39, 85.

11 Charles Darwin, *The Expression of the Emotions in Man and Animals*, 3rd edn, ed. Paul Ekman (New York: Oxford University Press, 1998), 7.

12 See especially Baron-Cohen, *Mindblindness*.

13 Damasio, *Feeling of What Happens*, 92–93.

14 Varela, Thompson, and Rosch, *Embodied Mind*, 180–88.

15 Varela, Thompson, and Rosch, *Embodied Mind*.

16 Sherry Turkle, "Romantic Reactions: Paradoxical Responses to the Computer Presence," in *The Boundaries of Humanity: Humans, Animals, Machines*, ed. James J. Sheehan and Morton Sosna (Berkeley: University of California Press, 1991), 224–52.

Bibliography

Aarsleff, Hans, *From Locke to Saussure: Essays on the Study of Language and Intellectual History*, Minneapolis: University of Minnesota Press, 1982.

The Study of Language in England, 1780–1860, Princeton University Press, 1967.

Abrams, M.H., *The Correspondent Breeze: Essays on English Romanticism*, New York: Norton, 1984.

"Keats's Poems: The Material Dimensions," in *The Persistence of Poetry: Bicentennial Essays on Keats*, ed. Robert M. Ryan and Ronald A. Sharp, Amherst: University of Massachusetts Press, 1998, 36–53.

The Mirror and the Lamp: Romantic Theory and the Critical Tradition, Oxford University Press, 1953.

Ackerknecht, Erwin H., "Contributions of Gall and the Phrenologists to Knowledge of Brain Function," in *The History and Philosophy of Knowledge of the Brain and Its Functions*, ed. F. N. L. Poynter. Oxford: Blackwell, 1958, 149–53.

"Anti-Phrenologia; a Plain Statement of Objections against the System of Drs Gall and Spurzheim," *Blackwood's Edinburgh Magazine* 13 (1823): 100–8, 199–206.

Appleyard, J. A., *Coleridge's Philosophy of Literature: The Development of a Concept of Poetry*, Cambridge: Harvard University Press, 1965.

Armstrong, Isobel. "The Gush of the Feminine: How Can We Read Women's Poetry of the Romantic Period?" in *Romantic Women Writers: Voices and Countervoices*, ed. Paula R. Feldman and Theresa M. Kelley, Hanover: University Press of New England, 1995, 13–32.

Atkinson, Henry George and Harriet Martineau, *Letters on the Laws of Man's Nature and Development*, London: John Chapman, 1851.

Austen, Jane, *Persuasion*, ed. D. W. Harding, London: Penguin, 1965.

Austen-Leigh, William and Richard Arthur Austen-Leigh, *Jane Austen: A Family Record*, revised and enlarged by Deirdre Le Faye, New York: G. K. Hall, 1989.

Averill, James, "Wordsworth and 'Natural Science': The Poetry of 1798," *Journal of English and Germanic Philology* 77 (1978): 232–46.

Baillie, Joanna, *The Dramatic and Poetical Works of Joanna Baillie*, 2nd edn, London: Longman, Brown, Green, and Longmans, 1853.

Baillie, Matthew, *Lectures and Observations on Medicine*, London: Richard Taylor, 1825.

Barker, Francis, *The Tremulous Private Body: Essays on Subjection*, London: Methuen, 1984.

Barker-Benfield, G. J., *The Culture of Sensibility: Sex and Society in Eighteenth-Century Britain*, University of Chicago Press, 1992.

Baron-Cohen, Simon, *Mindblindness: An Essay on Autism and Theory of Mind*, Cambridge: MIT Press, 1995.

Bate, Walter Jackson, *John Keats*, 1963; New York: Oxford University Press, 1966.

Beatty, Arthur, *Wordsworth: His Doctrine and Art in Their Historical Relations*, 2nd edn, Madison: University of Wisconsin Press, 1962.

Beddoes, Thomas, *Hygëia: or Essays Moral and Medical, on the Causes Affecting the Personal State of Our Middling and Affluent Classes*, 3 vols., Bristol: R. Phillips, 1802–3.

Beer, John, *Coleridge's Poetic Intelligence*, London: MacMillan, 1977.

Bell, Charles, *The Anatomy and Philosophy of Expression As Connected with the Fine Arts*, 7th edn, London: George Bell, 1877.

  Essays on the Anatomy of Expression in Painting, London: Longman, Hurst, Rees, and Orme, 1806.

  Idea of a New Anatomy of the Brain: A Facsimile of the Privately Printed Edition of 1811 With a Bio-Bibliographical Introduction, London: Dawsons, 1966.

  "Of the Nerves which associate the muscles of the Chest, in the actions of breathing, speaking, and expression. Being a continuation of the paper on the Structure and Functions of the Nerves," *Philosophical Transactions* 112 (1822): 284–312.

  "On the motions of the Eye, in illustration of the uses of the Muscles and Nerves of the Orbit," *Philosophical Transactions* 113 (1823): 166–86.

  "On the Nerves: giving an account of some experiments on their structure and functions, which lead to a new arrangement of the system," *Philosophical Transactions* 111 (1821): 398–424.

Review of Charles Bell, *An Exposition of the Natural System of the Nerves of the Human Body*, *Edinburgh Review* 47 (1828): 441–81.

Belsey, Catherine, "The Romantic Construction of the Unconscious," in *Literature, Politics, and Theory: Papers from the Essex Conference 1976–84*, ed. Francis Barker *et al.*, London: Methuen, 1986, 57–76.

Benjamin, Marina, "Elbow Room: Women Writers on Science, 1790–1840," in *Science and Sensibility: Gender and Scientific Inquiry*, ed. Marina Benjamin, Oxford: Blackwell, 1991, 27–59.

Benzon, William, "Articulate Vision: A Structuralist Reading of 'Kubla Khan,'" *Language and Style* 18 (1985): 3–29.

Bernal, Martin, *Black Athena: The Afroasiatic Roots of Classical Civilization*, vol. 1, *The Fabrication of Ancient Greece 1785–1985*, New Brunswick: Rutgers University Press, 1987.

Bewell, Alan, *Wordsworth and the Enlightenment: Nature, Man, and Society in the Experimental Poetry*, New Haven: Yale University Press, 1989.

Bialostosky, Don, "Coleridge's Interpretation of Wordsworth's Preface to *Lyrical Ballads*," *PMLA* 93 (1978): 912–24.

Birkett, Mary, *A Poem on the African Slave Trade*, Dublin: J. Jones, 1792.

Black, Joel, "Newtonian Mechanics and the Romantic Rebellion: Introduction," *Beyond the Two Cultures: Science, Technology, and Literature*, ed. Joseph W. Slade and Judith Yaroll Lee, Ames: Iowa State University Press, 1990, 131–39.

Blake, William, *The Complete Poetry and Prose of William Blake*, rev. edn., ed. David V. Erdman, Garden City: Anchor Press, 1982.

Blunden, Edmund, *Leigh Hunt: A Biography*, London: Cobden-Sanderson, 1930.

Boden, Margaret A., *The Creative Mind: Myths and Mechanisms*, New York: Basic Books, 1990.

Bornstein, George, "Constructing Literature: Empiricism, Romanticism, and Textual Theory," in *The Flight from Science and Reason*, ed. Paul R. Gross, Norman Levitt, and Martin W. Lewis, New York: New York Academy of Sciences, 1996, 459–69.

Brantley, Richard E., *Wordsworth's Natural Methodism*, New Haven: Yale University Press, 1975.

Brazier, Mary A. B., "The Evolution of Concepts Relating to the Electrical Activity of the Nervous System 1600–1800," in *The History and Philosophy of Knowledge of the Brain and Its Functions*, ed. F. N. L. Poynter, Oxford: Blackwell, 1958, 191–222.

[Brewster, Sir David], "The Connexion of Intellectual Operations with Organic Action," *Quarterly Review* 45 (1831): 341–58.

Brooks, Peter, "'Godlike Science/Unhallowed Arts': Language, Nature, and Monstrosity," in *The Endurance of Frankenstein: Essays on Mary Shelley's Novel*, ed. George Levine and U. C. Knoepflmacher, Berkeley: University of California Press, 1979, 205–21.

Brown, Thomas, *Observations on the Zoonomia of Erasmus Darwin, M. D.*, Edinburgh: J. Mundell, J. Johnson, and J. Wright, 1798.

  Review of *A Letter from Charles Villier to Georges Cuvier, Member of the National Institute of France, on a New Theory of the Brain, as the immediate organ of intellectual and moral faculties, by Dr Gall of Vienna*, *Edinburgh Review* 2 (1803): 147–60.

Burke, Kenneth, *Language as Symbolic Action: Essays on Life, Literature, and Method*, Berkeley: University of California Press, 1966.

Burwick, Frederick, "The Romantic Drama," in *A Companion to Romanticism* ed. Duncan Wu, Oxford: Blackwell, 1998, 323–32.

  "Sir Charles Bell and the Vitalist Controversy in the Early Nineteenth Century," *The Crisis in Modernism: Bergson and the Vitalist Controversy*, ed. Frederick Burwick and Paul Douglass, Cambridge University Press, 1992, 109–30.

Butler, Marilyn, "Introduction" and "Appendix C" to Mary Shelley, *Frankenstein or The Modern Prometheus: The 1818 Text*, Oxford University Press, 1993, ix-li and 229–51.

  Jane Austen and the War of Ideas, 2nd edn, New York: Oxford University Press, 1987.

Cabanis, Pierre-Jean-George, *On the Relations Between the Physical and Moral Aspects of Man*, trans. Margaret Duggan Saidi, ed. George Mora, 2 vols., Baltimore: Johns Hopkins University Press: 1981.

Caldwell, James Ralston, *John Keats' Fancy: The Effect on Keats of the Psychology of His Day*, Ithaca: Cornell University Press, 1945.

[Canning, George, George Ellis, and John Hookam Frere], "The Loves of the Triangles: A Mathematical and Philosophical Poem, Inscribed to Dr Darwin," 1798; rpt. in *The Anti-Jacobin, or Weekly Examiner*, 4th edn, revised and corrected, 2 vols., London: J. Wright, 1799, 2: 162–64, 200–5, 274–80

Carlson, Eric T. and Meribeth M. Simpson, "Models of the Nervous System in Eighteenth-Century Psychiatry," *Bulletin of the History of Medicine* 43 (1969): 101–15.

Chandler, James K., *Wordsworth's Second Nature: A Study of the Poetry and Politics*, University of Chicago Press, 1984.

Christensen, Jerome, *Coleridge's Blessed Machine of Language*, Ithaca: Cornell University Press, 1981.

Clark, David Lee, *Shelley's Prose or The Trumpet of a Prophecy*, Albuquerque: University of New Mexico Press, 1954.

Clarke, Edwin and Kenneth Dewhurst, *An Illustrated History of Brian Function*, Berkeley: University of California Press, 1972.

Clarke, Edwin and L. S. Jacyna, *Nineteenth-Century Origins of Neuroscientific Concepts*, Berkeley: University of California Press, 1987.

Coleridge, Samuel Taylor, *Biographia Literaria, or Biographical Sketches of My Literary Life and Opinions*, ed. James Engell and W. J. Bate, 2 vols., Princeton University Press, 1983.

    Collected Letters of Samuel Taylor Coleridge ed. E. L. Griggs, 6 vols., Oxford University Press, 1956–71.

    Table Talk, ed. Carl Woodring, 2 vols., London and New York: Routledge and Kegan Paul, Princeton University Press, 1990.

Combe, Andrew, "On the Effects of Injuries of the Brain upon the Manifestations of the Mind," *Transactions of the Phrenological Society* 1 (1825): 183–208; rpt. in George Combe, *A System of Phrenology*, New York: Colyer, 1841, 460–73.

Combe, George, *Essays on Phrenology, or, An Inquiry Into the Principles and Utility of the System of Drs. Gall and Spurzheim, and Into the Objections Made Against It*, 1819; ed. John Bell, Philadelphia: Carey and Lea, 1822.

    Letter from George Combe to Francis Jeffrey, Esq. in Answer to His Criticism on Phrenology, Contained in No. LXXXVIII of the Edinburgh Review, Edinburgh: John Anderson, 1826.

Condillac, Etienne Bonnot de, *Condillac's Treatise on the Sensations*, trans. Geraldine Carr, Los Angeles: University of Southern California School of Philosophy, 1930.

    An Essay on the Origin of Human Knowledge, trans. Thomas Nugent, 1756; rpt. Gainesville: Scholar's Facsimile Reprints, 1971.

Cooper, Astley, *The Lectures of Sir Astley Cooper, Bart. F.R.S. Surgeon to the King, &c. &c. on the Principles and Practice of Surgery; with Additional Notes and Cases, by*

Frederick Tyrell, Esq., 3 vols., London: Thomas and George Underwood, 1824–27.

The Twelve first Lectures of Mr Astley Coopers Anatomical Course delivered at St. Thomas' Theatre, A.D. 1817, taken by E[dward] Reynolds, MS, Countway Library, 1817.

Cooper, Barnsley Blake, *The Life of Sir Astley Cooper, Bart.*, 2 vols., London: John W. Parker, 1843.

Cooter, Roger, *The Cultural Meaning of Popular Science: Phrenology and the Organization of Consent in Nineteenth-Century Britain*, Cambridge University Press, 1984.

"Dichotomy and Denial: Mesmerism, Medicine, and Harriet Martineau," in *Science and Sensibility: Gender and Scientific Inquiry*, ed. Marina Benjamin, Oxford: Blackwell, 1991. 144–73.

Phrenology in the British Isles: An Annotated, Historical Biobibliography and Index, Metuchen: Scarecrow Press, 1989.

Crick, Francis, *The Astonishing Hypothesis: The Scientific Search for the Soul*, New York: Scribner, 1993.

Crook, Nora and Derek Guiton, *Shelley's Venomed Melody*, Cambridge University Press, 1986.

Cunningham, Andrew and Nicholas Jardine, eds., *Romanticism and the Sciences*, Cambridge University Press, 1990.

Dalton, Elizabeth, "Mourning and Melancholia in *Persuasion*," *Partisan Review* 62 (1995): 49–59.

Damasio, Antonio, *Descartes' Error: Emotion, Reason, and the Human Brain*, New York: Avon, 1994.

The Feeling of What Happens: Body and Emotion in the Making of Consciousness, New York: Harcourt, Brace, 1999.

Damasio, H. *et al.*, "The Return of Phineas Gage: The Skull of a Famous Patient Yields Clues about the Brain," *Science* 264 (1994): 1102–5.

Darnton, Robert, *Mesmerism and the End of the Enlightenment in France*, Cambridge, MA: Harvard University Press, 1968.

Darwin, Charles, *The Expression of the Emotions in Man and Animals*, 3rd edn, ed. Paul Ekman, New York: Oxford University Press, 1998.

Darwin, Erasmus, *The Poetical Works of Erasmus Darwin, M.D., F.R.S.*, 3 vols., London: J. Johnson, 1806.

Zoonomia: or, The Laws of Organic Life, 2 vols., London: J. Johnson, 1794–96.

De Almeida, Hermione, *Romantic Medicine and John Keats*, New York: Oxford University Press, 1991.

De Quincey, Thomas, *Collected Writings of Thomas De Quincey*, ed. David Masson, 14 vols., Edinburgh: A. and C. Black, 1896–97.

Devlin, D. D., *Jane Austen and Education*, London: Macmillan, 1975.

Diderot, Denis, *Rameau's Nephew and Other Works*, trans. Jacques Barzun and Ralph H. Bowen, Indianapolis: Bobbs-Merrill, 1964.

[D'Oyley, George], Review of John Abernethy, *An Enquiry into the Probability and Rationality of Mr. Hunter's Theory of Life*, etc., *Quarterly Review* 22 (1819): 1–34.

Eichner, Hans, "The Rise of Modern Science and the Genesis of Romanticism," *PMLA* 97 (1982): 8–30.

Ellenberger, Henri, *The Discovery of the Unconscious: The History and Evolution of Dynamic Psychiatry*, New York: Basic Books, 1970.

Ellis, F. S., *A Lexical Concordance to the Poetical Works of Percy Bysshe Shelley: An Attempt to Classify Every Word Found Therein according to Its Significance*, London: Bernard Quaritch, 1892.

"Essays on Cranioscopy, Craniology, Phrenology, etc., by Sir Toby Tickletoby, Bart.," *Blackwood's Edinburgh Magazine* 10 (1821): 73–82.

"Essays on Phrenology, etc.," *Blackwood's Edinburgh Magazine* 10 (1821): 682–91.

Eze, Emmanuel Chukwudi, *Race and the Enlightenment: A Reader*, Oxford: Blackwell, 1997.

Ferguson, Frances, *Wordsworth: Language as Counter-Spirit*, New Haven: Yale University Press, 1977.

Fernald, Anne, "Human Maternal Vocalizations to Infants as Biologically Relevant Signals: An Evolutionary Perspective," in *The Adapted Mind: Evolutionary Psychology and the Generation of Culture*, ed. Jerome H. Barkow, Leda Cosmides, and John Tooby, New York: Oxford University Press, 1992, 391–428.

Ferrier, Susan, *Marriage*, ed. Rosemary Ashton, Harmondsworth: Penguin, 1986.

Figlio, Karl M., "Theories of Perception and the Physiology of Mind in the Late Eighteenth Century," *History of Science* 12 (1975): 177–212.

Flanagan, Owen, *The Science of the Mind*, 2nd edn, Cambridge, MA: MIT Press, 1991.

Fodor, Jerry A., *The Modularity of Mind: An Essay on Faculty Psychology*, Cambridge: MIT Press, 1983.

Ford, Jennifer, *Coleridge on Dreaming: Romanticism, Dreams, and the Medical Imagination*, Cambridge University Press, 1998.

Fox, Christopher, "Defining Eighteenth-Century Psychology: Some Problems and Perspectives," in *Psychology and Literature in the Eighteenth Century*, ed. Christopher Fox, New York: AMS Press, 1987, 1–22.

Fruman, Norman, *Coleridge, the Damaged Archangel*, New York: George Braziller, 1971.

Galdston, Iago, "Freud and Romantic Medicine," *Bulletin of the History of Medicine* 30 (1956): 489–507.

Gall, François Joseph, *On the Functions of the Brain and of Each of Its Parts: With Observations on the Possibility of Determining the Instincts, Propensities, and Talents, or the Moral and Intellectual Dispositions of Men and Animals by the Configuration of the Brain and Head*, trans. Winslow Lewis, 6 vols., Boston: Marsh, Capen, and Lyon: 1835.

Gall, F. J. and J. G. Spurzheim, *Anatomie et Physiologie du Système nervaux en général, et du Cerveau en particulier, avec des observations sur le possibilité de reconnaître plusieurs dispositions intellectuelles et morales de l'homme et des animaux, par le configuration de leurs têtes*, 4 vols. and *Atlas*, Paris: F. Schoell, 1810–19.

Review of F. J. Gall and J. G. Spurzheim, *Anatomie et Physiologie du Système nervaux en général, &c., Critical Review*, 3rd series, 18 (1810): 487–98.

Galt, John, *The Entail or The Lairds of Grippy*, ed. Ian A. Gordon, Oxford University Press, 1984.

"The Idiot. An Anecdote," *Blackwood's Edinburgh Magazine* 26 (1829): 631–32.

Gaull, Marilyn, "Coleridge and the Kingdoms of the World," *The Wordsworth Circle* 22 (1991): 47–52.

"Joseph Johnson: Literary Alchemist," *European Romantic Review* 10 (1999): 265–78.

Gibbs, Raymond W., Jr., *The Poetics of Mind: Figurative Thought, Language, and Understanding*, Cambridge University Press, 1994.

Gilbert, Sandra and Susan Gubar, "The Mirror and the Vamp: Reflections on Feminist Criticism," in *The Future of Literary Theory*, ed. Ralph Cohen, New York: Routledge, 1989, 144–66.

Gittings, Robert, *John Keats*, London: Heinemann, 1968.

Godwin, William, *Enquiry Concerning Political Justice and Its Influence on Modern Morals and Happiness*, ed. Isaac Kramnick, Harmondsworth: Penguin, 1976.

Thoughts on Man, His Nature, Productions, and Discoveries, London: Effingham Wilson, 1831.

Goellnicht, Donald C., *The Poet-Physician: Keats and Medical Science*, University of Pittsburgh Press, 1984.

Golinski, Jan, *Science as Public Culture: Chemistry and Enlightenment in Britain, 1760–1820*, Cambridge University Press, 1992.

Gordon, George, Lord Byron, *Byron's Letters and Journals*, ed. Leslie A. Marchand, 12 vols.; Cambridge, MA: Harvard University Press, 1973–82.

Gordon, Ian A., *John Galt: The Life of a Writer*, University of Toronto Press, 1972.

[Gordon, John], Review of F. J. Gall and J. G. Spurzheim, *Anatomie et Physiologie du Système Nerveux en général, et du Cerveau en particulier*, *Edinburgh Review* 25 (1815): 227–68.

Gould, Stephen Jay, *The Mismeasure of Man*, New York: Norton, 1981.

Grabo, Carl, *A Newton Among Poets: Shelley's Use of Science in Prometheus Unbound*, Chapel Hill: University of North Carolina Press, 1930.

Grob, Alan, *The Philosophic Mind: A Study of Wordsworth's Poetry and Thought 1797–1805*, Columbus: Ohio State University Press, 1973.

Gross, Gloria Sybil, "Flights into Illness: Some Characters in Jane Austen," in *Literature and Medicine during the Eighteenth Century*, ed. Marie Mulvey Roberts and Roy Porter, London: Routledge, 1993, 188–199.

Hagelman, Charles, Jr., "Keats's Medical Training and the Last Stanza of the 'Ode to Psyche,'" *Keats-Shelley Journal* 11 (1962): 73–82.

Hale-White, William, Sir, *Keats as Doctor and Patient*, London: Oxford, University Press, 1938.

Hall, Jason Y., "Gall's Phrenology: A Romantic Psychology," *Studies in Romanticism* 16 (1977): 305–17.

Hamilton, Paul, "A French Connection: From Empiricism to Materialism in Writings by the Shelleys," *Colloquium Helveticum* 25 (1997): 171–93.

Harrington, Anne, *Medicine, Mind, and the Double Brain: A Study in Nineteenth-Century Thought and Culture*, Princeton University Press, 1987.

Harris, James, *Hermes: Or, A Philosophical Inquiry Concerning Language and Universal Grammar*, 1751; rpt. Menston, England: Scolar Press, 1969.

Harris, John, "Coleridge's Readings in Medicine," *The Wordsworth Circle* 3 (1972): 85–95.

Hartley, David, *Observations on Man, His Frame, His Duty, and His Expectations*, 2 vols., 1749; rpt. Hildesheim: Georg Olms, 1967.

Hatfield, Gary, "Remaking the Science of Mind: Psychology as Natural Science," in *Inventing Human Science: Eighteenth-Century Domains*, ed. Christopher Fox, Roy Porter, and Robert Wolker, Berkeley: University of California Press, 1995, 184–231.

Haydon, Benjamin Robert, *The Autobiography and Memoirs of Benjamin Robert Haydon*. ed. Tom Taylor, 2 vols., 2nd edn, New York: Harcourt Brace, [1926].

The Diary of Benjamin Robert Haydon, ed. Willard Bissell Pope, 2 vols., Cambridge, MA: Harvard University Press, 1960.

Hayles, N. Katherine, "Constrained Constructivism: Locating Scientific Inquiry in the Theater of Representation," *Realism and Representation: Essays on the Problem of Realism in Relation to Science, Literature, and Culture*, Madison: University of Wisconsin Press, 1993, 27–43.

Hays, Mary, *Memoirs of Emma Courtney*, ed. Gina Luria, 2 vols., New York: Garland, 1974.

Hazlitt, William, *The Complete Works of William Hazlitt*, ed. P. P. Howe, 21 vols., London, Dent: 1930–34.

Herder, Johann Gottfried von, "Essay on the Origin of Language," trans. Alexander Gode, in *On the Origin of Language*, ed. John H. Moran and Gode, Chicago: University of Chicago Press, 1966, 85–166.

Ideen zur Philosophie der Geschichte der Menschheit, in *Herders Werke in Fünf Bänden*, ed. Wilhelm Dobbek, vol. 4, Berlin and Weimar: Aufbau-Verlag, 1964.

Outlines of the Philosophy of the History of Man, trans. T. Churchill, 1800; rpt. New York: Bergman, 1966.

Herschel, John Frederick William, *Preliminary Discourse on the Study of Natural Philosophy*, 1830; rpt. University of Chicago Press, 1987.

Hirsch, E. D., Jr., *Wordsworth and Schelling: A Typological Study of Romanticism*, New Haven: Yale University Press, 1960.

Hobbes, Thomas, *Leviathan: Or the Matter, Forme and Power of a Commonwealth Ecclesiastical and Civil*, ed. Michael Oakeshott, New York: Collier, 1962.

Hodgson, John, *Wordsworth's Philosophical Poetry, 1797–1814*, Lincoln: University of Nebraska Press, 1980.

Home, Sir Everard, "The Croonian Lecture: Being Experiments and Observations on the Structure of the Nerves," *Philosophical Transactions of the Royal Society of London* 89 (1799): 1–12.

"Observations on the Functions of the Brain," *Philosophical Transactions of the Royal Society of London* 104 (1814): 469–86.

Review of Sir Everard Home, "Observations on the Functions of the Brain," *Monthly Review*, 2nd series, 76 (1815): 40.

Review of Sir Everard Home, "Observations on the Functions of the Brain," *Edinburgh Review* 24 (1815): 439–52.

Hoover, Suzanne R., "Coleridge, Humphry Davy, and Some Early Experiments with a Consciousness-altering Drug," *Bulletin of Research in the Humanities* 81 (1978): 9–27.

Hoyle, James F., "'Kubla Khan' as an Elated Experience," *Literature and Psychology* 16 (1966): 27–39.

Itard, Jean-Marc-Gaspard, *The Wild Boy of Aveyron*, trans. George and Muriel Humphrey, Englewood Cliffs: Prentice-Hall, 1962.

Jackson, Stanley, "Force and Kindred Notions in Eighteenth-Century Neurophysiology and Medical Psychology," *Bulletin of the History of Medicine* 44 (1970): 397–410.

Jacobus, Mary, "*The Idiot Boy*," in *Bicentenary Wordsworth Studies in Memory of John Alban Finch*, ed. Jonathan Wordsworth and Beth Darlington, Ithaca: Cornell University Press, 1970, 236–65.

Jeffrey, Francis, Review of George Combe, *A System of Phrenology*, *Edinburgh Review* 88 (1826): 253–318.

Johnson, Claudia L., *Jane Austen: Women, Politics, and the Novel*, University of Chicago Press, 1988.

Johnson, Mark, *The Body in the Mind: The Bodily Basis of Meaning, Imagination, and Reason*, University of Chicago Press, 1987.

Jones, John, *The Egotistical Sublime: A History of Wordsworth's Imagination*, London: Chatto and Windus, 1954.

Kagan, Jerome, *Galen's Prophecy: Temperament in Human Nature*, New York: Basic Books, 1994.

Keach, William, "Romanticism and Language," *The Cambridge Companion to British Romanticism*, ed. Stuart Curran, Cambridge University Press, 1993, 95–119.

"'Words Are Things': Romantic Ideology and the Matter of Poetic Language," in *Aesthetics and Ideology*, ed. George Levine, New Brunswick: Rutgers University Press, 1994.

Keats, John, *John Keats's Anatomical and Physiological Note Book*, ed. Maurice Buxton Forman, Oxford University Press, 1934.

The Letters of John Keats 1814–1821, ed. Hyder Edward Rollins, 2 vols.. Cambridge, MA: Harvard University Press, 1958.

King-Hele, Desmond, *Doctor of Revolution: The Life and Genius of Erasmus Darwin*, London: Faber & Faber, 1977.

Erasmus Darwin and the Romantic Poets, New York: St. Martin's Press, 1986.

Kitson, Peter J., *Theories of Race*, volume 8 of *Slavery, Abolition, and Emancipation: Writings in the British Romantic Period*, ed. Peter Kitson and Debbie Lee, London: Pickering and Chatto, 1999.

Kosslyn, Stephen, and Olivier Koenig, *Wet Mind: The New Cognitive Neuroscience*, New York: Free Press, 1992.

Kristeva, Julia, *Desire in Language: A Semiotic Approach to Literature and Art*, ed. Leon S. Roudiez, trans. Thomas Gora, Alice Jardine, and Leon Roudiez, New York: Columbia University Press, 1980.

    Revolution in Poetic Language, ed. Leon S. Roudiez, trans. Margaret Walker, New York: Columbia University Press, 1984.

La Mettrie, Julien Offray de, *Machine Man and Other Writings*, ed. and trans. Ann Thomson, Cambridge University Press, 1996.

Lakoff, George, "How Unconscious Metaphorical Thought Shapes Dreams," in *Cognitive Science and the Unconscious*, ed. Dan J. Stein, Washington, D.C.: American Psychiatric Press, 1997, 89–120.

    Women, Fire, and Dangerous Things: What Categories Reveal about the Mind, University of Chicago Press, 1987.

Land, Stephen K., "The Silent Poet: An Aspect of Wordsworth's Semantic Theory," *University of Toronto Quarterly* 42 (1973): 157–69.

Lane, Harlan, *The Wild Boy of Aveyron*, Cambridge: Harvard University Press, 1979.

Lau, Beth, *Keats's Reading of the Romantic Poets*, Ann Arbor: University of Michigan Press, 1991.

Lavie, Peretz and J. Allan Hobson, "Origin of Dreams: Anticipations of Modern Theories in the Philosophy and Physiology of the Eighteenth and Nineteenth Centuries," *Psychological Bulletin* 100 (1986): 229–40.

Lawrence, Christopher, "The Power and the Glory: Humphry Davy and Romanticism," in *Romanticism and the Sciences*, ed. Andrew Cunningham and Nicholas Jardine, Cambridge University Press, 1990, 213–27.

Lawrence, William, *An Introduction to Comparative Anatomy and Physiology; Being the Two Introductory Lectures Delivered at the Royal College of Surgeons, On the 21st and 25th of March, 1816*, London: J. Callow, 1816.

    Lectures on Physiology, Zoology, and the Natural History of Man, Delivered to the Royal College of Surgeons, London: Benbow, 1822.

Lefebure, Molly, *Samuel Taylor Coleridge: A Bondage of Opium*, London: Victor Gollancz, 1974.

Lempriere, J., *A Classical Dictionary*, 6th edn, London: T. Cadell and W. Davies, 1806.

Levere, Trevor H., *Poetry Realized in Nature: Samuel Taylor Coleridge and Early Nineteenth-Century Science*, Cambridge University Press, 1981.

    "S. T. Coleridge and the Human Sciences: Anthropology, Phrenology, and Mesmerism," in *Science, Pseudo-Science and Society*, ed. Marsha P Hanen, Margaret J. Osler, and Robert G. Weyant, Waterloo: Wilfrid Laurier University Press, 1980, 171–92.

Literature Online, 18 August 1999, Chadwyck-Healey, accessed 5 November, 1999 <http://lion.chadwyck.com/>.

Litz, A. Walton, "*Persuasion*: Forms of Estrangement," in *Jane Austen: Bicentenary Essays*, ed. John Halperin, London: Cambridge University Press, 1975.

Locke, John, *An Essay Concerning Human Understanding*, ed. Peter H. Nidditch, Oxford: Clarendon Press, 1975.

Lovejoy, Arthur O., *The Great Chain of Being: A Study in the History of an Idea*, 1936; Cambridge: Harvard University Press, 1974.

Lowes, John Livingston, *The Road to Xanadu: A Study in the Ways of the Imagination*, Boston: Houghton Mifflin, 1927.

Luke, Hugh J., Jr., "Sir William Lawrence: Physician to Shelley and Mary," *Papers on Language and Literature* 1 (1965): 141–52.

M., A., "The Craniological Controversy: Some Observations on the Late Pamphlets of Dr Gordon and Dr Spurzheim," *Blackwood's Edinburgh Magazine* 1 (1817): 35–38.

Macdonald, D. L. and Kathleen Scherf, "Introduction" to Mary Shelley, *Frankenstein: Or, The Modern Prometheus*, 2nd edn, Peterborough: Broadview Press, 1999, 11–38.

MacFarland, Thomas, *Coleridge and the Pantheist Tradition*, Oxford: Clarendon, 1969.

McGann, Jerome J., *The Poetics of Sensibility: A Revolution in Literary Style*, Oxford: Clarendon, 1996.

McKusick, James C., *Coleridge's Philosophy of Language*, New Haven: Yale University Press, 1986.

McMillan, Dorothy, "'Dr' Baillie," in *1798: The Year of the Lyrical Ballads*, ed. Richard Cronin, Houndmills: Macmillan, 1998, 68–92.

McNeil, Maureen, *Under the Banner of Science: Erasmus Darwin and His Age*, Manchester University Press, 1987.

Marcovitz, Eli, "Bemoaning the Lost Dream: Coleridge's 'Kubla Khan' and Addiction," *International Journal of Psychoanalysis* 45 (1964): 411–25.

Marshall, John C., "The New Organology," *Behaviorial and Brain Sciences* 3 (1980): 23–25.

Martineau, Harriet, *Harriet Martineau's Autobiography*, 2 vols., 1877; rpt. London: Virago Press, 1983.

Illustrations of Political Economy, no. V, *Ella of Garveloch. A Tale*, Boston: Leonard C. Bowles, 1832.

Matlak, Richard, "Wordsworth's Reading of *Zoonomia* in Early Spring," *The Wordsworth Circle* 21 (1990): 76–81.

Mazlish, Bruce, "The Man-Machine and Artificial Intelligence," *Stanford Humanities Review* 4 (1995): 21–45.

Meek, Ronald L., *Social Science and the Ignoble Savage*, Cambridge University Press, 1976.

Mellor, Anne K., *Mary Shelley: Her Life, Her Fiction, Her Monsters*, New York: Methuen, 1988.

Review of *Mémoires de l'Institut National, &c. Monthly Review*, 2nd series, 34 (1801): 298–309.

Miall, David, "The Body in Literature: Mark Johnson, Metaphor, and Feeling," *Journal of Literary Semantics* 26 (1997): 191–210.

"Coleridge on Emotion: Experience into Theory," *The Wordsworth Circle* 22 (1991): 35–39.

"'I see it feelingly': Coleridge's Debt to Hartley," *Coleridge's Visionary Languages: Essays in Honor of J. B. Beer*, ed. by Tim Fulford and Morton D. Paley, Cambridge: Brewster, 1993, 151–63.

"The Meaning of Dreams: Coleridge's Ambivalence," *Studies in Romanticism* 21 (1982): 57–87.

"Wordsworth and *The Prelude*: The Problematics of Feeling," *Studies in Romanticism* 31 (1992): 233–53.

Miller, Jonathan, "Going Unconscious," *New York Review of Books*, April 20, 1995, 59–65.

Modiano, Raimonda, *Coleridge and the Concept of Nature*, Tallahassee: Florida State University Press, 1985.

Monboddo, Lord James Burnet, *Of the Origins and Progress of Language*, 2nd edn, 5 vols., Edinburgh: J. Balfour, 1774–1809.

Moravio, Sergio, "From *Homme Machine* to *Homme Sensible*: Changing Eighteenth-Century Models of Man's Image," *Journal of the History of Ideas* 39 (1979): 45–60.

More, Hannah, *Slavery, A Poem*, London: T. Cadell, 1788.

Morris, Peter, "On the Nature of the Imitative Principle, and Some Other Faculties, Pointed out by Gall and Spurzheim," *Blackwood's Edinburgh Magazine* 6 (1819): 309–14.

Motion, Andrew, *Keats: A Biography*, 1997; University of Chicago Press, 1999.

Mullan, John, *Sentiment and Sociability: The Language of Feeling in the Eighteenth Century*, Oxford: Clarendon Press, 1988.

Nichols, Ashton, "The Anxiety of Species: Toward a Romantic Natural History," *The Wordsworth Circle* 28 (1997): 130–36.

Norton, Robert E., "The Tyranny of Germany over Greece?: Bernal, Herder, and the German Appropriation of Greece," in *Black Athena Revisited*, ed. Mary R. Lefkowitz and Guy MacLean Rogers, Chapel Hill: University of North Carolina Press, 1996, 403–10.

O'Donnell, Brennan, *The Passion of Meter: A Study of Wordsworth's Metrical Art*, Kent: Kent State University Press, 1995.

O'Farrell, Mary Ann, *Telling Complexions: The Nineteenth-Century Novel and the Blush*, Durham: Duke University Press, 1997.

Oppenheim, Janet, *"Shattered Nerves": Doctors, Patients, and Depression in Victorian England*, New York: Oxford University Press, 1991.

Owen, W. J. B., *Wordsworth as Critic*, University of Toronto Press, 1969.

Paivio, Allan, "The Mind's Eye in Arts and Science," *Poetics* 12 (1983): 1–18.

Patten, Janice, "Joanna Baillie, *A Series of Plays*," in *A Companion to Romanticism* ed. Duncan Wu, Oxford: Blackwell, 1998, 169–78.

Perkins, David, "The Imaginative Vision of *Kubla Khan*: On Coleridge's Introductory Note," in *Coleridge, Keats, and the Imagination: Romanticism and Adam's Dream; Essays in Honor of Walter Jackson Bate*, ed. John L. Mahoney and J. Robert Barth, S.J., Columbia: University of Missouri Press, 1990, 97–108.

Pettit, Henry, "Scientific Correlatives of Keats' *Ode to Psyche*," *Studies in Philology* 40 (1943): 560–66.

Phinney, A. W., "Wordsworth's Winander Boy and Romantic Theories of Language," *The Wordsworth Circle* 18 (1987): 66–82.

Pinker, Steven, *How the Mind Works*, New York: Norton, 1997.

The Language Instinct: How the Mind Creates Language, New York: Harper, 1994.

Piper, H. W., *The Active Universe: Pantheism and the Concept of Imagination in the English Romantic Poets*, London: Athlone Press, 1962.

Pittman, Charles, "An Introduction to Wordsworth's Reading in Science," *Furman Studies* 33 (1950): 27–60.

Poggi, Stefano, "Neurology and Biology in the Romantic Age in Germany: Carus, Burdach, Gall, von Baer," in *Romanticism in Science: Science in Europe, 1790–1840*, ed. Poggi and Maurizio Bossi, Dordrecht: Kluwer Academic Publishers, 1994, 143–60.

Pollin, Burton R., "Philosophical and Literary Sources of *Frankenstein*," *Comparative Literature* 17 (1965): 97–108.

Porter, Roy, "Medical Science and Human Science in the Enlightenment," in *Inventing Human Science: Eighteenth-Century Domains*, ed. Christopher Fox, Roy Porter, and Robert Wolker, Berkeley: University of California Press, 1995, 53–87.

Poynter, F. N. L., ed., *The History and Philosophy of Knowledge of the Brain and Its Functions*, Oxford: Blackwell, 1958.

Price, Bruce H., Raymond D. Adams, and Joseph T. Coyle, "Neurology and Psychiatry: Closing the Great Divide," *Neurology* 54 (2000): 8–14.

Priestley, Joseph, *Disquisitions Relating to Matter and Spirit*, London: J. Johnson, 1777.

Propp, V., *Morphology of the Folktale*, 2nd edn., trans. Laurence Scott and Louis A. Wagner, ed. Alan Dundes, Austin: University of Texas Press, 1968.

Putnam, Hilary, "Against the New Associationism," in *Speaking Minds: Interviews with Twenty Eminent Cognitive Scientists*, ed. Peter Baumgartner and Sabine Payr, Princeton University Press, 1995, 177–88.

Rajan, Tilottama, *Dark Interpreter: The Discourse of Romanticism*, Ithaca: Cornell University Press, 1980.

Rand, Benjamin, "The Early Development of Hartley's Doctrine of Association," *Psychological Review* 30 (1923): 306–20.

Read, Herbert, *Wordsworth: The Clark Lectures*, New York: Jonathan Cape, 1931.

Reed, Edward S., *From Soul to Mind: The Emergence of Psychology from Erasmus Darwin to William James*, New Haven: Yale University Press, 1997.

Reid, Thomas, *Essays on the Intellectual Powers of Man*, ed. Baruch A. Brody, Cambridge, MA: MIT Press, 1969.

An Inquiry into the Human Mind, on the Principles of Common Sense, 1785; rpt. Bristol: Thoemmes Antiquarian, 1990.

Restuccia, Frances L., *Melancholics in Love: Representing Women's Depression and Domestic Abuse*, Lanham: Rowman & Littlefield, 2000.

Richards, Graham, *Mental Machinery: The Origins and Consequences of Psychological Ideas*, Part I: *1600–1850*, Baltimore: Johns Hopkins University Press, 1992.

Richardson, Alan, "Coleridge and the Dream of an Embodied Mind," *Romanticism* 5 (1999): 1–25.

"Darkness Visible? Race and Representation in Bristol Abolitionist Poetry, 1770–1810," in *Romanticism and Colonialism*, ed. T.J. Fulford and Peter J. Kitson, Cambridge University Press, 1998, 129–47.

Literature, Education, and Romanticism: Reading as Social Practice, 1780–1832, Cambridge University Press, 1994.

"Romanticism and the Colonization of the Feminine" in *Romanticism and Feminism*, ed. Anne K. Mellor, Bloomington: Indiana University Press, 1988.

Ricks, Christopher, *Keats and Embarrassment*, Oxford: Clarendon, 1974.

Roberts, Daniel Sanjiv, "Exorcising the Malay: Dreams and the Unconscious in Coleridge and De Quincey," *The Wordsworth Circle* 24 (1993): 91–96.

Robertson, John Mackenzie, *New Essays Towards a Critical Method*, London: John Lane, 1897.

Robinson, Henry Crabb, *Diary, Reminiscences, and Correspondence of Henry Crabb Robinson*, ed. Thomas Sadler, 2 vols., Boston: Fields, Osgood, 1869.

Some Account of Dr. Gall's New Theory of Physiognomy, Founded upon the Anatomy and Physiology of the Brain, and the Form of the Skull, London: Longman, Hurst, Rees, and Orme, 1807.

Robinson, Mary, *The Poetical Works of the late Mrs. Mary Robinson*, 3 vols., 1806; rpt. London: Routledge/Thoemmes, 1996.

Roe, Nicholas, *John Keats and the Culture of Dissent*, Oxford: Clarendon, 1997.

The Politics of Nature: Wordsworth and Some Contemporaries, New York: St. Martin's Press, 1992.

Wordsworth and Coleridge: The Radical Years, Oxford: Clarendon Press, 1988.

Rosch, Eleanor, "Principles of Categorization," *Cognition and Categorization*, ed. Rosch and Barbara B. Lloyd, Hillsdale: Erlbaum, 1978, 27–48.

Rosch, Eleanor and Carolyn B. Mervis, "Family Resemblance: Studies in the Internal Structure of Categories," *Cognitive Psychology* 7 (1975): 573–605.

Rousseau, G. S. "Nerves, Spirits, and Fibres: Towards Defining the Origins of Sensibility," *Studies in the Eighteenth Century 3: Papers Presented at the Third David Nichol Smith Memorial Seminar, Canberra 1973*, ed. R. F. Brissenden and J. C. Eade, University of Toronto Press, 1976, 137–57.

"Psychology," in *The Ferment of Knowledge: Studies in the Historiography of Eighteenth-Century Science*, ed. Rousseau and Roy Porter, Cambridge University Press, 1980, 143–210.

Rousseau, G. S. and Roy Porter, "Introduction: Toward a Natural History of Mind and Body," *The Languages of Psyche: Mind and Body in Enlightenment Thought*, ed. G. S. Rousseau, Berkeley: University of California Press, 1990, 3–44.

Rousseau, Jean-Jacques, *Emile or On Education*, trans. Allan Bloom, New York: Basic Books, 1979.

"Essay on the Origin of Languages Which Treats of Melody and Musical Imitation," trans. John H. Moran, in *On the Origin of Language*, ed. Moran and Alexander Gode, University of Chicago Press, 1966, 1–74.

Rowe, M. W., "'Kubla Khan' and the Structure of the Psyche," *English* 41 (1992): 145–54.

Rzepka, Charles J., *The Self as Mind: Vision and Identity in Wordsworth, Coleridge, and Keats,* Cambridge: Harvard University Press, 1986.

Schaffer, Simon, "Self Evidence," *Critical Inquiry* 18 (1992): 327–62.

"States of Mind: Enlightenment and Natural Philsophy," in *The Languages of Psyche: Mind and Body in Enlightenment Thought: Clark Library Lectures 1985–1986,* ed. G. S. Rousseau, Berkeley: University of California Press, 1990, 233–90.

Schneider, Elisabeth, *Coleridge, Opium, and Kubla Khan,* University of Chicago Press, 1953.

Scott, Sir Walter, *The Journal of Sir Walter Scott,* ed. W. E. K. Anderson, Oxford: Clarendon Press, 1972.

The Letters of Sir Walter Scott 1826–1828, ed. H. J. C. Grierson, London: Constable, 1936.

Waverley, ed. Andrew Hook, Harmondsworth: Penguin, 1985.

Sejnowski, Terence J., "The Hardware Really Does Matter," *Speaking Minds: Interviews with Twenty Eminent Cognitive Scientists,* ed. Peter Baumgartner and Sabine Payr, Princeton University Press, 1995, 215–30.

Shelley, Mary, *The Last Man,* ed. Brian Aldiss, London: Hogarth Press, 1985.

Shields, Carol, "Jane Austen Images of the Body: No Fingers, No Toes," *Persuasions* 13 (1991): 132–37.

Shuttleworth, Sally, *Charlotte Brontë and Victorian Psychology,* Cambridge University Press, 1996.

Sloane, Eugene, "Coleridge's *Kubla Khan*: The Living Catacombs of the Mind," *American Imago* 29 (1972): 97–122.

Smith, Adam, "Considerations Concerning the First Formation of Languages, and the Different Genius of Original and Compounded Languages," *The Theory of Moral Sentiments; or, An Essay Towards an Analysis of the Principles by which Men Naturally Judge Concerning the Conduct and Character, First of their Neighbors, and Afterwards of Themselves, to which is Added, a Dissertation on the Origin of Languages,* 6th edn, Dublin: Beatty and Johnson, 1777, 389–426.

Smith, Hillas, *Keats and Medicine,* Newport, Isle of Wight: Cross, 1995.

Smith, Olivia, *The Politics of Language 1791–1819,* Oxford: Clarendon Press, 1984.

Sokolsky, Anita, "The Melancholy Persuasion," in *Psychoanalytic Literary Criticism,* ed. Maud Ellman, London: Longman, 1994, 128–42.

Southey, Robert, *The Life and Correspondence of the Late Robert Southey,* ed. Charles Cuthbert Southey, 6 vols., London: Longman, Brown, Green, and Longmans, 1849–50.

Sperry, Stuart M., *Keats the Poet,* Princeton University Press, 1973.

"Wordsworth and the Grounds of Human Consciousness," in *The Cast of Consciousness: Concepts of the Mind in British and American Romanticism,* ed. Beverley Taylor and Robert Bain, New York: Greenwood Press, 1987, 58–76.

Spevack, Marvin, *A Complete and Systematic Concordance to the Works of Shakespeare,* 9 vols., Hildesheim: Georg Olms, 1968–1980.

Spillane, John D., *The Doctrine of the Nerves: Chapters in the History of Medicine,* Oxford University Press, 1981.

Spurzheim, J. G., *Phrenology, or, The Doctrine of the Mind; and of the Relations Between Its Manifestations and the Body*, 3rd edn, London: Charles Knight, 1825.

  The Physiognomical System of Drs. Gall and Spurzheim; Founded on an Anatomical and Physiological Examination of the Nervous System in General, and of the Brain in Particular; and Indicating the Dispositions and Manifestations of the Mind, 2nd edn, London: Baldwin, Cradock, and Joy, 1815.

  A View of the Elementary Principles of Education, Founded on the Study of the Nature of Man, 2nd edn, Boston: Marsh, Capen, and Lyon, 1833.

Review of J. G. Spurzheim, *Observations sur la Phrenologie*, Monthly Review 94 (1821): 517–26.

Review of J.G. Spurzheim, *The Physiognomical System of Doctors Gall and Spurzheim*, Quarterly Review 13 (1815): 159–78.

Review of J. G. Spurzheim, *The Physiognomical System of Doctors Gall and Spurzheim*, Monthly Review 78 (1815): 147–65.

Stallknecht, Newton P., *Strange Seas of Thought: Studies in Wordsworth's Philosophy of Man and Nature*, Bloomington: Indiana University Press, 1958.

Stallybrass, Peter and Allon White, *The Politics and Poetics of Transgression*, Ithaca: Cornell University Press, 1986.

Staum, Martin S., *Cabanis: Enlightenment and Medical Philosophy in the French Revolution*, Princeton University Press, 1980.

Stein, Dan J., "Introduction: Cognitive Science and the Unconsious," in *Cognitive Science and the Unconscious*, ed. Stein, Washington, D.C.: American Psychiatric Press, 1997, 1–21.

Stevens, Scott Manning, "Sacred Heart and Secular Brain," in *The Body in Parts: Fantasies of Corporeality in Early Modern Europe*, ed. David Hillman and Carlo Mazzio, New York: Routledge, 1997, 263–82.

Stewart, Dugald, "Some Account of James Mitchell, a Boy Born Deaf and Blind," *Collected Works of Dugald Stewart*, ed. Sir William Hamilton, 11 vols., Edinburgh: Thomas Constable, 1854–60, 4: 300–61.

Review of Dugald Stewart, "Some Account of a Boy Born Blind and Deaf," *Edinburgh Review* 20 (1812): 462–71.

Stillinger, Jack, *Coleridge and Textual Instability: The Multiple Versions of the Major Poems*, New York: Oxford University Press, 1994.

Stockley, V., *German Literature as Known in England 1750–1830*, London: Routledge, 1929.

Stone, Lawrence, *The Family, Sex, and Marriage in England 1500–1800*, abridged edition, New York: Harper, 1979.

Sulloway, Frank J., *Freud, Biologist of the Mind: Beyond the Psychoanalytic Legend*, New York: Basic Books, 1983.

Sutton, John, *Philosophy and Memory Traces: Descartes to Connectionism*, Cambridge University Press, 1998.

Sweetser, Eve, *From Etymology to Pragmatics: Metaphorical and Cultural Aspects of Semantic Structure*, Cambridge University Press, 1990.

Tanner, Tony, *Jane Austen*, Cambridge: Harvard University Press, 1986.

Tatar, Maria, *Spellbound: Studies in Mesmerism and Literature*, Princeton University Press, 1978.

Taylor, Anya, *Bacchus in Romantic England: Writers and Drink, 1780–1830*, New York: St. Martin's Press, 1999.

Taylor, John R., *Linguistic Categorization: Prototypes in Linguistic Theory*, 2nd edn, Oxford: Clarendon Press, 1995.

Thelwall, John, *Poems Written Chiefly in Retirement*, 1801; rpt. Oxford: Woodstock, 1989.

The Peripatetic; or, Sketches of the Heart, of Nature and Society; in a Series of Politico-Sentimental Journals, in Verse and Prose, of the Eccentric Excursions of Sylvanus Theophrastus; Supposed to be Written by Himself, Southwark, 1793.

Thought, Not a Function of the Brain: A Reply to the Arguments for Materialism Advanced by W. Lawrence, in his Lectures on Physiology, London, Rivington, 1827.

Todorov, Tzvetan, *On Human Diversity: Nationalism, Racism, and Exoticism in French Thought*, trans. Catherine Porter, Cambridge: Harvard University Press, 1993.

Tooke, John Horne, Επεα Πτεροεντα, *or, the Diversions of Purley*, ed. Richard Taylor, 2 vols., London: Thomas Tegg, 1829.

Tronchon, Henri, *Le Jeune Edgar Quinet ou L'Aventure d'un Enthousiaste*, Paris: Publications de la Faculté des Lettres de Strasbourg, 1937.

Tsur, Reuven, *The Road to Kubla Khan: A Cognitive Approach*, Jerusalem: Israel Science Publishers, 1987.

Turkle, Sherry, "Romantic Reactions: Paradoxical Responses to the Computer Presence," in *The Boundaries of Humanity: Humans, Animals, Machines*, ed. James J. Sheehan and Morton Sosna, Berkeley: University of California Press, 1991, 224–52.

Turner, Mark, *The Literary Mind*, New York: Oxford University Press, 1996.

Reading Minds: The Study of English in the Age of Cognitive Science, Princeton University Press, 1991.

Van Peer, Willie, "Towards a Poetics of Emotion," in *Emotion and the Arts*, ed. Mette Hjort and Sue Laver, New York: Oxford University Press, 1997, 215–24.

Varela, Francisco J., Evan Thompson, and Eleanor Rosch, *The Embodied Mind: Cognitive Science and Human Experience*, Cambridge: MIT Press, 1991.

Waldoff, Leon, *Keats and the Silent Work of Imagination*, Urbana: University of Illinois Press, 1985.

Wardrop, James, *History of James Mitchell, A Boy Born Blind and Deaf, With an Account of the Operation Performed for the Recovery of His Sight*, London: John Murray and Archibald Constable, 1813.

Wells, Kentwood D., "Sir William Lawrence (1783–1867): A Study of Pre-Darwinian Ideas on Heredity and Variation," *Journal of the History of Biology* 4 (1971): 319–61.

Wheeler, K. M., *The Creative Mind in Coleridge's Poetry*, Cambridge: Harvard University Press, 1981.

White, R. S., "'Like Esculapius of Old': Keats's Medical Training," *Keats-Shelley Review* 12 (1998): 15–49.

Whyte, Lancelot Law, *The Unconscious Before Freud*, New York: Basic Books, 1960.

Wightman, W. P. D., "Wars of Ideas in Neurological Science – from Willis to

Bichat and from Locke to Condillac,"in *The Brain and Its Functions*, ed. Poynter, 135–48.

Willey, Basil, The *Eighteenth-Century Background*, London: Chatto and Windus, 1940.

Williams, Elizabeth A., *The Physical and the Moral: Anthropology, Physiology, and Philosophical Medicine in France, 1750–1850*, Cambridge University Press, 1994.

Wilson, Douglas B., "Psychological Approaches," in *A Companion to Romanticism*, ed. Duncan Wu, Oxford: Blackwell, 1998, 420–30.

Wiltshire, John, *Jane Austen and the Body*, Cambridge University Press, 1992.

Woodman, Ross, "The Idiot Boy as Healer," *Romanticism and Children's Literature in Nineteenth-Century England*, ed. James Holt McGavran, Jr., Athens: University of Georgia Press, 1991, 72–95.

Wordsworth, Christopher, *Memoirs of William Wordsworth, Poet-Laureate, D. C. L.*, 2 vols., London: Edward Moxon, 1851.

Wordsworth, Jonathan, "As with the Silence of the Thought," *High Romantic Argument: Essays for M. H. Abrams*, ed. Lawrence Lipking, Ithaca: Cornell University Press, 1981, 41–76.

William Wordsworth: The Borders of Vision, Oxford: Clarendon Press, 1982.

Wordsworth, William, *The Prose Works of William Wordsworth*, ed. W. J. B. Owen and Jane Worthington Smyser, 3 vols., Oxford: Clarendon Press, 1974.

Wordsworth's Literary Criticism, ed. W. J. B. Owen, London: Routledge & Kegan Paul, 1974.

Wu, Duncan, *Wordsworth's Reading 1770–1799*, Cambridge University Press, 1993.

Wylie, Ian, *Young Coleridge and the Philosophers of Nature*, Oxford: Clarendon Press, 1989.

Yolton, John W., *Thinking Matter: Materialism in Eighteenth-Century Britain*, Minneapolis: University of Minnesota Press, 1983.

Young, Robert, *Mind, Brain, and Adaptation in the Nineteenth-Century: Cerebral Localization and Its Biological Function from Gall to Ferrier*, Oxford: Clarendon, 1970.

Young, Robert J. C., *Colonial Desire: Hybridity in Theory, Culture and Race*, London: Routledge, 1995.

"Z" [John Gibson Lockhart?], "On the Cockney School of Poetry," no. 4, *Blackwood's Edinburgh Magazine* 3 (1818): 519–24.

Index

237

CAMBRIDGE STUDIES IN ROMANTICISM

General editors
MARILYN BUTLER
University of Oxford
JAMES CHANDLER
University of Chicago

Printed in the United Kingdom
by Lightning Source UK Ltd.
106286UKS00002B/126